LOSING THE LIGHT

Other Books by Andrew Yule:

HOLLYWOOD A GO-GO

FAST FADE: David Puttnam, Columbia Pictures and the Battle for Hollywood

THE BEST WAY TO WALK

LOSING
THE LIGHT

Terry Gilliam
and the
Munchausen Saga

by

ANDREW YULE

APPLAUSE BOOKS

211 W. 71st St, New York, NY 10023

An Applause Original
LOSING THE LIGHT: Terry Gilliam and the Munchausen Saga
Copyright © 1991 by Andrew Yule

Library of Congress Cataloging-in-Publication Data

Yule, Andrew.
    Losing the light: Terry Gilliam and the Munchausen saga/
Andrew Yule.
        p. cm.
    "An Applause original" — T.p. verso.
    Includes bibliographical references and index.
    ISBN 1-55783-060-6 : $22.95
    1. Adventures of Baron Munchausen (Motion picture)
2. Gilliam, Terry. I. Title.
PN1997.A31143Y8 1991
791.43'72—dc20   91-28212
                                          CIP

Copyrighted photographs.

APPLAUSE BOOKS
211 W 71st Street
New York, NY 10023

Phone: 212-496-7511
Fax: 212-721-2856

First Applause Printing: 1991

FOREWORD
&
ACKNOWLEDGMENTS

The reconstruction of the *Munchausen* misadventures was the next best thing to a trip back in time. Every conceivable movie-making hazard was encountered in the process. What began to emerge as the *Munchausen* story unfolded was even a larger picture of the minefield peculiar to Hollywood and the movie industry. The result, apart from being its own incredible tale, represents a crash course covering all aspects of movie-making: from the conception of the original idea, to script writing and financing, through the pre-production, production, post-production stages, the final release strategy, and box office peril.

I, like the reader, never actually alighted on the *Munchausen* set. With the inspiration for this book came a wave of regret that I had missed the hard-core journalistic heat that the immediate experience would have offered. But as my excavation and reconstruction proceeded, I began to think that even as an observer, the experience might have been intolerable. Part of me wonders how I or anyone else might have survived the *Munchausen* gamut. Of course, many did not.

I have relied on the candor of thirty-three of the film's principal participants who shared their experiences with me in interviews at various locations around the world, including London, Rome, Munich, Paris, Venice, Stratford Ontario, New York City and Los Angeles. I'm grateful to all who supplied another piece of the alluring *Munchausen* puzzle.

If Terry Gilliam's *The Adventures of Baron Munchausen* proves to be a lasting masterpiece, as some contend, it will be against all conceivable odds. With the budget escalating out of control, and reportedly heading for $50 million, Gilliam came close to being fired. Columbia promptly threatened to reject the picture. Everything that could go wrong had gone wrong. Stampeding elephants had laid waste to expensive props and equipment. Filming at Rome's Cinecitta had proceeded at an agonizing snail's pace. Infighting between the director and producer had come close to physical violence.

The genesis of Gilliam's involvement with the affairs of the notorious Baron came about during a visit in the summer of 1979 to ex-Beatle George Harrison's magnificent nineteenth-century house. Harrison first mentioned the character as they strolled together through the manicured grounds and rose-trellised pavilions. Later that day, he showed Gilliam his leather bound collection of Rudolph Raspe's Munchausen editions, complete with illustrations by the French painter Gustave Doré. To the captivated Gilliam they looked exactly like movie storyboards.

That Christmas, Ray Cooper of Handmade Films gave Gilliam a book on the Baron's adventures as a gift. "You're the only one who could turn this into a movie," was Cooper's deliberately challenging inscription.

Looking again at Doré's vivid illustrations and rereading sections of Raspe's stiffly anarchic text, Gilliam gradually became intrigued with the prospect of putting the Baron's adventures on screen. He needed something lighter after the dark corners he had probed in *Brazil*. Was it possible that Munchausen could complete the trilogy that had begun with *Time Bandits* and *Brazil*?

Baron Karl Friedrich Heironymous von Munchausen, born to the Hanoverian nobility in 1720, had enlisted in the Russian army as a soldier of fortune and fought with them against the Ottoman empire of the Turks. His exploits provided the springboard for many of his fantastically tall tales, which were later recounted in book form by Raspe, one of Munchausen's drinking companions. Since their first publication in 1785, the tales of the Baron's adventures had held an entire continent of children spellbound, and today they are recognized as classics of German literature.

As for Karl Friedrich Heironymous himself, some say that he died grief-stricken at having been branded an incorrigible fabricator of tall tales, albeit a romantic one. Others say he died in a state of utter bliss, supremely content in the knowledge that through the retelling of his tales he had achieved the bright, keen flame of immortality, the ultimate goal of which most men can only dream.

"Your 'reality,' sir, is lies and balderdash, and I'm delighted to say that I have no grasp of it whatsoever," the Baron had once declared. The more Gilliam discovered about the Baron and his origins, the more he became smitten. He began to see that in the Baron's imaginative inconsistency lay the magical stuff of dreams.

Gilliam's intrepid efforts to translate the free-spirited, dramatic and romantic adventures of Baron von Munchausen to the screen is in itself a fascinating tale of the "reality" of Hollywood filmmaking — and a lesson in the price of achieving a dream. Through the words of those involved — from hours of taped interviews, correspondence files opened by the companies themselves, and months of research, the untold story of the making — and unmaking — of "one of the most expensive Hollywood films ever made" begins to unfold . . .

CHAPTER ONE

The main kick for Milchan is in the glamour aspect, getting to schmooze movie stars and power brokers, the 'starfucker' phenomenon.
—Steve Abbott

Gilliam and Abbott are breaking my balls! For $500 and $1,000 they are breaking my balls!

—Arnon Milchan

Arnon Milchan, Gilliam's Israeli-born producer on *Brazil* once portrayed himself with typical modesty as "young, slim, good-looking, amiable and clever." Sporting tinted spectacles, he is often carelessly well-dressed in a fashionable welter of double-ply cashmere and scuffed leathers, an open-necked silk shirt exposing his hairy chest. He is given at times to affecting a rather touching, furtively adolescent grin of the caught-behind-the bicycle-shed variety. Although designated as the heir to a large chemical manufacturing fortune by London's *Sunday Times* in 1985, Milchan describes himself as a self-made millionaire.

He found a temporary home for *Munchausen* at 20th Century-Fox, the only company in Hollywood, Gilliam maintains, who had ever heard of the Baron. The four-page *Variety* advertisement that trumpeted the deal seemed to him to represent the apex of Milchan's enthusiasm. In true Munchausen style, it promised the most outrageous, the most fantastic — and the most expensive — film ever made. Not, as it turned out, from Fox. Their agreement was soon invalidated by a "key man" clause in the contract when Alan Hirschfield and Norman Levy left the company and Fox's new chief, Barry Diller, evidently no Munchausen scholar, deflatingly opted to pass.

Milchan promptly began negotiations at Tri-Star Pictures. He arranged a meeting with Gilliam, Steve Abbott of Prominent Features (a company representing the film interests of various ex-Monty Python members) and Tri-Star's team of David Matalon and Jeff Sagansky. Twelve million dollars was offered by Tri-Star subject to the participation of an outside producer, Keith Barish. While Milchan and the Prominent Features group realized this would not be enough, they decided to wait out Barish's decision.

Steve Abbott began working with Gilliam in 1979. Still in his late twenties, he had entered the business originally through accountancy school, which explains his meticulous approach to business affairs. He dresses casually, talks frenetically, and wears his fair hair long and tousled. He remembers first hearing about the *Munchausen* project as early as 1980. Once *Brazil* was out of the way, there was no doubt in Abbott's mind that *Munchausen* would be pushed to the forefront.

He soon was brought into regular contact with Arnon Milchan, whom he describes as "a producer of the no-hands-on school": "He knows the heads of Hollywood studios and major heads of finance in Europe and puts people together. That's his forte. He's never pretended to be interested in running his financial and business life by the book. As an individual he's charm itself and hops around almost for the sake of it. If he's in London or Paris and he's got a free afternoon, he'll take the Concorde over to see what's happening in New York. He managed to get everything together for *Brazil*, but I don't know how he did it. He's delivered the goods — some good

films like *Once Upon a Time in America* and *King of Comedy* —
and some not so good, like *Legend*."

Although Gilliam was ostensibly a partner on *Brazil*, it soon
became clear that legally he was working for Milchan. Abbott became
upset and angry by the cavalier attitude Milchan adopted throughout
the production period. Perhaps because he was Gilliam's man, Abbott
was allowed to look after *Brazil*'s entire financial structure. "Milchan
was incredibly trusting in a perverse way," Abbott admitted. "At any
time I could have stolen his money! Then it kind of backfired on him
when I was able to go through all the expenses on the movie with my
auditor's eye and point out to him the items that were his own
personal things and had absolutely nothing to do with the film. He
was furious. It was the beginning of the end of the partnership. Terry
had trusted Arnon implicitly and it began to irritate him that money
had been spent in a frivolous way."

Abbott was particularly disturbed to find that Milchan was
paying Charles McKeown, Gilliam's co-writer, out of *Brazil* funds —
for work he was doing on the projected *Munchausen* project. When
confronted about this, Milchan's response was simply to suspend all
payments to McKeown.

A gentle, scholarly man of medium height and slight build,
McKeown is perhaps the perfect foil for Gilliam. He is often seen as
the ballast that prevents his friend from rocketing into orbit, or at the
very least, the space control that talks him back down again.

McKeown sees Milchan as a Munchausen character himself.
"You just never know whether he was telling the truth or not. The
kind of deals he was in, the level of finance and the way he operated,
seemed to me like a world upside down. I felt we were dealing with a
sort of dangerous, shady quality. He boasts enormous wealth and
clearly wants to be seen as the most generous individual.

"Arnon took Terry and me along once to the Victoria Sporting
Club, which was full of Arabs. He told us he was very amused at
being the only Jew there. We were given champagne with the meal,
which was complimentary since some months earlier he had won
£120,000 in the club. The visit gave us a superb example of Arnon's
generosity and unlimited largesse — when someone else's money was
being used!

3

"I came away from that scene with no sense of envy whatsoever. While he was capable of being very generous in an obvious way, when it came to getting £10,000 out of him for some work he actually owed me, forget it. My agent spent months phoning him all over the world and getting no reply. He seemed to be quite pathological in his desire not to part with money."

• • •

German-born Thomas Schuhly is an unashamed product of years of bodybuilding, now maintained at Cinecitta through daily workouts at his specially built gym. In his middle thirties, he is decidedly handsome from certain angles. Schuhly seems to divide the world into two classes — those who can be useful to him, and those who cannot. With his slate-blue eyes, aquiline nose, and the corners of his mouth slightly downturned, he exudes equal measures of desperation and earnestness.

The culmination of his years in the German movie industry came with his "executive producer" credit on *The Name of the Rose*. Although the movie version of Umberto Eco's monumental best seller bombed in the United States, where most observers agreed it was dismally handled by 20th Century-Fox, it took in a record-breaking $100 million in Europe. *The Name of the Rose* offered watershed proof that a major movie could go into profit without reliance on the U.S. market, up until then regarded as vital. The multilingual Schuhly refers constantly to his contribution to *The Name of the Rose*, and of how he pulled all the vital elements together — ignoring the fact that Bernd Eichinger of Neue Constantin produced the movie and exercised total day-to-day control. "I'm the Rambo of film production," Schuhly boasts proudly. "If anyone got out of line on that production, I just *smooshed* them up against a wall!"

He claims as his mentor Horst Vendtland, a major German producer, whom he compares to producer, Dino De Laurentiis. "Horst always wanted me as his heir," Schuhly blithely maintains. "For many years on the Continent I had the best reputation of all as regards running a production, because I have worked with very complicated directors, and maybe I had the luck to do it very well."

As cigarette after cigarette is smoked and discarded through the open side window, he retraces the path that led him to take over the production reins of *Munchausen* from Arnon Milchan. He had first met Milchan in the editing rooms of Cinecitta: "Arnon is a character I basically like a lot. The movie industry is to a large extent built on these adventurers, these people who can create images in the minds of bankers. He is very charming, always flying very high. I know a lot of stories about him" — a hearty chuckle — "like I do about De Laurentiis, but I still like him a lot. Stories like these are always linked to brilliant people.

"Arnon comes from one of the oldest Jewish families in Israel and was brought up with a first class sophisticated education. He's an excellent salesman; he can sell you a piece of shit for a piece of gold. Both of us like Italy, because if you are bright you can make a very substantial business there. There is a lot of money and the Italians like this kind of *condottiere*. You meet these people in Los Angeles and Rome, but the style doesn't work in London.

"Arnon heard about how I'd finished *The Name of the Rose* $1 million under budget, and with a shooting schedule of 14 weeks that was originally estimated to be 18 weeks, and asked me if I was interested in running the *Munchausen* show. I said I wasn't interested in running *someone else's show*; I run my *own* shows. Eventually we agreed between us that he would be executive producer and I would be the producer."

At this stage Gilliam was asked to fly out to Lake Como to visit Milchan and Schuhly on the set of Milchan's *Man on Fire*, a movie featuring Jonathan Pryce and Ray Cooper, both friends and colleagues of his. Milchan introduced Schuhly to Gilliam as the line producer he had settled on for *Munchausen* and swiftly and amicably established the connection.

Schuhly was based at Cinecitta and knew his way around. It made perfect sense, therefore, to produce *Munchausen* in Italy, both from the artistic and economic viewpoints. Gilliam loved the idea of working in Italy. The baroque influence, the tremendous, crackling atmosphere, and the sensuality all seemed ideal for the outrageous, chaotic and romantic concept he had of *Munchausen*.

Ray Cooper, instigator of the *Munchausen* challenge, noted that Schuhly kept referring to himself as Rambo. "And he looked the part," he noted, "at least when he had his dark glasses on. Without them he was a bit less effective; his eyes gave him away — they were a fraction anxious and weak. Still he was pretty impressive, especially with his claim that he'd brought *The Name of the Rose* in virtually single-handed."

Schuhly was soon privy to Milchan's account of the stormy meetings with his director and Abbott over *Brazil*'s finances, and his allegations of "ball-breaking." "I can't stand it any more," Milchan raged as he strode up and down Schuhly's office at Cinecittà. "This *fucking Abbott*, he says, 'Arnon, you live in a first-class suite and this was not foreseen in the budget. Arnon, you flew Concorde from Paris to . . .' Thomas, this is out of my concept of life!"

Schuhly watched as the impending split approached and cannily bided his time. He knew that the brilliantly devious Milchan had taken a calculated risk bringing him on board in the first place. He was aware that he and Milchan were similar types and that Milchan half expected him to take over when he bowed out. All Schuhly had to do was watch as the entire constellation broke down, seeing it as "this noble Jew" on the one hand and "this accountant and Terry" on the other.

Gilliam recalls that finally matters became too complicated with Milchan. "He eventually told me to go and take *Munchausen* with me. He didn't want anything for it. 'Let's just call it a day,' he said." Steve Abbott recalled a similar parting of the ways: "We met in a hotel in Rome. Very clearly on two occasions, both that evening, then again on the following day when he and I had a separate meeting, he said, 'It's free and unattached. I just want to help. All I want is that if you're going to speak to any of the people I've already spoken to, let me know what they're offering and how your negotiations go, because I want to retain a position with them. Otherwise, it's yours to go with.'"

Having only once in his life actually glimpsed Milchan's signature on *anything*, Abbott had some difficulty in believing this apparent magnanimity. As if to dispel any lingering doubts, Milchan chose to expand even further. "Yes, I *like* jetting about," he admitted. "No, I *don't* like things on paper. I like to move things about from one country to another. With your background as an accountant, you like things in writing, formalized, things for the tax authorities to look at. We're never going to see eye to eye. I want to stay friends with Terry, but not if he replaces me with someone else who controls the picture. I can't live with that joint control. *I've* got to have it, otherwise it's yours and I wish you good luck. I'll only make a fuss if you go to someone else and you're working for *them*. If you're running your *own* production company, that's fine."

Gilliam and Abbott wasted no time in setting up their own production entity, The Munchausen Partnership, with Anne James, a colleague of Abbott's, brought in as a third partner. Schuhly saw his chance and phoned Gilliam to suggest that they continue to collaborate on *Munchausen*. A meeting was set up at Cinecitta.

Schuhly anticipated there could be potential pitfalls in their future relationship and had no intention of being "trapped" like Milchan. "I developed my system to hook Terry. I played more or less to his and Steve's philosophy," he admitted. "I wanted to make *Munchausen*, but I quickly realized that I was going to get the same shit as Arnon, since Steve and Terry are coming from the same background, the *petit bourgeoisie*. I am from the *big bourgeoisie*, same as Arnon. The two sides have different life-styles.

"On the one hand, we have the sensuous Latin style and on the other the stiff Calvinistic Protestant life-style that Terry embodies. Not to mention Abbott, the converted Jew who hates nothing more than Germans, which was the background to many problems later. A screenplay depends on how you sell it, do the backers believe in it, do they believe in you — it's money, business, *corruption* even! When I had the first meeting with Abbott, I couldn't believe it. I forced myself to keep my mouth shut, knowing that once I'd taken over, the production would run as *I* was used to run a show."

Steve Abbott came back from the rendezvous in Rome with many reservations. He could see that Schuhly was very bright. The naked ego and ambition he displayed did not in themselves disconcert him. What did put him off was what he perceived as Schuhly's abnormally high "bullshit quotient."

"That's not necessarily an insult for a film producer," he conceded. "You need it to get finances, but the other fact that disturbed me was his lack of any genuine enthusiasm for the project, except maybe as some kind of stepping stone to work with Terry. He did a wonderful public relations job for himself, impressing Terry no end. He knew absolutely everybody in Rome and introduced the two of us to Fellini, Sergio Leone, to the top technicians there, to actors like Marcello Mastroainni. It was fine as far as it went, but there was something . . ."

"What do you think of him?" Gilliam asked Abbott on their return. For a while Abbott was silent. Then he startled Gilliam with his reply. "I don't mind the bullshit," he said, "but why would he want to bullshit *us*?"

Obsessed with this notion, Abbott spent two full afternoons at the British Film Institute's library looking up the records on Schuhly. Schuhly had claimed he had qualified as a lawyer in Germany and had gone on to become managing director of Bernd Eichinger's movie company, Neue Constantin, where he produced four Werner Fassbinder films. He had also cast himself as Fassbinder's right-hand man and confidant, working on scripts with him, as well as performing duties of lighting cameraman and assistant director.

Carefully examining every reference to Fassbinder and Schuhly in German Film Year Books and other sources, Abbott discovered that while Schuhly *had* been producer on Fassbinder's documentary *Theatre In A Trance*, and on *Veronika Voss*, as well as production manager on one of his other films, his credits fell far short of his claims. Schuhly's truth seemed to result from an unequal contest between agreeable fantasy and disagreeable fact.

When Abbott pointed this out to his partner, Gilliam argued that he knew how films worked, that credits were not really significant. "I let things slide because of Thomas's energy," he later admitted. "It was a sloppiness I would pay for later."

Despite misgivings on all sides, the die was cast. *The Adventures of Baron Munchausen* would be co-produced by the newly-created Munchausen Partnership arm of Prominent Features, and by Schuhly's Rome-based Laura Films. All they needed to start the ball rolling was a little development money.

CHAPTER TWO

I'm working class, yes, and so is Steve, but I thought I was closer to Thomas in being more of a buccaneer. Steve is very cautious. He very much plays by the rules. I'm willing to bend all sorts of rules and do outrageous things to make things happen, which is the connection between Thomas and me. I sensed that he was someone who would go all the way to get something done. Where I differ from Thomas is my belief in the work ethic and actually doing the job, *beyond* bullshit.

That's an important part of the process, but you then have to have other skills to make a movie, and that's where we split. I feel guilty if I don't work extremely hard.

—Terry Gilliam

Twenty-five million dollars is the psychological barrier beyond which we'll find no takers for Munchausen.

—Jake Eberts

Gilliam's main reaction was one of enormous relief that the project was not going to collapse because of his parting with Milchan. Schuhly's undeniable charm and energy having won the day, he moved quickly to set up a meeting with Gilliam, Abbott and Allied Filmmakers' Jake Eberts, to pursue seed funding for what was already designated a "$25 million project." He declined a $1 million development fee offered by his old company, Neue Constantin, on the basis of previous conflicts with NC's head, Bernd Eichinger.

Although Eberts and Schuhly were co-executive producers on *The Name of the Rose*, they had managed to accomplish this feat without ever actually meeting. If the reader considers this strange, perhaps it tells us something of the multifaceted nature of producers' titles in films. All sorts of "producers" carry out all sorts of functions, some of them extremely limited in scope and duration. Eberts' usual role is to provide, through his company Allied Filmmakers, the seed financing to fuel a project until a major U.S. studio is coaxed on board. In *The Name of the Rose*, Eberts' primary contribution was to acquire the participation of 20th Century-Fox.

In the gospel according to Schuhly, the tag "executive producer" on the Continent signifies the individual who runs the physical production. Specifically, he claims to have acted as first assistant director, production manager, production supervisor, line producer, co-producer and financier on *The Name of the Rose*, active and on the set from morning to midnight with the director.

Ebullient fireball Bernd Eichinger, physically a match for his muscle-laden ex-colleague, unhesitatingly described all of Schuhly's proclaimed functions as "bullshit," save for his working title of production manager. As head of Neue Constantin, Germany's leading production and distribution company, whose international credits range from *Christiane F* through *Never Ending Story* and *The Name of the Rose* all the way to *Me and Him* and *Last Exit to Brooklyn*, Eichinger is in a unique position to assess Schuhly's claims.

The two men first met back in Munich, where Eichinger knew Schuhly as producer of a single Fassbinder movie, *Veronika Voss*. They remain good friends. "Thomas has good energy and he's very positive," Eichinger informed me. "His *problem* is that he's a constant mixture of reality and hyper-reality. On the one side he's so strong, very ambitious. But his mind is always ten steps ahead of him! On *The Name of the Rose* he'd say a problem was taken care of, then more often than not I'd find some loose ends that hadn't been properly tied up. It took me some time to realize that. Another thing is that he's no good at follow-up. And if you say, 'I'll consider it,' he thinks he's got a signed deal."

As for Schuhly's claim that he brought in *The Name of the Rose* one million dollars under budget and finished it in fourteen weeks instead of the original eighteen weeks scheduled, Eichinger gives a deep-throated chuckle. "We brought the movie in under budget because of savings and adjustments *I* was able to make as we went along," he maintains. "Regarding the schedule, this, I'm afraid, is an example of Thomas's hyper-reality. *The reverse is true.* We went four weeks *over*, from 14 to 18 weeks! Yes, I offered Thomas $1 million to develop *Munchausen*, and he turned it down. But I didn't offer it as an investor; I wasn't interested except as distributor, for Germany. I offered it as a friend to help him, a personal gesture."

Eichinger had a word of advice for Schuhly, his erstwhile protégé, after a close study of *Munchausen*'s script and the projected budget. "You'll never make it for $25 million," he told him. "$40 million would be more like it."

"You're crazy!" was Schuhly's response. "Costs at Cinecitta are lower —"

"Thomas, there's just *no way*, whether you make it in Cinecitta, Calcutta or on the moon. Let's go through the script together and I'll explain this to you."

"Bernd, there's no need. I tell you you're crazy . . ."

Shrugging his shoulders, Eichinger handed Schuhly back the script. "Fine, OK, I'm crazy. Thomas, I wish you the best of luck in this venture."

• • •

A Canadian-born business graduate, Jake Eberts was an investment banker for ten years before entering the shark-infested waters of movie making. The modest, unassuming Eberts quickly earned himself a reputation as a man of his word, a rare phenomenon in the movie world. Tall, bespectacled and sandy-haired, Eberts resembles a college professor more than a movie mogul. But beneath that exterior there beats the heart of a born hustler. What sets Eberts apart is the passion he feels for the goods he hustles.

His account of the sale of *The Name of the Rose* to Barry Diller at 20th Century-Fox illuminates Eberts' honest but very much maverick style: "I'd spoken to Barry many times about the movie. I was in the middle of this do-or-die trip to Hollywood to conclude the deal. One of the contending studios provided me with a car fitted with a telephone. I called Barry Diller and told him once again what a magical property *The Name of the Rose* was and what a feather it would be in the cap of whoever got it. 'All right, I'm convinced,' Barry finally agreed. 'How much are you asking?' 'Five million dollars,' I replied. 'OK, it's a deal,' said Barry. I said, 'Look, I'm pushed for time. Do we have to meet or could I just follow this up with your business affairs guy?' 'Sure,' he told me, 'no problem. I'll let him know and he'll expect your call.' When I phoned an hour later, I was told that the contract was already being prepared. Barry had been as good as his word. The deal for $5 million with Fox was done without even having to go through the studio gates!"

Eberts was extremely impressed with the *Munchausen* script Gilliam and McKeown had produced. Nothing like it had been seen on the screen for a long, long time. They had woven individual tales of the Baron's swashbuckling exploits and Herculean deeds into a single dazzling yarn.

"The movie's about lies," Gilliam enthused. "It's about the greatest liar the world has ever known. It's about flying to the moon and meeting 60-foot-high people with detachable heads. It's about falling into the center of the Earth and meeting Vulcan and Venus. It's about being swallowed by whales and flying on cannonballs. It's about dancing in the sky. In other words, a normal, everyday sort of film."

Delighted as he was with Munchausen, Eberts immediately realized there was a "$25 million way of making it and a $50 million way." Schuhly insisted that his was the $25 million way, boasting that in Italy the movie could be made for 40 percent less than the cost of shooting in England. "Just as well," Eberts noted, "for that is the psychological limit beyond which we'll find no takers."

The bulk of the finance would inevitably have to be found in America. Eberts' concern in pitching the movie was the lack of familiarity with the Baron legend in most countries outside of Germany and Italy . . . and particularly in America.

It was true that some of the Baron's tales had been translated for American children at the turn of the century. In the early thirties a comic strip featuring the Baron ran in U.S. newspapers but, along with other German-related strips, like *The Katzenjammer Kids*, the Baron was quietly dropped with the rapid buildup of anti-German feeling. In 1933, Metro-Goldwyn-Mayer produced a B film, *Meet the Baron*. Directed by Walter Lang, it starred radio comedian Jack Pearl, Jimmy Durante, Ted Healy, The Three Stooges, Edna May Oliver and Zazu Pitts. Pearl also played the Baron on a weekly radio series, signing off each episode with "Vas you dere, Charlie?" Clearly a major, skillful campaign would be needed to rekindle awareness of the Baron in the America of today.

Despite his reservations, Eberts was excited by the prospect of working with a filmmaker of Gilliam's standing. The dynamics of his association with Schuhly and the refreshing absence of any showbiz flamboyance in Steve Abbott clinched the deal. He had one last crucial question at that first meeting: "Are all the rights clear? I mean, Milchan's out and you're in, Thomas, is that correct?" He was assured that that was indeed the case.

Gilliam was impressed by Schuhly's skill at working "the triangle" with Eberts: "Jake thought Schuhly was with me and I thought he was with Jake! Steve was in my corner and new to the world of finance. He wasn't as comfortable as I was and kept asking all these awkward, embarrassing questions, which I kept brushing aside. Jake was a great choice. That was the main outcome as far as I was concerned."

In October 1986, Eberts agreed to put up $350,000 development money. "You'll need a large part of that for our pitch to the studios," he told the *Munchausen* team. "To sell this project we'll need to put together a stunning visual presentation, set paintings, models, *the works*."

When Gilliam announced that he would be able to finish the definitive storyboards within a couple of months, Schuhly responded that he would conclude precise budget calculations at the same time. Gilliam called him several weeks later only to discover that the calculations had never even begun. For the first time he saw that although Schuhly was supposed to be the starting motor, he was way ahead of him. That situation was never to alter.

Schuhly's major contribution to keeping Gilliam's enthusiasm level high was to introduce him to artists with whom Gilliam had previously only dreamt of working. One such artist was production designer Dante Ferretti, a dynamically charming ball of energy whose most recent work was on *The Name of the Rose*.

Ferretti had moved to Rome in 1959 at the age of 16 to study at the Academy of Fine Arts and the Faculty of Architecture. He entered the movie area a year later, first as an assistant and then as a full-fledged production designer in 1969. He has worked with the Italian directors Elio Petri, Marco Bellochio, Luigi Comencini, Marco Ferreri, Liliana Cavani, Ettore Scala and Dino Risi, on Pasolini's *Medea*, *Decameron*, *Canterbury Tales*, *Arabian Nights* and *Salo*; and on Fellini's *Orchestra Rehearsal*, *City of Women* and *Ginger and Fred*.

"Everyone was asking why I wasn't working with Fellini any more," says the cheerful, bald Ferretti, with the gleeful chuckle that is his trademark. "I jokingly replied it was because I had to work with Terry Gilliam, because I had seen his wonderful movie *Brazil*! Ten days after that Thomas Schuhly called me and asked if I would like to work on *Munchausen*!"

As far as Gilliam was concerned, the match was made in heaven. He had tried to emulate the look of Pasolini's films when making *Monty Python and The Holy Grail* and *Jabberwocky*. Now at last here he was meeting the man behind it all. And Ferretti wanted to work with *him*! Gilliam fondly remembers this as the movie's honeymoon period.

The designs and models that began to roll off Ferretti's assembly line were stunning exhibits to give potential backers an idea of the unique look of the film. Gilliam confidently indicated to Eberts that their presentation and script package would be ready for the big push to a Hollywood studio by the end of the year. The question was: would a proper budget be ready, courtesy of Schuhly? As the meetings in Los Angeles drew near, Steve Abbott repeatedly tried to extract some concrete figures but without success. In the meantime, with the bulk of Eberts' money already invested in Ferretti's presentation,

Prominent Features/Munchausen Partnership had to advance $250,000 of their own to keep the pot boiling.

A major area of disagreement between Schuhly and Gilliam began to arise over the casting of the Baron. Schuhly wanted Sean Connery, arguing that he would make a sexy, romantic hero. "Sean's great, but he's not our Baron," Gilliam argued. He wanted someone less well-known; older; someone whom the movie would endow with its own personality rather than the other way around. Priding himself on what he saw as his close relationship with the actor after *The Name of the Rose*, Schuhly next proposed Connery for the key cameo of King of the Moon. "Now you're talking," Gilliam agreed, "Sean would be terrific as the King."

With the push to achieve a suitably impressive presentation almost complete, Eberts arranged for a trip to Hollywood in late December of 1986. The timing was crucial if the starting date of July 1987 was to be kept; any later than that, the unit might run into weather problems in Rome. Eberts was on the verge of completing a U.S. video deal with Vestron Pictures for $8 million, and $3 million already had been raised between the brothers Cecchi-Gori of Italy and Germany's Neue Constantin for rights in their territories. That left $14 million to be found in Los Angeles.

As they set off in search of their Hollywood fortunes, the party of Eberts, Schuhly, Gilliam and Abbott was in for an unexpected legacy from the Milchan era.

CHAPTER THREE

The one thing I know about films is that when the motor's running you've got to go with it. It looked as though it had all come together.

—Terry Gilliam

Thomas is very much like a powerful gun in action. If you don't aim it correctly, it'll destroy your own army.

—Bernd Eichinger

The group's first meeting in Los Angeles was a 3 p.m. appointment at Columbia Pictures' Burbank headquarters in the San Fernando Valley. Gilliam had already called David Puttnam after his takeover of the studio and asked, "Do you have $25 million for *Munchausen*?" Puttnam's somewhat discouraging response was, "I'm not doing that sort of film, but come and talk to David Picker when you get here."

Eberts was aware of Puttnam's coolness, and worried that an

accusation of cronyism might be leveled because of their association on Goldcrest's *Chariots of Fire*, *Cal* and *The Killing Fields*, and more recently on Allied Film's *Hope and Glory* and *White Mischief*. Eberts says he, in fact, never considered Puttnam a close friend in the mold of Richard Attenborough, John Boorman and other British filmmakers with whom he has also done business. "David is not the kind of guy you ever become intimate with. He's the kind of guy you parry with all the time, a professional colleague."

Gilliam had worries of his own about Puttnam's reaction to the project. He had, after all, turned *Brazil* down when it was offered to him years earlier. His feeling was that Puttnam understood neither his movies nor the man who made them. Maybe he was smart enough, though, to see that other people liked them . . .

David Picker *was* an old friend of Eberts. A seasoned old hand in the movie business as ex-president of both United Artists and Paramount, Picker's career gets mixed reviews in Hollywood. "The attention span of a gnat," said one source. "One of the great survivors," countered another. Portly in build, curt in manner, the pinkly prosperous Picker represents Old Hollywood. His appearance at Puttnam's side at Columbia, after years out in the cold as an independent producer, was regarded as probably his last hurrah in Hollywood's corridors of power.

Picker warmly embraced Eberts on his arrival at Columbia's Plaza East. Before the rest of the party could even sit down he declared, "Let me tell you, I think *Munchausen* is the most wonderful script I've ever read."

"Follow that!" Eberts thought, even as he tried to choke back his delight. It looked like they were home free at their very first port of call. It seemed that Puttnam had left his second-in-command to either pick up or drop the project. The group hoped Picker's enthusiasm would prove contagious.

The next meeting on their schedule was across the Burbank Studio lot with Terry Semel at Warner Brothers. Eberts had a "first look" deal in exchange for covering Allied's overhead. The forthright Semel immediately cut to the heart of the matter. "Twenty-five million dollars," he pondered. "Terry Gilliam. No, it's not our type of picture. I don't like period pictures *of this kind*."

Gilliam's reaction was, "What the hell does he mean, *of this kind?*" His ruffled feathers were smoothed by Eberts as they drove away. "There's nothing worse than being endlessly dangled," he suggested. "Terry Semel's always the same; he comes right to the point. It's a quality I've always deeply appreciated in him."

A few blocks away at Disney's Touchstone Pictures on Buena Vista Boulevard, Jeffrey Katzenberg declined even to meet the party, maintaining that his company was not in a position even to discuss a $25 million picture. At the time *Who Framed Roger Rabbit?* was in production and reportedly already over budget. Ned Tanen at Paramount agreed to a meeting, but also found the price tag too steep. At M-G-M Alan Ladd Jr., who had his own *Roger Rabbit* in the wings in the shape of *Willow,* mentioned that he had a "problem with the script," and the project was far too expensive as well.

The group next visited Tri-Star, Columbia's sister company under the Coca-Cola umbrella, where the $12 million deal Milchan had originally negotiated was still theoretically on the table. Or was it? Eberts did the "serious speech" as a prelude to Gilliam's "floor show" of the pastel artistry of Dante Ferretti's sketches and models. "It was like going into one lion's den after another," Gilliam said, with an involuntary shudder. "I don't trust these people, I don't know what it is they want. And whatever it is, I don't know how to sell it!"

David Matalon, the blandly smiling head of production at Tri-Star, seemed unmoved by the presentation. So did producer Keith Barish, whom he had asked to join them. "A very cold fish," was Eberts' impression of Barish. Gilliam went further. "He looked to me like a man composed of razor blades. I actually got him to laugh at one point, which I thought was a major achievement. But I'm very wary of getting involved with guys like that."

Far from being ill at ease during the Universal meeting, Gilliam felt that the whole thing was just too outrageous. Thomas Pollock, an entertainment attorney and another longtime friend of Eberts, had taken over the company's movie operation since the battle between Sidney Sheinberg and Gilliam over handling of *Brazil.* Sheinberg was still around as president and chief operating officer of Universal's corporate parent MCA. "Oh, we're all professionals here," Pollock joked, in a vain attempt to lighten the atmosphere. *"Sure we are!"*

was Gilliam's unspoken reaction. Perhaps predictably, no deal was struck.

For Schuhly the Hollywood trip won him some new introductions, as well as the opportunity to renew some old acquaintances including Dino De Laurentiis. "Sell all this shit and come join me here in Los Angeles," Dino told him. "I will make you big and famous and rich — because I like you!" Schuhly decided not to take up the offer, a smart move since a year later De Laurentiis' DEG went bankrupt.

Eberts and his little band were surprised when 20th Century-Fox's Scott Rudin called out of the blue to suggest a meeting. "What's the point?" was the question on everyone's mind, knowing the studio had abandoned the project. Rudin insisted that they had unfinished business to discuss and invited them to lunch at Fox's commissary. While Abbott's impression of young Rudin was of a very earnest rabbinical student, matters soon took on a decidedly secular tone as the bill for their modest lunch was produced. "Two years ago we paid Arnon Milchan $150,000 to develop *Munchausen*," Rudin informed the astonished party. "We've no objection to you guys going elsewhere with it, but naturally we'd like our money back."

Gilliam could scarcely believe his ears. He was supposed to have been Milchan's partner, yet this was the first he had heard of any $150,000 payment from Fox. His mind raced back to the incredible difficulties that Charles McKeown had experienced in getting money out of Milchan to develop *Munchausen*, the eventual grudging part payment by Milchan out of *Brazil* funds, then finally having to pay McKeown out of his own pocket to finish the script.

"That sure was an expensive lunch," Eberts muttered, as he, Schuhly, Abbott and Gilliam emerged into the still blinding late afternoon sunshine of Pico Boulevard.

Stunned as he was, Gilliam was determined to take Milchan to task. He had a dinner date that very evening with Milchan, along with Schuhly, actor Christophe Lambert and several other guests, at an Italian restaurant in Malibu. Gilliam kept himself in check throughout the meal, awaiting the right opportunity. Schuhly knew what was in the cards and kept looking over the dinner table and smiling conspiratorially, as if enjoying a private joke. Finally, as the party was leaving the restaurant, and the rest of the group reached the door, Gilliam and Milchan trailed behind.

"By the way," Gilliam said quietly, "Scott Rudin wants the $150,000 back Fox paid you."

In an instant the smile was wiped off Milchan's face. The veins on his neck began to bulge. His face, says Gilliam, turned purple with rage. For a moment Gilliam imagined he was watching outtakes from a Rick Baker remake of *Dr. Jekyll and Mr. Hyde*. He had seen nothing like Milchan's reaction outside of a movie. The guests froze at the door. It was as if the very ions in the atmosphere had changed. "You think you're *so smart*, Terry," Milchan finally blurted out. "You think you know everything." Then he stormed past everyone and out into the night.

Gilliam has not spoken to Milchan since. "I still don't understand him," he said. "We had a partnership. He'd been demanding ridiculous things from Charles and not paying him, and all the time he'd quietly pocketed Fox's money. Arnon can be great, but when it comes to money there's something — I don't know — bits just don't seem to connect."

• • •

Meanwhile Puttnam expressed serious reservations about a Columbia commitment. He was not prepared to give a final cut to Gilliam. In terms of the script, the relationship between the Baron and some of the other characters, young Sally in particular, didn't strike Puttnam as dynamic enough. And whom was the picture for, anyway? Kids or adults? For a $25 million adventure, he pointed out, the answer had better be both. Then there was the *overriding* question: could the movie be made, as scripted, for $25 million?

The *Munchausen* party's visit to Los Angeles ended with a rendezvous at David Puttnam's Coldwater Canyon home above Studio City. Gilliam was disconsolate, unable to deal wth Puttnam, whom he could see was less than fully behind the project. Only Picker's enthusiasm was keeping *Munchausen* alive. There were faint, chilling echoes of Universal and Sheinberg in Puttnam's attitude. If Puttnam went ahead, he would demand control over *Munchausen*. In that event, the whole deal with Columbia was about to unravel.

Under the impression he was giving *Hollywood Reporter* an "off-the-record interview," Gilliam waxed lyrical over drinks at the Chateau Marmont. He contrasted the small budget films Puttnam had professed he would make at Columbia with the studio's "intention" to back *Baron Munchausen*. "What we are doing is very perverse," Gilliam explained, unaware that every syllable would be reported the following day, "because the mood in Hollywood, particularly with David's arrival, is to make everything controllable. We're taking the *opposite* tack. This is flamboyance, big budget, *spectacle*. But the advantage we have is that come 1988 there will be all these little films around and then this *thing, Munchausen,* will come along!"

The repercussion from Columbia, and a clearly furious David Puttnam, was immediate. "We have no knowledge of any deal on *Munchausen* at this time," was the studio's terse announcement.

CHAPTER FOUR

Munchausen was meant to be a light, fantastic comedy. This is something that leans more to Italy than to a garage in London, where Terry made Brazil. I had to promise Picker and Puttnam not to produce a heavy, dark film with the Baron becoming Freud. If you want to do an auteur's film, then you must do it for $3 million, and maybe we're back in that garage in London!

—Thomas Schuhly

We should all look at Disney's Return to Oz before too long, just to see why it didn't work for the modern public. It might contain a message.

—David Puttnam

Puttnam nonetheless followed through, and sent a detailed analysis of the script to Jake Eberts a few weeks later. The first reel of any movie is potentially the most confusing, he pointed out. The first fourteen pages of the *Munchausen* script would be a special challenge to assimilate. He acknowledged the enormous richness in the script, comparing it with *Alice in Wonderland, Gulliver's Travels, The Wizard of Oz*, George Melies and Jules Verne, as well as Raspe and Doré. But there was, in his opinion, an overabundance of riches. "All good ideas, but too many of them, so that the story line wobbles and wanders into too many cul-de-sacs." Puttnam, in a 16-page plot summary, detailed the scenes he disputed. The Baron's horse, Bucephalus, for example, which had been cut in half by a hastily lowered portcullis, was shown with the front half grazing contentedly in a field before being stitched to its rear quarters by a peasant. "Too much embroidery," Puttnam inadvertently punned. With any deal from Columbia dependent on a sympathetic response to his "suggestions," this scene and others was unceremoniously ditched.

• • •

While waiting for Columbia to make up its corporate mind, Schuhly claims to have received a barrage of gypsy's warnings, centering on one T. Gilliam, Esq. The *Brazil* shooting, he was told, had gone on for nine solid, arduous and often acrimonious months. "Someone older and wiser than me would not have gone ahead," he told me in his offices at Cinecitta, "but I had to get *The Baron* off the ground. I wanted to surround Terry with first-class people. My idea of taking the movie to Rome was to secure the film under my wing. Columbia said they were very happy with the choice of Italy. We were all aware that for the figure we were discussing, we had to produce a light film for a big audience. I'm not Italian myself, so there was no selfish reason for me to choose Italy, except perhaps that I love the country, I'm based at Cinecitta and I'm married to an Italian girl. But that apart — "

As Columbia deliberated, Jake Eberts had his own reasons to reflect on Allied's investment in the Baron. His company's deal was to have their investment repaid with interest at the start of principal photography, and to get profit points in the finished picture. If the movie failed to get the green light, however, Allied stood to lose every penny.

"I have not expressed astonishment at how many of the effects indicated in the script will be obtained," Puttnam noted in the letter attached to his script comments. His next sentence was suspiciously ecclesiastical in tone. "One simply has to assume they will be achieved as described, so an act of faith is required."

The crunch, and the explanation for the biblical approach, came in the eventual terms of the deal Puttnam offered. On Columbia's behalf, he felt emboldened to invest only to a limited extent in the faith department. Where Eberts had asked for the movie to be made as an in-house Columbia picture, Puttnam was prepared only to look at a "negative pickup" arrangement. This boiled down to, "You make the movie independently, then the studio will guarantee to buy it from you, *at a fixed price.*" This turned out to be $11.5 million for worldwide theatrical and television rights, excluding Italy and Germany.

With an $8 million video top-up from Vestron Pictures confirmed, the total Eberts had achieved from all sources was $22.5 million: $2.5 million less than his target. There was yet another snag to Puttnam's deal. "We want U.S. video rights for our partnership company, RCA/Columbia," he told Eberts. "We'll pay you the same as you're talking at Vestron — $8 million — but we want the two deals *crossed.*" Eberts felt he was in trouble on all fronts.

First, could they live with the $2.5 million shortfall?

Second, at the last moment, he had withdrawn from a similar video deal with Vestron on *The Name of the Rose.* Now, going back to them at this advanced stage with a similar letdown on *Munchausen* would be a real embarrassment.

Third, Columbia's proposed "crossing" clause meant that if the theatrical release of *Munchausen* was a loser, the money could be recouped from the RCA/Columbia video side. "Over my dead body," Eberts vowed.

Fourth, under the terms of a "negative pick-up", a bank loan would have to be obtained to fund the day-by-day production costs of the movie. Columbia's guarantee was only the first part of the essential collateral required; the second was the procurement of a completion guarantor's services. Their bond would ensure that a *finished* picture would be delivered to Columbia, no matter what eventualities might arise.

The first bullet was bitten by Gilliam and Schuhly, who agreed that if this was the best, indeed, the *only* deal on the table, they would simply have to cut their cloth accordingly and live with $22.5 million. Unless, of course, Eberts could squeeze a little more out of the studio. The second bullet Eberts had to bite on his own. It meant facing the prospect of being banished forever from Vestron's portals, but it was either that or good-bye, Columbia. The third bullet he was *not* prepared to bite. Theatrical and video rights *must* remain uncrossed, Columbia was told, or there was no deal.

The condition that accompanied the "negative pick-up" arrangement was also tough to accept. The bank interest charges, plus the fee and contingency allowance which a completion guarantor would demand (none of which *Munchausen* would have had to bear had it been adopted by Columbia) would now deplete an already diminished budget.

Puttnam had astutely ensured that Columbia would not be responsible for any budget overages of the movie. *Heaven's Gate* had gone $30 million over its original $11.6 million budget and directly resulted in the sale of the United Artists studio by Transamerica. If another tragedy of similar proportions should develop with *Baron Munchausen*, it would be a *Heaven's Gate* for the completion guarantor, *not* the studio. With two previous crippling blows — from *Ishtar* and *Leonard Part VI* — Columbia, and Puttnam, were in no mood to make it three in a row.

There was also the delicate matter, especially in light of Gilliam's epic tussle with Sheinberg at Universal, over who would have the final cut. A compromise was ingeniously devised by Puttnam. Gilliam had told Puttnam that he was making the picture "for my grandfather, father, and daughters, Amy and Holly." He had unwittingly sprung his own trap. "Fine," said Puttnam, "then you'll be happy to go with the preview verdict of an all-age audience. If your first cut gets awarded 55 percent or more of the top ratings at two research screenings, we'll go with that. If not, the studio will have the right of final cut. Contractually we'll have it anyway, but I'll make up a side letter that'll spell out your rights."

When the contract was eventually drafted, Gilliam bemusedly tried to absorb the formal wording, which basically gave him the traditional two chances at the cherished final cut: slim, and none:

"If, using a questionnaire with a six point scale (a) less than fifty-five percent (55%) of the audience surveyed at such screening rate the Picture in the top two categories (currently 'Excellent' and 'Extremely Good') or less than forty-five percent (45%) of the audience surveyed rate the Picture as 'Recommended Definitely,' Columbia shall continue to have final cutting authority on the Picture, or (b) fifty five percent (55%) or more of the audience rates the picture in the top two categories and not less than forty five percent (45%) of the audience surveyed rate the Picture as 'Recommended Definitely,' notwithstanding anything to the contrary contained in the Agreement, Terry Gilliam shall have final cutting authority on the Picture for its initial theatrical release in the United states of America.

"Notwithstanding anything in this Letter Agreement to the contrary, if Columbia objects to or requests changes in certain specified scenes included in the Picture as delivered by Prominent Features, the questionnaire utilized at the screening shall also survey the reaction of the audience to such scene or scenes and with respect to each scene so surveyed if a statistically significant number of the audience surveyed (i) 'like' such a scene, the scene shall remain in the Picture or (ii) 'dislike' such scene, the scene shall be changed in accordance with Columbia's instructions."

A longtime advocate of audience surveys, Puttnam had effectively covered his tracks in legal gobbledegook. For Gilliam, it was the most personal bullet of them all. "At the end of the day, when all the dust settles, there's no doubt that we'll strike a deal with Columbia," Eberts assured his team. "It might not be the one we wanted, but there'll be a deal. If we're to have any chance of making our July start, we have to proceed on that assumption and start pre-production immediately." Eberts' practical contribution to making sure this happened was to increase Allied's contribution to $850,000.

● ● ●

After seeing the sterling work both men had executed on *Brazil*, Gilliam wanted Jim Acheson as costume designer on *Munchausen*, and Roger Pratt for cinematographer. He was aware of the practical budgetary problems in bringing them from London to Rome; since their stay would cost a fortune in hotels and "per diems." Schuhly breezily dismissed the problem. "A drop in the bucket," Gilliam was assured, "compared to the enormous savings we'll make by shooting in Italy."

Schuhly's "anything you want" assurances soon began to sound like a sick joke. Frustration rapidly set in when virtually none of the sets and models Gilliam asked for appeared on their due dates. His sketch of a cannon was a case in point. It took a month to become a tiny scale model. A month later, instead of the full-size version being produced, Cinecitta wheeled out an almost identical, albeit slightly enlarged, scale model.

Gilliam is the first to admit that some designs had to be changed when they were ready. This was often the result of the time lag between conception and execution, the norm on any large-scale production where the creative concept requires physical translation. *Munchausen* was, after all, at the opposite end of the scale from domestic or courtroom dramas, with their conventional sets. Even so, each delivery promise seemed made only to be broken.

Another cause of increasing concern was Schuhly's budget breakdown. His estimates were always on the brink of being produced, but they seldom made it to the finish line. And the individual costings that were eventually produced worried Gilliam.

English special effects wizard, Richard Conway, a soft-spoken individual who has managed to weather his way through a series of tough movie assignments including Gilliam's *Brazil*, got his first taste of the way events were likely to proceed when he wanted to build a scaffolding tower 20 feet square and between 20 and 30 feet high. Cinecitta's technicians demanded a special drawing for their construction department. When this was produced, the tower was costed out at almost $7,500. Conway was staggered at the estimate and sent the drawing to England. Back came a quote for $1,400, which included the construction, dismantling and hire of the scaffolding for the period required.

Conway said he came across numerous examples of individuals being invited to add fictitious extras to bills and was even, on several occasions, asked personally to join in the scam. Beyond what he saw as rampant corruption, Conway's concern was how this would affect

Gilliam. "None of them had any idea back then what Terry's like," he assured me. "He's a *tornado*. If he hasn't got a strong structure around him things just fly off and big gaps appear. It was bound to happen, and happen it did."

Dante Ferretti spent weeks working on set designs on the assumption that everything was being shot in the relatively controlled environment of Cinecitta. After producing elaborate models for costing purposes, various alternative locations around Rome were suggested by Schuhly.

Applications for permission to shoot at Villa D'Este and Villa Adriana were made to the Ministry of Arts. "Dante kept designing and redesigning sets while we waited for 'yes' or 'no' on Schuhly's locations," said Gilliam. "Jim Acheson began work on the costumes, Irene Lamb on the casting in England and Marjorie Simkin in the States. Jake Eberts and Thomas Schuhly were *still* negotiating with Columbia and trying to push the deal forward so we could start in July as scheduled. When I asked Thomas about the budget, which I did constantly, it was always 'being worked on,' but there was 'no problem.' "

The Ministry of Arts gave the unit's applications short shrift. In no way, it seemed, were they anxious to have their Eternal City redesigned, whether free of charge or not. "Several substantial changes would have been necessary," Ferretti concedes. "We found a nice place in the Appian Way where we wanted to film the battlement scenes. Again they refused to consider the rebuilding we proposed." With time and money rapidly slipping away, it was back to Cinecitta and the drawing board.

Apart from the embarrassment of *Hollywood Reporter*'s premature announcement of the movie as a Columbia picture — thought by many to be the reason for its subsequent downgrading to a negative pick-up on Puttnam's slate — another aspect that rankled was Schuhly's deal for German rights that he had negotiated with Bernd Eichinger. Puttnam called Eichinger personally, telling him "We're negotiating for *Munchausen* but we want it for the world; otherwise there's no deal. You'll have to give it up."

"My dear David," replied Eichinger, "with all due respect, you can't say that. Neue Constantin has a signed deal with the producer."

"Surely you wouldn't want to prejudice their chances of getting a deal at Columbia?"

"That would be the last thing I'd want to do, but a deal's a deal. Maybe we can find another way around this — "

The eventual, simplistic version of the agreement that was struck was for Eichinger to retain German distribution rights to *Munchausen* as a sub-distributor of Columbia, while Puttnam agreed in exchange to pick up Doris Dorrie's new "talking prick" production, *Me and Him*, from Neue Constantin.

CHAPTER FIVE

*When Schuhly got us into Italy by telling us
how much money we'd save, I assumed that
he meant doing everything 'straight.'*
                                   —Steve Abbott

*The problem with movies is that you're in
with the most bizarre group of people.*
                                   —Terry Gilliam

As late as Easter weekend, the deal with Columbia was far from
complete. Eberts was still trying desperately to increase Columbia's
total contribution, as well as to avoid the dreaded "crossing" clause.
The studio's negotiating tactics were simple: "We cannot commit
beyond this amount. And the rights *must* remain crossed." A
Columbia executive phoned Eberts in London on Good Friday with a
real shock-horror: "The deal's off." By Monday, however, after some
blunt talking on both sides, they were back on track. It was the end of
April before the deal was confirmed, and the end of May before it was
signed.

Columbia had increased its offer by $1 million to $12.5 million ; in return the $8 million Vestron video deal was transferred to RCA/ Columbia as Puttnam had requested. Eberts could still boast the achievement of two key conditions. First, the Munchausen Partnership was to enjoy an unusually high 60 percent of the film's eventual profits, rather than the standard 50/50 split with Columbia. Second, in a rare, hard-won concession, theatrical and video remained uncrossed.

The unit had to move fast, for the funds intended for preproduction were all but gone. In view of the disorganization at Cinecitta, a July start was now out of the question. With September 7 pencilled in instead, Eberts began to conduct talks with banks for production funds, and invited quotes from completion guarantors.

The Long Term Credit Bank of Japan offered the lowest interest rates. Inexperienced with movie deals as they were, they had loaned money to the industry before through their subsidiary, the Bank of California. Now they were looking for a more direct involvement in movies.

A Los Angeles-based bonding company, Film Finances, Inc., run by expatriate Englishman Richard Soames, took on the mantle of completion guarantor. Film Finances had been Gilliam's completion guarantor back in 1976 on *Jabberwocky*. Alarm bells went off at the mention of Film Finances. When he had gone all of £60,000 over budget, Film Finances had fired him, his producer and editor; all three were re-hired on the same day to finish the film. Now, apart from their $1 million fee for *Munchausen*, Film Finances was insisting on a $2 million contingency fund being set aside from the budget to cover "unforeseen expenses."

Between Columbia and Film Finances, funds from the movie had shrunk from the original $25 million requested — first to $22.5 million with Columbia's first offer, then up to $23.5 million with their second. And with Film Finances' fee and contingency allowance deducted, the net haul was only $20.5 million.

Gilliam's only yardstick in the budgetary debate was *Time Bandits* which he turned out for $5 million in 1980, and *Brazil*, costing $13.5 million in 1984. Based on Schuhly's repeated claims that shooting in Rome would be forty percent cheaper than in

England, he anticipated no problem in bringing *Munchausen* in for the revised target.

Since Gilliam was not yet fully resident in Rome, he had never become properly acquainted with Robert Coca, the film's first production supervisor. To this day, Gilliam remains unsure why Schuhly fired him. Pre-production was indeed reeling in chaos, and clearly this might be reason enough. But was it Coca's fault or had he been hamstrung by inadequate financial support? With no Columbia money on the table, Schuhly had of necessity obtained commitments from many firms, both inside and outside of Cinecitta, with the bare minimum of cash changing hands and very little in writing. For whatever reason, Coca would be only the first of *Baron Munchausen*'s many "fallen" warriors.

To replace him, Schuhly turned to American Robert Gordon Edwards, a German resident with whom he had worked on *Never Ending Story*. With his wild-man handlebar moustache and shoulder-length hair, Edwards resembled an extra straight from the set of *Annie Get Your Gun*. Surprisingly, his first pronouncement was that *Baron Munchausen* was seriously under-budgeted. When Schuhly's answer was to stoutly defend his figures, the one-note response quickly engendered an insidious, "Fine, but don't hold *us* responsible." The "We *told* you" attitude soon permeated the entire production staff. Gilliam found himself hard pressed to discern any improvement dating from Edwards' appointment, especially since his major contribution was to turn down the English crew he wanted. In an effort to coax cinematographer Roger Pratt into joining him, Gilliam brought Pratt to Rome for the weekend. Negotiations fell apart when Edwards coolly informed Pratt that he would be unable to bring his right-hand man with him. Costume designer Jim Acheson, who had already started work, was next to be snubbed.

Gilliam began to feel a disturbing sense of isolation. Keen as he was to film in Rome, he had assumed he would have his key English crew members aboard. Now it looked as if Schuhly's plan was to get rid of them completely, either directly or through Edwards. Small wonder he had been so comfortable about the "per diems" problem! "I *needed* these people," Gilliam protested, "and you assured me going into this thing that we could afford to bring my team. Suddenly there's no team around me."

From his Prominent Features headquarters in London Steve Abbott could see Schuhly's *modus operandi* from a distance, and was convinced that Gilliam's isolation had been deliberately orchestrated. Abbott's intuitive reservations re-emerged with a vengeance as he saw glimmerings of what he considered the producer's master plan to keep costs down on *Munchausen*. To him, Prominent's "hands-on" days were now numbered. "He wanted to do business," Abbott told me, "in a way I could never condone as a professional. I could never have sanctioned the payment methods he proposed when engaging people in Italy. Suddenly it became all too clear how he proposed to save up to forty percent of the costs of shooting the film in England. The final straw as far as I was concerned came when he turned around and said scornfully, 'If you want to do everything *properly* and *by the book*, then it's going to cost you *more* in Italy than it would in England.' Terry may or may not criticize Prominent Features from shrinking back from this arrangement, as I immediately did. That's up to him. Yes, we were the senior partner, but not in terms of the Italian production. Prominent wasn't a party to that aspect at all; we had no control over what was happening there."

The legal position was that Prominent Features/Munchausen had a co-production deal with Schuhly's Laura Films. As the rights were created by Laura, they were to be passed on to Prominent, who would in turn deliver the film to Columbia. Prominent had direct contracts for the underlying rights, and for the script with Gilliam and McKeown, as well as Gilliam's deal as director and Schuhly's as producer. The original intention had been for Prominent to be the production company in the post-production phase. "What's amusing," Abbott ruefully recalled, "is that at our first meeting, when Thomas was pushing to get himself in, he told us, 'Watch this Milchan guy, he doesn't pay our taxes!'"

Schuhly smiled enigmatically at Abbott's recollection, then laughed out loud, amidst a welter of flying cigarette butts. "When I told him that from time to time in this business you have to *buy* a deal, he nearly fainted! I always had to juggle between Steve and Anne James, his partner. Her main problem was not to sign away her house as security! This is where I'm *different*. I was brought up by

Fassbinder, who taught me to take the risk and conceal my different faces. My major aim was to get the film off the ground no matter what. Once the ship was sailing, *then* I could influence it. Ya?"

"I understand why Steve backed off," admits Gilliam, "but I wasn't there to change the system. Money in movies comes from all different sources and to me the end often justifies the means. The notion that just because it's corporate money it's clean is bullshit. I don't know how you take a moral ground on these kinds of things. For all Arnon's faults, I don't think his money was any more tainted than from any other source. I probably don't buy Outspan oranges or Cape apples if I can help it, but I don't spend my whole life thinking about it. I *would* draw the line at money coming from drugs; that would be unacceptable, but if you're dealing in art in Italy, the money's at least going to the people who are doing the work. I don't, in the end, know how to justify the new world we live in."

• • •

At the height of set construction Dante Ferretti had no fewer than 100 carpenters working under his supervision, although they were directly employed by Cinecitta. Dante can look incredibly quizzical, a bit like a bemused gnome. "Does that sound like a lot?" he asked me. "Well, you have to remember this was a *big* film, we were building for a grand total of 67 sets!"

The rabbit Schuhly pulled out of his hat to replace Roger Pratt was an indisputable class Italian act. Enter: Giuseppe Rotunno, one of the top cameramen in the world, and one of the few non-Americans to be a member of ASC. Rotunno began his career at the age of 15 as a photo lab technician at Cinecitta.

He made his first contact on American productions as lighting cameraman on the second unit of Henry King's *Prince of Foxes*. In 1952 he was appointed director of photography on Dino Risi's *Bread, Love And . . ..* He went on to photograph *Senso* for Visconti in sumptuous color, then won worldwide acclaim for his magnificent monochrome photography on *White Nights*. Since then he has worked with Visconti on several other films, including *Rocco and His Brothers* and *The Leopard*, together with Lina Wertmuller, Monte Hellman, Martin Ritt, Vittorio De Sica and Stanley Kramer; for John Huston on Dino De Laurentiis' *The Bible . . . In the Beginning*; for

Fellini on *Satyricon, Roma, Amarcord, Casanova, Orchestra Rehearsal, City of Women* and *Juliet of the Spirits;* for Robert Altman on *Popeye;* for Alan J. Pakula on *Rollover;* for Fred Zinnemann on *Five Days One Summer;* and for Mike Nichols on *Carnal Knowledge.* For his work on Bob Fosse's *All That Jazz* he was nominated for an Academy Award. Fair to say, then, that Rotunno knows his way around a camera!

Gilliam was deeply impressed, surprised and assured by the Italian's grave, modest demeanor when they met. A short, handsome man in his mid-sixties, with a head full of neatly combed greying hair and a slightly anxious, apprehensive expression on his otherwise passive features, Rotunno was equally impressed by Gilliam.

"I look forward to working with you, Giuseppe," Gilliam told him. The reply came in charming broken English. "And for me too, Terry. Please, you call me Peppino. Everybody else do this."

As with Dante Ferretti, it seemed that Gilliam had found another soul mate. Schuhly had substituted for the English contingent in the best tradition of Milchan's "putting people together." He had acted fully in line with his declared intention to surround Gilliam with first-class people.

CHAPTER SIX

As far as I was concerned the organization of the production was ratshit from the start. Thomas constantly assured me the way you worked in Italy was different. You saw nothing at first, then it all happened.

—Terry Gilliam

All publicity is good, as long as they spell your name right.

—Thomas Schuhly

As the weeks passed, Gilliam felt more and more detached from the production side of *Munchausen*. He had previously always worked within clearly defined limits, but the Italian approach was not to impose any limits. As far as the Italians were concerned, he was "Il Maestro," for whom everything was possible. Schuhly was announcing to the world the advent of the biggest film in Europe since *Cleopatra*. The Italians began to smell money a mile off. Although Schuhly was advised to keep quiet, there was no holding him down. To the local press *Munchausen* became "Un Kolossal."

With the prospect of Rome locations now abandoned and time running out, Schuhly decided that certain scenes should be shot in Spain. He wanted Almeria for the beach location, then the ruined city of Belchite, which had been levelled during the Spanish Civil War siege, and which Dante Ferretti remembered already had an unused set from a previous film. Then Robert Edwards was dispatched to look over the Alhambra where several other films had already been made. "Yes, we *can* use the site," he reported back, "but we *can't* use lights or smoke. And we *can't* stop any of the public walking anywhere. Nor can we put any film equipment on the floor, not even a tripod . . ."

Special effects expert Richard Conway took in Gilliam's pained reaction to this litany as he mentally ticked off the scenes they had hoped to capture on the site: Berthold's running-man stunts, charging horses and exploding cannon. Gilliam felt like weeping. Apart from being extraordinarily expensive, much precious time had been wasted on the abortive expedition. Why hadn't Edwards discovered these restrictions earlier? It was back to Cinecitta to redesign yet again.

Schuhly began to absent himself from Cinecitta for long periods, intent on pursuing his dream of casting Marlon Brando as Vulcan. Gilliam accompanied him on one trip to Los Angeles and was told by Brando's agent, Jay Kanter, that a meeting had been set up with The Great One at the Chateau Marmont Hotel, where Gilliam and Schuhly were both staying.

On the appointed day, Schuhly and Kanter anxiously stood guard at the hotel's main entrance just off Sunset Boulevard. Brando arrived at the entrance on Sunset itself and made his way straight to the desk, announcing that he was there to see "Terry Gilliam and his party."

Gilliam was upstairs reading a book, affecting tremendous cool, when the phone rang. "Mr. Brando is downstairs to see you," the clerk at reception whispered in suitably reverential tones. Gilliam gulped, "Send him up to my room."

In Brando came, a huge man wearing a lightweight linen suit that seemed to go on forever. The only subject he wanted to talk about at first was English houses. Then he switched to his "awful experience" with Charlie Chaplin and Sophia Loren while making *Countess from*

Hong Kong. "Sophia and I loathed each other," Brando confided. "One day I bet her she couldn't touch her toes and lay both hands flat on the ground, which I could. You don't believe me, Terry? Watch."

To Gilliam's astonishment Brando proceeded to demonstrate the feat, and with the greatest of ease. The show over, Brando grinned broadly and resumed his tale. "Well, she took the bait and bent over. Quick as a flash I grabbed her from behind and began banging her ass."

When Gilliam stopped laughing at the mental image conjured up, he remembered that Schuhly and Kanter were still pacing around outside. "Christ, Marlon," he exclaimed. "Let me call them up. They'll be going crazy down there."

Schuhly's initial aggravation at what had happened soon melted into obsequiousness in front of his idol. "Let's go down to my room now, Marlon," he suggested, with a final sideways glare at Gilliam. "I've laid on a buffet for you."

At the mere mention of food, Brando's eyes lit up. Soon he was making an excellent attempt at demolishing the fine spread. Schuhly's own brand of small talk proved initially successful, since Brando, an ex-boxer himself, seemed to enjoy hearing of Schuhly's college prowess in the sport. It was Kanter who finally suggested they talk about the movie and the role they had in mind for his client. Brando's final word was: "Let me think about it."

For the next few days Gilliam watched as Schuhly desperately tried to pin Brando down. Countless calls were made but none were returned. Gilliam was so incensed that he himself left a message on Brando's answering machine, the gist of which was: "Give Thomas an answer, one way or another. You know he's in awe of you, but that's no excuse for you to bully the guy. You'd be terrific as Vulcan, but we need an answer." He was unrepentant when he met Brando at a party the following night. Brando had clearly listened to the message and was decidedly cool — as well as totally noncommittal.

Gilliam was preparing for bed that evening when Schuhly burst into his room. "Brando's prepared to talk for $3 million," he declared, beside himself with excitement. "But I think I can get him down to $1 million! You know how crazy he is to make his pet project, the Indian rights movie? I've offered to set it up with Italian money if he plays Vulcan."

Gilliam looked at Schuhly. "He's jerking you around," he replied. "Tell him if he's really serious, he'll do *Munchausen* for nothing and give *all* the money to the Indians."

By the end of May Schuhly was convinced Brando would do it for $1 million. He even telexed his confidence to David Puttnam, with whom he had explored the possibility of extra money if the star said, yes. Gilliam was present when the almost inevitable telex arrived from Brando, saying that he had decided to pass on the project after all. Schuhly was crushed by the news.

Returning to the set in Italy, Gilliam continued to regard Robert Edwards as a woefully ineffective production supervisor. The natural evolution of sketches to models to full-size sets was simply not happening. The suspicion was that, like Coca before him, he was being hamstrung by lack of money, even though Columbia had advanced $1 million in advance of signed contracts. Edwards was also clearly unwell. Although he had come on all tough and strong it turned out he had recently undergone a major operation for cancer. Schuhly continued to insist, however, that Edwards would surprise them all in the end.

The appointment of Don French, a wiry, deep-voiced Englishman, as Gilliam's First Assistant Director, brought fresh hope. Although the direct line of responsibility for the production side was still first with Schuhly, then Edwards, French would be another presence. "Don should be perfectly at home here," was the standing joke. "He knows all about disasters. He was on *Ishtar*." For that matter, so was Lee Cleary, the Second Assistant Director French brought with him.

As French attempted to tackle the multitude of problems that preceded his appointment, he and Gilliam gravitated to each other as fellow sufferers in the chaos. Both men were alarmed that the usual sequence of events which move a production forward was not being followed. They also found many of the Italians extremely difficult to deal with — at times canny, clever and devious; yet also capable of loyalty and dedication. If only they could tap into these latter qualities . . .

Gilliam admits to sweeping many questionable issues under the carpet, allowing Schuhly full power to make the equation work. He had rationalized that by going to Italy and placing himself completely in Schuhly's hands, he could absolve himself of responsibility for the nuts and bolts of the film's day-to-day organization. Once there, he knew he would be unable to second-guess Schuhly. All he could say was, "*This* is wrong, it isn't *working*, we need *this*, we need *that*," and hope that Schuhly would make it happen. After all, wasn't Schuhly, by his own account, the archetypal strong producer, the veritable Rambo of the movies?

Gilliam still felt deep down that he could trust Schuhly and that in the long run everything he had promised would appear. As the weeks passed, however, he looked in vain for any sign that of the gap narrowing between Schuhly's promises and their delivery. Schuhly kept claiming he was in charge of the day-to-day details, but there was little sign of it, and he seemed totally unprepared to delegate. There was no one carrying out the vital functions to make the production come together. Edwards was a lost cause, and if French or anyone else appeared to overstep their authority, Schuhly seemed to take a perverse delight in chopping these individuals off at the feet so they were unable to compete with him. Although ostensibly trying to do everything, he was in fact achieving very little.

Gilliam watched with concern as French became increasingly frustrated with the crossed lines and misrepresentations. He was unable to reconcile the budget Schuhly had finally produced with what he saw as the schedule necessary to shoot the film. His original schedule called for twenty-five weeks, which he then agreed to melt down to twenty-one weeks, then 101 working days. Meanwhile Schuhly had led Film Finances to believe that eighteen weeks was possible — a claim Gilliam and French viewed as outrageous, especially bearing in mind the move to Spanish locations.

Because *Time Bandits* and *Brazil* had been made so cheaply, Gilliam found that people believed he could do extraordinary things. For a while, he did, too. "The problem was doing it in *Italy* with Schuhly's so-called organization," he recalled. "Thomas just kept on talking nonsense. He would never say, 'We can't do this, Terry.' It was *always*, 'I've got Dante Ferretti down from 7 million lire to 4 million lire to 2 million lire for Vulcan's dining room and we've screwed the studio charges down!' And there was always the hope that if we did go over budget, David Puttnam would come in with a little more. Dante was the only one who was behaving like a producer should at this stage, bending and twisting and doing everything to push things along, but he was getting little or no support. One of the things that drove him crazy was that he was carrying this burden on his own. Schuhly kept relying on him and Don French to solve all the problems at the studio."

While Schuhly could be extremely convincing in meetings, Charles McKeown had occasion to observe the lack of follow-through noted by Bernd Eichinger. It became increasingly evident that, despite his claimed credits and track record, Schuhly lacked the ability to push *Munchausen* along. More and more pressure fell on Gilliam, who had his own problems in terms of directing the picture without worrying about the budget and logistical details.

McKeown watched as *Munchausen* fell further and further behind its pre-production schedule. "That was the beginning of Terry's anger," he told me, "and it got worse and worse the deeper in the shit we sank."

CHAPTER SEVEN

Up until Munchausen *I'd always been very smart about Terry Gilliam films. You don't ever be in them. Go and see them in the cinema by all means — but to be in them,* fucking madness*!!*

—Eric Idle

Terry, are you serious! You're going to make a movie epic about a 75-year-old man and an 8-year old girl set in the eighteenth century! Give up now, kid!

—Mel Brooks

At the start Terry and I were standing together. Ya! Then the big waves came! Whoomp!

—Thomas Schuhly

Gilliam's ex-Monty Python partner Eric Idle had been working for some time in Hollywood turning out scripts for movies that never seemed to get made. While this had proved lucrative, it could hardly be described as creatively satisfying.

Munchausen's script had arrived at exactly the right strategic moment. Accustomed to wrestling with unfinished material, Idle was delighted by the beginning, middle and end of the Baron's complex story, as well as the intriguing way McKeown and Gilliam had chosen to tackle it. He promptly volunteered to be in the movie.

Apart from being extremely funny both on and off the screen, Idle is serious and erudite, and given to listening as much as talking. His prominent eyes, especially when he fixes his audience with a concentrated stare, his lanky body and swirling limbs, suggest elements of ex-Python John Cleese and Bloomsbury's Lytton Strachey.

"Instead of taking a small part that would just involve a few days, take the money and run," he reflected ruefully, "I volunteered to play Berthold, who's in the movie all the way through. *Major error!*"

Idle tasted Schuhly's ostentatious style when his lawyer was specially flown to Rome by the producer to settle what he calls "my little deal." "Schuhly was charm itself and took all of us, Terry included, down to the coast to have dinner. He invited Nastassja Kinski and her husband for an extra bit of show business. During the meal he went into a huddle with my lawyer and signed our agreement on a napkin. Then he pocketed the napkin, which was never seen again!

"The next night he put on another dinner. This time with Ursula Andress. Now I was on board, committed. Gilliam turns up, I turn up, Ursula turns up, my lawyer turns up. The only one who *doesn't* turn up is Schuhly, who doesn't turn up all night! It was bizarre, as though now that I was 'in the bag' my usefulness was over. That's when I realized that Schuhly was a flake."

While Idle was making this discovery, English casting director Irene Lamb selected the Baron's other three henchmen. Gilliam's co-writer Charles McKeown was set for the role of Adolphus. Diminutive Jack Purvis was to be Gustavus. Winston Dennis, of London club bouncer fame, was cast as the black giant Albrecht. Jonathan Pryce was to play Horatio Jackson, the marshall of the besieged town; Peter Jeffrey, the Sultan; ex-Python Michael Palin,

Prime Minister on the Moon; Harry Andrews, the Captain inside the Sea Monster; Bill Paterson, Henry Salt; and Alison Steadman, Daisy. U.S. casting director Marjorie Simkin chose the statuesque 17-year-old Uma Thurman for the roles of Rose and Venus.

When Gilliam asked Lamb to get the legendary, inimitable Max Wall to play a dead man cameo, the comedian turned the part down with a rheumy eye-roll. "I know I'm *old*, Irene, but are these bloody directors trying to tell me something?" It seemed that someone else had just offered him the role of a corpse in another movie!

Lamb had cast *Jabberwocky*, *Time Bandits* and *Brazil* for Gilliam. "And there was no way I wouldn't come into *Munchausen*," she bravely declared. "Even if I'd been in the middle of something else I'd have walked out of it! You know, Terry must have made less out of *Time Bandits* than most of us. I made more on my percentage than I did on the film, and I was well paid on the film. Very few people do that, especially without telling you. Nobody knew until the check showed up in the mail, and that sum came off Terry's own percentage, no one else's.

"His films always start miles before anything ever happens. As soon as he begins writing he wants to start casting. He loves actors with tremendous timing. He wants people to literally *become* his parts; he doesn't want somebody just to be *themselves*."

Lamb quickly ascertained that Gilliam would only settle for an English actor to play the Baron. Ideally he wanted a man of around 70 or so, who could adapt to the changes of age he had in mind for the Baron's various adventures. When Michael Hordern came in, he seemed like a dream come true — until Gilliam went into his description of the part. "You ride through the ranks of the Turkish troops, then run up the ramparts, cannons firing all around you —" Hordern chortled. "Look, Terry, I'm 73." A pause. "And I'd *very much* like to see 74!"

Richard Vernon, who also has a deliciously dry wit, arrived next. At the end of an hour, he suggested that Gilliam write a list of things he *wanted* him to do. Then Vernon would check the few he *could* do!

In the end, Gilliam conceded to Lamb that it would be unrealistic to expect an older man to cope with months of physically demanding work.

• • •

After her film debut in 1941 at the age of 16, titian-haired Valentina Cortese found herself in great demand as a petite, attractive ingenue during the war years and the Nazi occupation of Rome. Her English-speaking debut came in *The Glass Mountain* opposite Michael Denison and Dulcie Gray. It was followed by her acclaimed performance in *Secret People*, about which one critic wrote: "First Garbo, then Bergman — now Cortese!" When four teenagers were auditioned for the role of Valentina's younger sister in that movie, Cortese was so taken by young Audrey Hepburn that her pleading with the director resulted in Hepburn's film debut.

Now in her late sixties, the slim and elegant Cortese remains enchantingly attractive, with saucer-shaped emerald eyes set on alabaster-pale skin, with high cheekbones and a wide, generous smile. "I have never read my critics," she disarmingly confided. "If they are bad I feel as though my legs have been cut off, and if they are good, then I'm stupid enough to think I'm a star! In my career I probably disappointed my critics, because I always took more care of Valentina than I did Cortese — but this is life! From 1959 to now I have done some of the best theatre in Italy. I was more serious over my stage career than I ever was with my film career. I worked with Fellini and Zeffirelli on stage and managed to make some good films with them, too — *Juliet of the Spirits* with Federico, *Day for Night* for darling François Truffaut. What a lovely man he was and what a wonderful director!"

In June, 1987, she received a phone call from Cinecitta to say that Terry Gilliam was looking for an actress to play the Queen of the Moon and double as Violet in *Munchausen*. "I thought it would be such an experience to work with him. I *adored Brazil.* My agent showed him some photographs and Terry wanted to see me right away. He came here to Venice and we had lunch in Harry's Bar, where Hemingway used to go. We laughed so much. It was wonderful. We knew we were *simpatico* immediately. If I can echo my critic, darling, I felt, 'First Fellini, then Truffaut — now Gilliam!' Oh — I forgot about Zeffirelli, but he won't mind. I regard Franco as my naughty older brother!"

Gilliam had snared his Queen Ariadne. Meanwhile, Schuhly was stoutly maintaining that Sean Connery was *The Man Who Would Be King.*

• • •

Having gone in so many directions to cast the Baron, Gilliam was continually hearing the name of John Neville. Thirty years earlier Neville had conducted a series of earnest discussions with his friend, boozing companion and fellow Old Vic actor Richard Burton, about establishing a theatrical partnership, but Burton changed his mind and decided his future was in the cinema.

Although Neville also appeared in several movies — *Billy Budd*, *Topaz*, and what he refers to wryly as "the *other* Oscar Wilde movie," he set his course for a theatrical career. He took up management of Nottingham's Repertory Theatre. By the time he came to Gilliam's attention he was in his third season as Artistic Director of the Stratford Festival Theatre in Ontario, Canada. The soundings began with a phone call from Gilliam's colleague Pam Meager, a make-up artist and an old friend of Neville's from his days at the BBC.

Gilliam was in Canada interviewing young Sarah Polley for the role of Sally, and so followed up Meager's call with a visit to Stratford. After asking Neville to read the script, he offered him the role on the spot. Neville was overwhelmed.

Tall and distinguished, Neville looks every inch the Shakespearean thespian, albeit one stranded halfway between the worlds of the aesthete and the voluptuary. The mellifluously flowing locks of silver-grey hair, the superb sweep of the aristocratic nose and piercing blue eyes are instantly complemented by his warmly courteous demeanor.

"I thought it was an enormous act of courage for Terry to offer me the Baron. When you think how huge the movie is, and how little my name means at the box office! That's part of the enormous stubbornness in him that I would see all through shooting."

At the time of Gilliam's offer Neville was in the midst of a particularly heavy season at Stratford, with the unexpected added chore of directing a production of *Othello*. Permission was obtained from his board of directors. "They saw it as a big chance for me and felt it would reflect well on the theatre if it turned out any good. If it didn't they could disclaim me, since I was leaving at the end of the

1989 season anyway."

Neville had no idea at the time just what an extraordinary mission he was taking on. Neither, for that matter, did his agent — otherwise he would have asked for a far more substantial fee! As with many others, *Munchausen* would become for him an endless odyssey and its eventual completion a seemingly impossible dream.

Irene Lamb swiftly observed that Neville's casting wrote *finis* to the prospect of obtaining European superstars for cameo roles. Schuhly had wooed Gilliam on the prospect of the participation of his "great friends" Jean-Paul Belmondo, Gerard Depardieu and Marcello Mastroiainni. Lamb could now see that their eyes had been firmly focused on the plum role of the Baron. With the advent of Neville, it was exit stage left for all those under "cameo" consideration.

Since Lamb had been allocated a relatively modest cast budget for the movie, she was appalled to discover the salaries some of the Italian cast had negotiated. Someone walking across the screen and saying a couple of lines seemed to her to be vastly overpaid. When she questioned this, Schuhly stiffly informed her they were simply paying the "going rate." It was a rate with which Lamb was totally unfamiliar.

CHAPTER EIGHT

I told Thomas Schuhly three things: "You call me now, which is too late. The preparation you have made up to now is very poor. And the main thing is, the budget is not realistic."
—Mario Pisani

The terrible mistake we can all look back on was in not getting Arnon to sign something.
—Steve Abbott

The longer Gilliam watched Don French and Schuhly interact, the more he realized the extent of the animosity that had grown between them. French had worked with Schuhly on Neue Constantin's *Never Ending Story*. "He's all *bullshit*," he repeatedly warned Gilliam, echoing Abbott's earlier sentiments. While one side of Gilliam suspected that French was right, and every passing day produced fresh incriminatory evidence, he still clung to the increasingly tattered vestiges of faith he had in Schuhly. The friction only increased as French began to escalate his demands and insist on prompter action.

By June it became clear to everyone, Schuhly included, that Edwards was indeed a lost cause. Mario Pisani, a highly regarded Italian who had worked on many American films, seemed a logical replacement as production supervisor. An ebullient man in his fifties, distinguished by watchful owl-like eyes and a mane of graphite hair, Pisani then spent a month of precious time deciding whether or not to accept the assignment.

"Thomas explained 'the situation' to me and I told him that the first thing I had to do was make my *own* budget. I went to Spain with Dante Ferretti to see the locations, checked all the figures, then spoke with Thomas again. I told him his budget was no good for me. He replied that I could adjust the items *inside* the budget, but that the present total must remain the *limit*. At one time, in the movie *National Lampoon's European Vacation*, we were going to shoot this terrible sequence in which we had to drive a car into a real fountain in the middle of Rome.* I said why do we have to shoot here when we can shoot the same scene in the quiet little town of Frascati? So we built a fountain there and shot the scene with no permits and no problems. Unfortunately, there was nothing to suggest like this in *Munchausen*. It was established to build everything from the beginning. I declined the job, preferring to lose money rather than my reputation."

Lee Cleary was dispatched to Madrid by Don French to work with the Spanish unit. There was little work to supervise. Almost no money had been forwarded to pay for it. Due to the lack of funds, no building had begun in Almeria, although some work was underway in Belchite. The Spanish contingent, distrustful of Schuhly, was loath to commission new work without the certainty of being paid for it. Cleary sat tight for weeks on end in an office overlooking the capital's main thoroughfare.

On his return to Rome Cleary heard a similar lament. The Italians complained that they had been unpaid for several weeks. One night he saw Schuhly accosted by the crew in the bar of the Savoy

---

* "I was in that movie," Eric Idle recalled. "Come to think of it, I was in the fountain as well!"

Hotel while having a drink. "Why don't you share the money you have amongst yourselves?" he suggested. "And stop bothering me!"

● ● ●

Bernd Eichinger visited Schuhly at Cinecitta in July 1987 on his way to begin filming *Me and Him* in New York. He was hoping to disperse growing doubts and rumors which were now pouring out of the studio. When Eichinger asked to see the sets constructed so far, Schuhly took him downstairs and waved airily at a few rooms. Some spaces had pictures and sketches pinned to the walls; some contained paintings and models that had been prepared. To Eichinger, Vulcan's underground munitions factory looked tremendous, but would have been equally at home in a toy shop window. He was astonished. "Thomas," he said, "you're less than two months away from principal photography on a huge production and you have no sets ready. This is surely very worrying."

"It'll happen, Bernd," Schuhly assured him. "The money's been late in coming, but everything's organized now and ready to go."

Eichinger could see nothing either "organized" or "ready to go" and reflected once more on his friend's tenuous grip on reality. Schuhly had once told Eichinger that his hero was Alexander the Great. Like Alexander, Schuhly seemed convinced that destiny was his partner in every enterprise and that the partnership rendered him invincible. Unfortunately, Eichinger reflected, ordinary mortals with whom Schuhly was partnered had to survive in the real world. As he left Cinecitta's portals for the airport, the fears he arrived with were in no way diminished.

● ● ●

All the troubled production needed now was a further fly in the ointment. Sure enough, a particularly awkward specimen was about to emerge in the shape of 63-year old Lithuanian-born Allan Buckhantz.

Buckhantz burst on the scene in July with the assertion that he owned the remake rights to a previous *Munchausen* incarnation, the 1943 *Die Abenteuer Des Baron Munchausen*, produced by UFA. Back in 1985, Buckhantz claimed, he made a presentation to Guy McElwaine at Columbia, via Marty Baum at Creative Artists, for a remake of the German movie. The proposal had been supported by a

218-page script, more than 3,000 storyboard illustrations, a budget, and detailed financing suggestions. This was no capricious claim, but a serious proprietary challenge to the work. Noting that his submission had been made fully a year before David Puttnam took over as head of Columbia, Buckhantz was infuriated when the studio, with Puttnam now at the helm, informed his attorney in March 1987 that they had no intention of proceeding with his proposed remake. Three months later Columbia had announced its backing of Gilliam's film, adding that it was based on materials "in the public domain, and not subject to copyright protection."

Buckhantz's lawyer, Stanley Caidin, made his client's position crystal-clear: If Gilliam's completed *Munchausen* project had any material in common with the UFA version, they well might find themselves landed with a suit charging copyright infringement. Columbia, he maintained, was already violating Buckhantz's rights to the title of the movie. Furthermore, he alleged that the studio had unfairly impaired his client's chances of striking a deal elsewhere. Much was made of the fact that Buckhantz had received a producer credit on Blake Edwards' *Victor/Victoria*, a remake of another German film to which he owned the rights.

Columbia issued a crisp rebuff to Buckhantz's complaint. "We have complete faith in the integrity of the screenplay by Terry Gilliam and Charles McKeown and the production that is committed to by Terry Gilliam and Thomas Schuhly," they announced. "We look forward to distributing this movie at Christmas, 1988."

Buckhantz dispensed with his lawyer's relatively prosaic style in his own more evocative communication with David Puttnam: "*Now come on . . . !*" he wrote. "*Get off it, Puttnam!* The fact is, Columbia Pictures . . . has been deceptive, manipulative, evasive, circumventive, etc., thus maybe cunning — from Columbia's point of view — not very smart, I say . . . In the end (*Munchausen*) will be a 'legacy' both Columbia Pictures and its parent will be left to deal with long after you're gone."

Never having seen the Buckhantz version, Gilliam was startled at the time and credence Columbia's phalanx of lawyers afforded his claim. Although it was ultimately deemed "without merit" by the studio Columbia was only prepared to live with the situation if indemnities were provided by the triumvirate of Gilliam, Eberts and Schuhly through an "Errors and Omissions" policy with a division of the Fireman's Fund insurance company.

What they were *not* prepared to live with was the still-unresolved Arnon Milchan situation. With 20th Century-Fox looking to him for a refund of their $150,000, Milchan chose to dispute that he had ever relinquished the project. The *Munchausen* team was staggered by his new settlement terms.

They, not he, were obligated to repay the $150,000 to Fox, with an extra $75,000 settlement for Milchan himself, plus *profit points* in the picture! Outraged, Gilliam wrote to his ex-partner: "I hate having to listen to everyone with whom I argued saying to me, 'See, we told you so. He *is* a crook. Money is the only thing he cares about.' Certainly the way you are behaving makes a total mockery of everything we ever talked about. I think it's absolutely pathetic behavior and unworthy of you to try to get us to pay back the money you got from 20th Century-Fox, which none of us has ever seen, and certainly was never spent on *Munchausen*. It's laughable."

Laughable or not, the Munchausen Partnership ended up acquiescing to all of Milchan's demands, as well as having to settle profit points on 20th Century-Fox. "Ultimately I don't know what got to Arnon," Steve Abbott reflected, "other than his love of money. Our lawyers' advice was to hang on, since nothing had been signed with either party. If we had, we'd probably have won our case. The problem was that everyone knew the film had a momentum and money spent on it and deals signed, and basically we had a gun at our heads. It was nothing short of absolute extortion."

Even after four years of learning how Hollywood and film financing worked and the outrageous way key players were capable of behaving, the outcome deeply upset the ultraconservative Abbott. He had spent a year at Gilliam's side while he was going through the *Brazil* battle and knew that Milchan was not unique in the brand of standards and morals he observed. He still found it a shock to be the target of such tactics.

Milchan remained unrepentant, choosing to glibly overlook the original fee paid him by Fox, *and* the percentage he now owned of *Munchausen*. "I told my attorney to make the deal as painless for

Terry as possible," he claimed. "We had a signed working relationship, he and I. I had 50 percent of the movie and I didn't have to give it up. Selling 50 percent of a movie for $75,000 isn't being difficult."

• • •

Although Puttnam had advanced $1 million of Columbia's $12.5 million before final signatures were applied to the contract, Schuhly maintains he still felt it necessary to virtually set up camp at Columbia's Burbank headquarters until the deal was formally promulgated at the end of July. Only then could he get the balance of the funds from the Long Term Credit Bank of Japan. With the start of principal photography barely six weeks away, and tents threatening to fold in Spain and Italy, the schedule looked hideously tight.

The production was to initiate at Cinecitta, where interiors of the giant fish and Vulcan's ballroom and factory sequences were to be shot from September 7 to 11, and the theater scenes from September 14 to 25. Location filming at Almeria for the Turkish camp episode was set for September 28 to October 8, to be followed by a move to the besieged city in Belchite until October 27. The unit was then scheduled to return to base at Cinecitta until completion of filming on January 22, 1988.

Even with the vast number of sets and costumes, location work, complicated makeup and special effects, it looked possible that French's tightened schedule of 101 days could be achieved. This would require, however, superlative organization from the top, total harmony among the principals, and brilliant coordination on the floor. If any *one* of these three elements broke down, the result would seriously handicap French's optimism. If *all three* disintegrated, the production would descend into bedlam.

• • •

Schuhly was painfully aware of the skepticism in Rome — not least among his closest associates — that the deal would ever be consummated. According to Gilliam, the Hollywood establishment would take great pleasure in giving this super confident German producer the grand runaround. Dante Ferretti was firmly convinced that his sets would never see lights, camera or action.

Schuhly's call to say they had a "done deal" was greeted,

therefore, with a mixture of enormous relief and stunned disbelief. Nevertheless, he was not to have a hero's welcome. Schuhly's ego, now hungry for laurels and applause, was shattered by what he perceived as the ungrateful reaction to his financial tour-de-force. "The first day after I signed the deal, I was still recovering from the stress of it," he told me. "*Not one person* called me from Rome to say 'congratulations.' The bets for the failure would have been much more in favor than for success. Then, when I got back to Rome, the atmosphere was one of complete indifference. I was attacked for all the difficulties and problems that had arisen. I started pulling out that week because I cannot imagine how it is possible to work closely with somebody who doesn't appreciate the impossible odds I'd just overcome. I'm used to a different kind of behavior. Terry was not supportive. As for Jake Eberts, he just left me in the shit! *He* was in Canada, writing his fucking memoirs!

"It was *Terry's* job to motivate people while I wasn't around for all those weeks. They were just sitting around saying, 'Schuhly will get fucked in Hollywood.' As soon as I came back Terry expected me to take over production management. When I told him I was too tired, he retorted that when we had first met in England, I had said I would run the show. That was true, but when we talked about that *Arnon* had been the financier! Now *I'm* the financier, and if you're involved in that it consumes an enormous amount of energy. I know I have tremendous strength, but this was too much!"

Schuhly's image of himself as the paternalistic "Great Producer" in the mold of Dino De Laurentiis, was in for a considerable battering. He attended a few of the production meetings Don French set up. Held in Gilliam's modest ground-floor office instead of Schuhly's power center known to everyone at Cinecitta as The Black Tower, the purpose of these meetings was to bring expectations and responsibility down to earth.

Don French, in his bulldog-terrier fashion, launched an attack on Schuhly at the very first session, taking him to task for his string of broken promises. The Italian contingent left as soon as they saw their producer's face darken. "How dare you talk to me like that!" he sputtered, before going on to mount his sole line of defense: the lack of finance to date. "Besides," he taunted French, "you were on *Never*

Ending Story, weren't you, so you must know all about fucking inefficiency!"

Gilliam watched as the barb struck its intended nerve. Schuhly was fully aware that French had only been given responsibility for bringing *Never Ending Story* under control toward the end of the production, and that he had nothing to do with the movie's previous overruns. Yet it was a well-aimed salvo that deflected attention, if only for a moment, from his own purported inadequacies. When both men had calmed down, Gilliam watched Schuhly lose concentration and drift off. Clearly the producer had decided it was not his function to submit to questioning on the minutiae of production matters.

French relentlessly returned to the assault at the second meeting. Again most of the Italians filed out. Only Rotunno chose to remain. This time Schuhly was in no mood to justify himself. Flinging his chair aside, he rose to his feet and pointed at French. "If you raise your voice to me a third time," he roared, "you'll finish here — your career, *maybe even your life*! In any case you'll wind up in the hospital, because I'll knock your teeth out. Nobody, *but nobody*, talks to me that way."

For a moment French looked poised to leap across the table and tear his tormentor's head off. Instead, some degree of discretion prevailed. White-faced with anger, he stormed out. "Thomas, that was uncalled for," said Gilliam. "Don's only trying to get this mess sorted out." Schuhly raged at Gilliam, "If you don't like it, I'll kick you out of town as well. I didn't break my balls for months, sweating to get Columbia's money, to get fucked now. Don French is *bullshit*. Do we get three or four elephants? So a model is a few days late? What the fuck do I care about details like that?"

It was Rotunno's turn. "Terry, without Thomas we would not be here having this meeting," he pointed out. "The film would have been cancelled long ago."

"I wonder if that would have been such a bad thing," Gilliam questioned, wearily shaking his head.

"Look, it has not been *possible* for me to have sets built without money," Schuhly declared, calming down and slumping back into his seat. "I *know* the film is not ready to start, I haven't had any *money*. Even so, a lot of things have been done. If I hadn't kept it running and had let it stop, it would never have restarted. Believe me, I have enough experience to know this trap!"

With the meeting adjourned, Rotunno accompanied Schuhly back to his office. "You know, Thomas," he said, "Terry may never forgive you for making this film possible." As far as Schuhly was concerned, the remark was not far from the mark. He valued the psychological support he had from Rotunno, whom he considered one of the most intelligent people in the business.

With the deadline for the scheduled start of principal photography rapidly approaching, Gilliam received another nasty shock a few days after the meeting. Don French had been unusually silent and withdrawn at breakfast, and as the two of them drove to an appointment in Rome, Gilliam attempted to lighten the tone. "Which of the characters in the film are we all most like?" Gilliam asked. "Well, you're the Baron," French offered, "that's clear for a start. Only someone with enormous unputdownable optimism would ever have embarked on a project like this."

"In that case, Don," Gilliam replied, "you've got to be Sally. You're the one who pushes the Baron on, keeps him going, providing the driving force."

"Thanks," said French. "I appreciate that, Terry. But I'm sorry, I'm not going to be made Schuhly's scapegoat. In all the years I've worked in films I've never come across anything like this. I've been asked to do false budgets and underschedule the film. I can't *do* that to a crew. I hate walking out on you like this, but there's no way I can work with that *jerk*!"

Days before the scheduled start of production, Gilliam's right-hand man bailed out and handed him his letter of resignation. Exit French.

CHAPTER
NINE

Communication with Terry became more and more difficult. Every day there was some different bullshit and I just wasn't interested. He kept on complaining about the problems of communication and the difference in language. But it wasn't only my decision to shoot in Italy.

—Thomas Schuhly

Of course I was in love with the idea of Italy. And to have it much cheaper on top, as Thomas claimed! Great! What we didn't know about was the terrible inefficiency and the multitude of scams.

—Terry Gilliam

Terry Gilliam spent a fitful night after Don French's resignation; the few moments of sleep he was granted incorporated a recurring nightmare. In it he was twenty-one years old and back in Los Angeles, acting as counselor in a summer camp that catered exclusively to the children of Hollywood stars such as Hedy Lamarr's and Danny Kaye's. He was known to both the clients and their progeny as "Gillie the Goy."

The annual highlight for the parents' visiting day was a play staged by the drama committee. Drama coach Gilliam used his influence to push for the selection of *Alice Through the Looking Glass*. With only one week to prepare, he saw that the choice had been over-ambitious. None of the young players seemed able to remember their lines, apparently due to an impenetrable lack of understanding of the text. Painted hardboard sets collapsed with unfailing regularity, lighting cues caused a power overload that blacked out a neighboring village, and in the heat, greasepaint refused to stick, reducing the players' features to unrecognizable streaky blobs.

Gilliam found himself summoned before a white-faced chief scout. "You fuck up with *this*," he was informed, "with all these Hollywood kids running to tell their moms and dads what a *shithead* you are, and you can kiss any Hollywood ambitions goodbye."

He felt squeezed between the certainty of failure and the inevitability of admitting defeat. "It won't be ready," he heard himself say. "We'll have to cancel the show this year. We'll have to cancel . . ."

Gilliam awoke in a heavy sweat with the sound of the word "cancel" reverberating in his brain. An identical chain of events had actually occurred when he was a summer camp counselor back in the early sixties. A production of *Alice Through the Looking Glass* had indeed been canceled. Parents were offered a multitude of inadequate excuses, all of which were torpedoed by their offspring.

The nightmare highlighted the dilemma he now faced in reality with *Munchausen*. It was a situation he had spent the last twenty years assiduously avoiding. "Gillie the Goy," he mused, "you've well and truly fucked up."

A chaotic twenty-four hours followed Don French's resignation. Rumor was chased by counter-rumor, culminating in a report from Bob Edwards informing Schuhly that French was taking Lee Cleary with him. The team so carefully recruited was now beginning to break up. Schuhly immediately phoned Cleary, who, it turned out, was on the other line with French. "Lee, even after what has happened here today, we would like you to stay on and see this film through," Schuhly said, while Cleary put French on hold. Cleary was mystified. "What's happened today, Thomas?" he asked. "Don quit the film," Schuhly replied.

"Hang on a minute," said Cleary, going back to French. "Thomas just told me you're leaving."

"That's right, Lee. I was just about to tell you and say that Terry has asked you to stay on."

When Gilliam realized what a total distortion Edwards' accusation had been and its possible consequences for the project, he felt something snap. "If *I'm* losing Don," he raged at Schuhly, "*you're* losing Bob Edwards."

"But he's crucial to the Film Finances deal," Schuhly replied.

"Is he? Well, only you know how, Thomas."

"Terry, they *know* the guy, they've worked with him before, they *trust* him — "

"Fuck it, I don't *care*. As far as I'm concerned, Edwards is *going*! And I still intend to speak to Don and try to change his mind."

Despite his protests Schuhly fell into reluctant agreement that Edwards should be dismissed. A letter was promptly dispatched to the production supervisor he had hired only three months earlier. "You do not comply with the requirements of your contract," Edwards was advised. "Please think this over and we'll discuss it. In all friendliness, Thomas." Although the honeymoon itself was over, Edwards was retained for a while as adviser on the unit's blue-screen installation at Cinecitta. Schuhly then wrote to Gilliam to lay down the conditions for a reinstatement of Don French:

"Dear Terry,

Just a few words to take in consideration: I accept that the Assistant Director should be in the first place your choice, but if you come back with Don it will be to a certain extent a decision against me. (And this is *not* an ego problem!) As you know, I really get along with all our people/crew, but going back to Don *will* mean, and about this I'm 100 percent sure, programming conflicts!

When you *accepted* that Don "went away," I saw this somehow as a "compromise" between you and me, but maybe this was a wrong interpretation. Anyhow, I won't make an issue out of this story. If you think that Don is necessary, then you should get him. I will try my best to avoid conflicts. You have to make it *clear* to him that if he goes another time on the producer of this film I'll charge him heavily.

Cordially, Thomas.

P.S. This is, as I have said, *no* ego bullshit, but I see basically no strong reason to work with people *who hate me deeply*."

Gilliam could see from the whole tone of Schuhly's letter that the situation was hopeless. In any case, he had already tried unsuccessfully to cajole his friend into staying, and French had been adamant in his decision to leave.

"Your note troubled me considerably," Gilliam's reply ran, "in particular the sentence that when Don 'went away,' I saw this as a compromise between the two of us. The implication of this is that there was a fight between us. I didn't realize there was. That also made me feel that my gut feeling was right, that you in fact *engineered* Don's resignation, that you placed him in a position that forced him to quit. Don and I had been pushing for a long time against what, I have said time and time again, is *one of the worst production departments I have ever been involved with*. My only fight has been to get a decent organization to run this film."

In retrospect, Schuhly readily admitted that Edwards had proved a major disappointment. "He fucked up many things. I took him on to begin with because he is American, Film Finances felt comfortable with him, and he spoke fluent Italian. I realized my mistake too late."

Replacing Edwards with another Italian, the genial Mario Di Biase, Schuhly's attention next turned to the gap left by French. He chose David Tomblin, one of the most experienced First Assistant Directors in the world, who had skillfully steered several big-budget ventures through to their successful conclusions, among them *A*

Bridge Too Far, Gandhi, Raiders of the Lost Ark and *Out of Africa*. Gilliam and Schuhly had passed him over for *Munchausen* in February only because he had been tied up on Spielberg's *Empire of the Sun*. Tomblin had gained the distinct impression at the time that they were wary of him. Now here was Schuhly calling him again, asking if he knew of any first assistants who would take over the project. And in two weeks' time! Tomblin asked Schuhly if by any chance he wanted him to do it, which he surmised was the intention all along.

A visit to Rome proved to Tomblin how pathetically unprepared the movie was. His first reaction after reading the script and consulting the storyboards and schedule was to give the whole deal a quick pass. Gilliam went for a completely up front, candid appraisal of the situation. "Sure," he agreed, "Italy's a rat's nest. Yes, the film's in total chaos. That's why we need *you*, David, to sort the whole bloody lot out. We've got the makings of a great film here and it would be criminal to let it die."

Gradually Tomblin began to be infected with the *Munchausen* virus. Like so many before him, Tomblin was becoming captivated by the lure of the wild, improbable adventure. "Give me a week to think it over," he suggested. "Then I'll come back and talk."

Gilliam was in Madrid and preparing to fly back to see Tomblin when a call came from Schuhly in Rome. "There's a problem with one of the crew," he reported.

"One of the crew? Who?"

"Dave Tomblin. He's decided not to join us after all."

To Gilliam, Tomblin was not just "one of the crew" — he was supposed to save the entire show! Stunned by Schuhly's cavalier description of Tomblin's apparent change of heart, Gilliam rang Tomblin direct. "It's impossible," he was now told. "I've taken a closer look back in Rome, Terry, and it's just not going to work."

"Stay right there," said Gilliam, "I'm flying back."

Gilliam made an offer even the resolute Tomblin found impossible to refuse. He would be given the coveted title of the movie's Line Producer. His regular assistant, Roy Button, would join him. Reaction in the film community was muted. Tomblin as First Assistant Director? Of course, none better! Tomblin as Line

Producer?? Many saw the "move upstairs" as illogical, rather like hiring a goal scorer and then putting him to work as a linesman. The unit had nonetheless secured the individual Gilliam would come to describe as his "man of the match."

With Tomblin's appointment came another dramatic upgrading. The young Spanish first assistant, Jose Luis Escolar, was moved into Don French's shoes as overall First Assistant Director. One ominous note: he could not speak a word of Italian.

• • •

As with any insurance risk, Film Finances' batting average told the story. Out of 1,800 films they had insured since their inception in 1950, collecting an average fee of around 5 percent of each budget, only a handful had gone into serious cost overages.

Like most completion guarantors, Film Finances transfer much of their insurance risk to Lloyd's of London. In the case of *Munchausen* their liability was initially confined to the first $2 million of any cost overage, with Lloyd's taking over for the next $8 million. Any additional overage above this $10 million total — *utterly unthinkable* though it might be — would boomerang back to Film Finances.

Concerned that such an eventuality might bankrupt the company and leave them with an unfinished movie on their hands, the Japanese lenders insisted that Film Finances enter into an unusual "cut-through endorsement" with Lloyd's, bringing them back, in a "worst case" scenario, with ultimate responsibility to deliver *Munchausen* complete.

Film Finances insisted on signed assurances from Schuhly and Gilliam before they would go ahead. In Gilliam's case they also asked for a deferment of salary, to which he agreed. They both acknowledged that they had approved the screenplay and production schedules and reviewed the budget, and that these were considered adequate. "I understand," they both further confirmed, "that in certain circumstances you have the right to take over control of the production and to replace personnel. In the event that you exercise such rights I agree to cooperate fully."

By July the full capitalization was at last in the pipeline, courtesy of signed contracts with Columbia Pictures Corporation (United States), RCA/Columbia Video (United States), the Cecchi-Goris

(Italy), Neue Constantin (Germany) and Long Term Credit Bank (Japan). Side letters covering the Allan Buckhantz indemnification and the 20th Century-Fox and Arnon Milchan settlements were lodged with Columbia. Accident insurance was with Fireman's Fund. Film Finances was the movie's completion guarantor, and through them Lloyd's of London.

• • •

In July animal trainer Pierre Lechien received a telephone call in Paris from a friend on the *Munchausen* crew. They had been auditioning for Argus, the Baron's canine companion, but thus far only "cowboys" had been sent for consideration. Until now, the unit had been looking at red setters. Something different and scruffier was needed: an anxious, old, frail-looking animal, decrepit and feeble enough to match the Baron in his old age. Something with a long nose, Lechien was told; greying, almost with a beard. He felt that a wire-haired lurcher — an English breed resembling a greyhound — would be ideal.

Being half-Romany himself, he knew of a gypsy encampment near Chantilly that actually used the breed for poaching. There was only one problem: as poachers' dogs the lurchers were not allowed to bark. No matter, Lechien thought, he would soon train one of the beasts to bark on cue.

After being shown the animal on a video Lechien had prepared, Gilliam was sold on the breed. Word was relayed to Paris that the deal was on. With only eight days' filming of Argus on the schedule, Lechien was first assured that there would be no need for a back-up dog. A few days later, however, the still-resident Bob Edwards, astonished that anyone could have thought one dog was enough, declared that Argus would require an understudy. For Lechien it was back to Chantilly to audition a second lurcher. After ten years of disciplined silence, both dogs were soon barking — and on cue — as if they'd been born to it, thanks to Lechien's secret-formula vocal lessons.

On the basis of eight days' shooting Lechien had asked $150 per day per dog, which would include his services as keeper and minder. In addition he wanted return air fare from Paris, freight charges and "per diems" on top. The assistant in charge of Lechien's contract reckoned his fees were expensive, but Lechien was in no mood to haggle. The deal signed, Lechien and his lurchers left Paris in time for the start of the filming.

• • •

Schuhly began waving checks at everyone connected with costumes, set construction and props in a frenzied effort to meet the revised September 7 start date. The assembled cast and crew would be eating into the film's budget at the rate of $700,000 a week by then, and if the film started any later, weather problems were virtually certain on the Spanish locations. Gilliam and others expressed grave doubts as to the practicality of September 7, but Schuhly would have none of it. The deadline would be met, he averred.

Schuhly put it to me that his attitude was entirely justified: "I knew that neither Jake nor Terry really understood my policy, because it was so complicated, and if you involve other people they could get scared shitless. I had to spend a lot of Columbia's money *quickly* so nobody could back out. There are no saints in this business.

"You want to know the truth? At the end of the day, as a producer, you have to play this chess game alone. It changes every five minutes, therefore it makes no sense to involve somebody who sees only 10 percent. I wanted this film made under any circumstances, no matter what. Jake is a very honest person, but he's not a warrior; he makes his figures up in London and I could not explain to him the theory and chemistry of our situation. I knew he would get scared. Peppino Rotunno knows everything; he smells it, but he has 40 years experience. Maybe he said 'yes' to the film because he couldn't imagine somebody who's crazy enough to play this game!

"Since we could not shoot without the costumes, they came first. And as they could not be finally commissioned until the money was available, there was an almost inevitable delay. What you have to understand is that Rome virtually shuts down for a month in August. Gabriella Pescucci tried very hard, but I realized it was unlikely the costumes would be ready. And the theatre set construction was running behind as well. Why didn't I stop the film or delay it at this point? Because once you stop a film like this, it's the most dangerous situation. If you lose the momentum, people have time to change their minds and say 'OK, let's back away now before any more money is wasted.' I was determined not to give anybody that chance!

"This film was always a potential pain in the ass and everyone knew that at Columbia. I had to use the momentum, *whatever* the circumstances and at *whatever* price, to keep it going — convincing here, seducing there."

One week before the scheduled start, there still were no costumes, no sets and no props. Gilliam felt all dressed up with no place to go. The sea monster's interior and Vulcan's cave still only existed in miniature; completed sets seemed weeks away. Rehearsals started. Salaries and per diems were dutifully devoured. A few congratulatory telegrams arrived. With 20th Century-Fox's coffers replenished, their message ran: "Dear Terry: Congratulations/Have a great shoot/I can't wait to see the movie. Scott Rudin."*

Jake Eberts phoned Cinecitta from London on the evening of the 7th to find out how the first day's shooting had gone. "We didn't start today." Schuhly reported. "The set we required was not quite finished." "When *will* you be ready?" asked a shocked Eberts.

"September 14," Schuhly promised.

• • •

Eric Idle arrived from France only to be told that the shooting had been postponed. "Couldn't you have called me before I left?" he asked Schuhly.

A period of what John Neville would ruefully dub "the make-work program" followed. The cast would assemble and read the script for an hour or so each day. In preparing for their coming-ashore scene after the escape from the sea monster's belly, the actors involved were also put through their swimming and diving paces. "There was John Neville," Idle recalled, chuckling, "a seasoned Shakespearean, learning to *scuba dive* with me. It was quite mad. And Winston

---

*With perfectly ironical timing, another message arrived from Universal. After the acrimonious tussle over the theatrical release of *Brazil*, they were adopting a more conciliatory approach over the preparation of the television version. They would be happy to work with Gilliam on any additional editing, "if that were thought to be necessary." Gilliam refused to have anything to do with it; he felt truly on the cusp. Would the *Brazil* saga ever be finished? And more importantly, would the *Munchausen* saga ever get *started*?

Dennis, little Jack Purvis, Charles McKeown and Sarah Polley as well. It was like a holiday program or an outwardbound course.

"Charles had his head shaved very oddly, worse than being totally bald; there was a cross left there. With my wife away for the weekend they shaved my head, and I got home to this empty villa, completely bald and alone, with no food in the house. It was a choice of either going out for a meal or ending it all! I decided to brass it out and hit the streets of Frascati. People backed off as I walked along, thinking either that I'd escaped from a mental institution or I was a football hooligan. The good side is that you get an extra yard or so in the street — especially when Jack and Winston and I, all totally bald, walked down the street together! In restaurants we got great service; it was like a badge.

"Of course, the *real* reason for shaving all our heads was pure sexual jealousy on Gilliam's part. He doesn't want anybody more handsome or virile appearing on the set. If he can possibly stick warts all over your face and shave all your hair off, he will!"

• • •

As September 14 approached, Lee Cleary was asked to prepare a call-sheet, requesting all the actors to turn up in full makeup. The crew was mystified by this, since there was no evidence that the theater set on which shooting was now scheduled to start would be ready in time.

Winston Dennis remembers being at lunch on Saturday, September 12, when he heard the devastating news that a crane and some scaffolding had collapsed, causing considerable damage. Shooting was promptly postponed for *one more* week, to September 21.

"We knew full well the costumes weren't going to be ready," Dennis said, "so *someone* was certainly let off the hook by the accident. There was even a rumor that Schuhly himself was behind it, but I'm *sure* that's not true!" (Dennis had experienced a taste of Schuhly's style when his weekly stipend had been delayed. "Listen, I tell you your money is safe," Schuhly had assured him. "It is right here in the computer and we Germans are *very* efficient!" To Dennis the scene carried overtones of a B-movie.)

Speculation of sabotage was rife over the collapse of the crane and the suspicious inconsistency of the damage it caused. "The accident was not unconnected with the fact that Cinecitta is in Rome," one member of the crew volunteered. "I don't believe it wasn't pushed," Gilliam declared. When Fireman's Fund was asked to pay for the week's delay, they refused to settle in full. The "accident," in their view, was *no* accident.

• • •

The next week brought three further waves of depressing news, the gravity of which seemed to escalate as the new starting date approached.

On September 15 equestrian Tony Smart, who for months had been training four horses to carry out the difficult stunts involving the Baron, broke the news to Gilliam that Spain, where the stunts were to be performed, had been hit by African horse fever. No horses, it had just been decreed, were to be allowed either in or out.

The next day Pierre Lechien reported that Argus I and Argus II were both laid low with a liver ailment. The two lurchers would be out of commission for several weeks. So much for back up!

Then came the third and even more crushing piece of news. After one turbulent year as head of the studio, David Puttnam had just announced his "resignation" from Columbia. How his successors would view the studio's involvement in *Munchausen* remained an apocalyptic question.

No horses, no dogs, no Puttnam — and with the delayed start, the production was already $2 million over budget. All this before Gilliam had had a chance to expose a single foot of film. "We were beginning to realize," said Idle, "that *Munchausen* was Schuhly's concentration camp. We were *never* going to get out!"

Gilliam's reaction to Puttnam's departure was relatively sanguine; he had always regarded Picker as Columbia's main advocate for *Munchausen*, and Picker was still in place. "Certainly, though, the low moments were mounting up," he concedes. "I just steeled myself, and this gigantic turtle that was our movie kept edging forward. No matter what happened, it seemed to be part of the process. Things were going to go as wrong as they possibly could — but we'd just keep marching on. I didn't talk that much to anybody at this point. I just kept going step by step. A numbness took over. I felt like Job, being punished for taking on too much."

Terry Gilliam, Thomas Schuhly

Photo by F. Bellomo
Sting

Photo by S. Strizzi
David Taylor

Photo by F. Bellomo
Terry Gilliam, Charles McKeown, Gene Rizzo, Jonathan Pryce

Gene Rizzo and friend

Mario Pisano, Dante Ferretti

Stratton Leopold, Terry Gilliam, Gene Rizzo

Dante Ferretti, Giuseppe Rotunno

Thomas Schuhly

Terry Gilliam, Giuseppe Rotunno

by F. Bellomo

Terry Gilliam, John Neville

Giuseppe Rotunno meters the moonlight

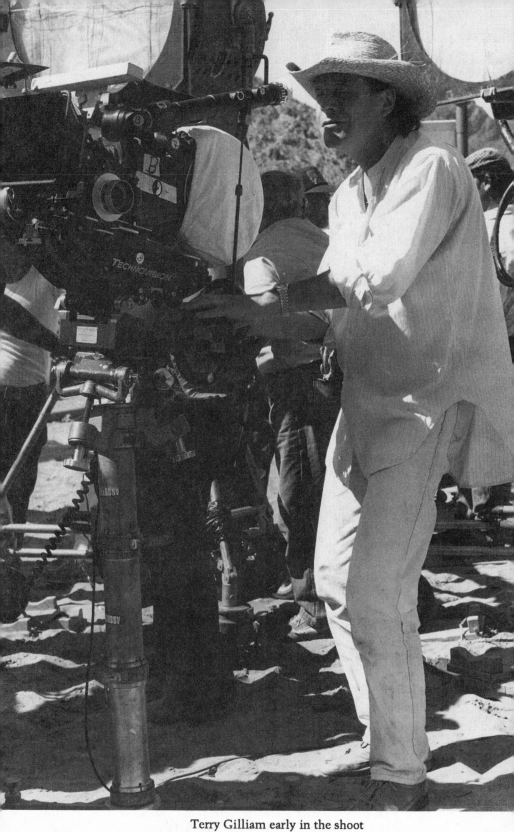

Terry Gilliam early in the shoot

Uma Thurman, Valentina Cortese, Allison Steadman, John Neville

John Neville, Eric Idle, and Charles McKeown
attempt contact with the outside world

CHAPTER
TEN

If you start a movie unprepared you never catch up. You lose morale and there's an instant sense of failure, no matter how hard everyone works. On Munchausen *nothing was ready, nothing was right!*
—Charles McKeown

The big worry for me was that after the first week of shooting I could see how Terry was doing his job. Up until then it had been all theory. Now I knew the worst!
—Thomas Schuhly

Schuhly wrote to Richard Soames at Film Finances several days before shooting finally began to explain the delays which had already encumbered the production's budget. Before Day One of the scheduled shoot, the producer — without consulting his director — was already offering up sacrificial cuts in the script. Schuhly made it pointedly clear to Soames, whose company would bear the brunt of the overages, that these would *certainly* occur unless major surgery was contemplated.

"I realize that you are rather nervous in your L.A. office," he began, before launching into a dissertation on the foibles of moviemakers and their budgets. He conceded there was a "grave discrepancy" in the case of *Munchausen* between the script and the finance available. "For this picture," he explained, "the budget should more or less be considered *a rough guide for cost-checking.*"

"Estimated to complete" would always refer to pure theory, he continued. Then he came out with the staggering admission: *"I cannot complete the picture according to the script,"* citing the Vulcan and the Moon sequences as prime candidates for amputation.

His next suggestion was perhaps the one complete betrayal of his director of which he was guilty throughout the proceedings. Gilliam would be allowed a time limit for each of the sequences, forcing him to concentrate on "necessary shots." There would be no time for what Schuhly tantalizingly termed "decorative additions." It was a phrase Soames would carefully digest and regurgitate several months later as "enhancement." "I still have the picture under control," Schuhly concluded his epistle, with what Soames may have perceived as something less than total conviction.

• • •

A picturesque Cinecitta sound stage, roofless since World War II bombings, was pressed into service by Dante Ferretti for his construction of Gilliam's eighteenth-century war-ravaged theatre.

While the existing shell promised the right backdrop, it had limitations. Such niceties as theatrical wings were out of the question. What you saw was what you got. Idle protested, complaining that the whole set should have been built right from scratch on a soundstage inside the studio. "Who's doing the planning around here?" he asked.

Gilliam defended the structure because of its day and nighttime utility as a set. The roofless shell was also ideal for the balloon escape sequence. What everyone failed to anticipate was the deadly heat buildup inside the covered set during the day. The soaring temperatures rendered the first day of shooting impossible. Everyone was sent home in a sweat and told to report back at 6 o'clock that evening. *Day* one became *night* one.

Bill Paterson as Henry Salt seemed to suffer the most that first night under the myriad set and scenery problems. Surrounded by the whirling and cranking *deus ex machina* of eighteenth-century stage wizardry that Ferretti had faithfully recreated, Paterson struggled valiantly with his ripest Scottish accent intact as artificial suns whirled, papier-maché moons rose and sank, galleons disappeared beneath cut out waves and a giant whale snapped its jaws in his vicinity.

"There I was on that stage in Rome," he recalled, safely back in London, "with the moon rising over Terry's blessed island of cheese. No sooner had I bade a fond farewell to a three-horned monster than I was greeting a whale entering stage left, then walking on top of these heavy artificial wooden waves that hit me in the goolies every time they rocked up and down. Just that going on was enough to make me think I was earning my money on this one! Fantastic though the set was, it was far too small to accommodate the thirty-odd crew plus thirty-odd cast all crammed into it. The madness of those first few nights will stay in my mind forever! The special effects group was English, the stage crew was Italian, the actors were English, American and Italian, the first assistant director was Spanish. The combination produced this absolutely *incredible* babble." "Here we were trying to make this film with all these nationalities," Idle observed, "when the only thing they'd made successfully together for the last 400 years was war!"

At midnight the first "set-up" was finally completed, eliciting a somewhat hysterical cheer from the assembled cast and crew. The bottle of champagne which had forlornly waited since September 7 for its debut popped its cork to celebrate the event. Paterson was content to limp out of sight, grateful to be clear of the spotlight.

Scheduled to be dismissed at 6 o'clock each morning, the weary troupe soon discovered that if the shoot over-ran by even half an hour they would be plunged into the frenzy of Rome's morning rush hour traffic. Paterson recalled arriving back at his hotel feeling like a rag doll and falling asleep until midday. Then, devoting the afternoon to pulling himself together, he would again have to face the bracing drive through the evening rush hour to Cinecitta and another twelve hours of hectic night shooting.

Robin Williams, who had just completed *Good Morning Vietnam*, was visiting Rome at the time of the *Munchausen* shooting. Invited by his friend Eric Idle to visit the set, he was introduced to the much-harassed Gilliam. Williams was already familiar with many of the crew, including Peppino Rotunno, with whom he had worked on Robert Altman's *Popeye*. At 2 o'clock in the morning Williams performed his impromptu shtick as Rotunno: "Terry, I will-a be ready in another hour. Don't-a worry, don't-a worry. We need-a just a *leetle* more darkness. I tell you in just another two hours we will get it perfect. Yes, *perfect*! Just a *leetle* more darkness!"

Next to arrive in Rome was singer/songwriter Gordon Sumner, aka Sting. Sumner, a neighbor of Gilliam's, polished off his tiny cameo role of a misguidedly heroic soldier in a single day. Oh, lucky Sting!

Another visitor was Peter Asher, late of the Peter & Gordon singing duo, brother of Jane Asher, and one of the top names in the rock industry. By coincidence, his professor father was the person who had discovered and named the medical Munchausen Syndrome, describing patients who learn the symptoms of a disease and then reproduce them in order to fool medics.

Idle later became convinced that everyone in the unit was affected by this condition. He recalled how "this motley crew with all our heads shaved" assembled in the Green Room, a hideous modern version of a Nissen hut with concrete floor, hardboard walls and a tin roof. "There we'd have to wait for our call. A typical night I'd be in costume from 7:00, then get called about 3:30 a.m, in one case to do a shot in which we were all escaping inside wickerwork baskets — out of sight, mind you, but still in full makeup and costume! You couldn't *see* me. There were just these baskets running across the stage. Then the scene was cut from the finished film! Thanks a *lot*! That was the evening's work, and eight hours of hanging around. Complete madness. You'd get home in the morning and the wife would say, 'Well, dear, what did you do last night?' and all you could say was. 'I ran about inside a basket for twenty minutes.'

"I don't think Terry ever had time to get an overview. Schuhly? He was all talk, and never there anyway. Basically he just fitted up his office with spotlights to give interviews. He was only interested in empire building. He told us that what you need for filmmaking was balls. And that's all he ever talked — balls."

Schuhly proved himself the master of surprise in an interview he gave Giovanni Grassi, the Rome-based correspondent of *Hollywood Reporter.* "The one director I felt I could entrust this material to was Terry Gilliam," he rhapsodized while Gilliam was putting his cast through their early paces. "Terry asked to be permitted to work on the screenplay with Charles McKeown and the final script I received seemed full of inventiveness . . ."

As Gilliam ran his eyes over Schuhly's communiqué, he could feel his temperature soaring. "Full of inventiveness" certainly seemed to perfectly sum up Schuhly's summary.

Later that same week Schuhly summoned the publicist in charge of stills photography. He insisted that on every photographic release where Gilliam was named in connection with the film, his own name be given equal prominence. Even "Terry Gilliam's *The Adventures of Baron Munchausen,* a Thomas Schuhly production" was rejected; "A Thomas Schuhly production, Terry Gilliam's *The Adventures of Baron Munchausen*" finally sanctioned.

McKeown saw at first hand the effects of the late start and organizational shambles on Gilliam. "It was very demoralizing. The costumes for the soldiers in the theater scene were delivered all freshly pressed and brand new — and these were supposed to be soldiers in the midst of a bloody battle! Nobody had thought of that. We had to dirty them all down. And while the theater set *looked* extraordinary, nothing *worked.*"

"The famous Monty Python foot had come down," Gilliam recalls, "and it was finally crushing me. I started becoming more and more superstitious about everything that happened. The problem is, once you've started off on a path and planned something, and then each day you fail to achieve that, every day is a failure; each day you get into a deeper depression. It doesn't matter that it's still good, it just wasn't what you set out to do. You must remember that the film is always complete in my head and that I am measuring what we're doing daily against that and coming up short every time. The summer camp episode certainly left a scar that has haunted me. I'd set my own rules and gone against the system and pulled it off with small budget movies time and again. Now I felt that *Munchausen* was the one I was going to get caught on. It was my worst nightmare come true."

By the end of the first week David Tomblin announced that they were already one full week behind. In other words, the unit had been scheduled to shoot *twice* as much material as they had actually achieved. At the present rate, he calculated that if all went smoothly they might complete the movie in 26 weeks; if not, it could stretch to 31. Fresh waves of despondency and alarm swept away the prevailing mixture of delirium and exhaustion. Everyone knew that 31 weeks would never be authorized. Tomblin had one answer: script cuts.

Without delay Film Finances' chief Richard Soames flew from Los Angeles to meet his Rome representative, Umberto Sambucco, for crisis talks. A minimum over-budget figure of $4 million was already considered a certainty — and this could quickly escalate. If the figure could at least be *contained* to $3 million, Soames knew this would be covered by the $2 million contingency fund and their $1 million fee. He also reminded Schuhly of Film Finances' prerogative of abandoning *Munchausen* altogether. "If the picture proceeds," he argued, "it could go $10 million over budget before it's finished, maybe even $15 million."

Schuhly pleaded that containment, rather than abandonment, should be the keynote. He insisted that it was too late to turn back. "I have $16 million either spent or fully committed," he claimed, "and if you abandon now, that money is lost. You will have nothing to show for it."

Soames' next suggestion, when he had recovered from Schuhly's staggering news, revealed a distinct flair for gunboat diplomacy. They could always bring in another director to replace Gilliam. Although Schuhly was protecting what he saw as the corporate beast rather than the individual, it is to his credit that he declared this option out of the question as far as he was concerned. Soames was successfully disabused of the notion, at least for the time being.

Schuhly claims that these crisis meetings took up such an inordinate amount of his time that there was none left to visit the set. "Plenty of opportunity, though, for his daily bodybuilding and photo sessions," one of the crew observed.

Following his meeting in Rome with Schuhly and Gilliam, Soames wrote to both men from his London office, formally advising them to revise their storyboards and method of shooting to manageable proportions in order to achieve the agreed schedule. "It does not take a genius," he suggested, "to see how overlength the movie will be if you shoot the proposed storyboard in its entirety."

Referring to the "potentially disastrous" overcost that would arise if progress continued at the present snail's pace, he reminded them that his company had only taken on the project based on their personal representations, made on several different occasions, that the script could be achieved within the constraints of budget and schedule. *"I need hard evidence that this is still the case,"* he concluded.

Schuhly's solution was presented to David Picker on his arrival in Rome. "Let's face realities," he claims to have suggested. "We're going to have a major problem. Five million more from Columbia will solve everything. It makes no sense to close your eyes and hope that Terry will come up with a genius idea; that's not possible because of the nature of the screenplay. Terry is a very experienced director and he knows how to modify and simplify a film, but he cannot *change* a film."

For his part, Picker adopted the well-known Burbank Stand-off: "Thomas, we all know you're very experienced in production. Columbia has a deal for $12 million, plus $8 million for video and that's *it*. And if anyone can bring in this movie on budget, it's you!"

One thing Schuhly did ascertain from his meeting with Picker was that Columbia would only accept a film by Terry Gilliam — perhaps the one legacy from Puttnam that was adopted by his successors. "The idea of a Terry Gilliam film without Terry Gilliam is ridiculous!" was their constantly reiterated theme.

Schuhly's overture to Picker was only the beginning of a determined assault to capture the active sympathy of the new post-Puttnam regime at Columbia. He was the producer, after all, he reasoned, and he had profit points in the picture. He could offer Columbia something, but what could they offer him in return to ease Film Finances' growing sense of exposure? Nothing, came the answer in short order from Victor Kaufman, Puttnam's successor.

"This was the fuck-up," Schuhly recalled. "Kaufman and the new management were only interested in hiding behind the contracts and sticking to the letter of the law. I said we should forget the contracts and try to get the film made, but it was hopeless. If Puttnam had still been around it might have been different, but I just couldn't get Kaufman and the rest to sit around a table with Film Finances. They simply didn't want to know. I found it hard to accept that only Soames was in the shit; at least he should have had offers he could live with."

CHAPTER ELEVEN

Terry always wanted me to be the mother of the show, but I didn't have the time or the energy, nor was I interested. It wasn't my business.

—Thomas Schuhly

Schuhly knew damn well there was no way that we could transfer Munchausen *to Pinewood or anywhere else without his cooperation.*

—Eric Idle

I always identify with my lead characters. I was Sam in Brazil. *"What will become of the Baron? Surely this time he cannot escape" began as the movie's theme tune. It soon became mine.*

—Terry Gilliam

At the end of the first week of shooting, Gilliam met with McKeown, Tomblin and co-producer Ray Cooper to discuss cuts they might offer. The extraordinarily shy, retiring and erudite Cooper has at various times in his life been a musical child prodigy, a member of the pop group Blue (Melting Pot, Banner Man) Mink, a classical actor, Elton John's percussionist, a director of Handmade Films — and, for many years, a staunch friend of Gilliam's. And after all, the original challenge that only Gilliam could turn Baron Munchausen's adventures into a movie had come from Cooper.

He is easy to spot in a crowd. Cooper's the one with the shaven head (pre-*Munchausen*), wearing a white Grandad shirt, black waistcoat and trousers. His credits on *Munchausen* serve to demonstrate further his versatility. As well as his co-production credit on the movie he would jointly produce the score with Michael Kamen *and* play the role of Horatio Jackson's functionary. What even this list fails to illustrate is his marvelous ability to pour oil on troubled waters and deal amicably with all sides in a dispute. This knack would be stretched to the limit at several stages in *Munchausen*'s history.

Gilliam entered into earnest, if somewhat desperate, discussions with his friend and colleague. Instead of cuts, was there a way of vacating Italy and taking the whole show back to England? Many of the scenes could be rethought and translated into models, which would dramatically cut costs. When this was put to Schuhly he ostensibly agreed. He would remain producer, while responsibility for setting up facilities in England and recruitment of the new crew would be assigned to Prominent Features.

Schuhly's "agreement" may have been a tactical, shrewd move along the lines of "Let the children play." He probably knew that Prominent lacked the capacity to cope with such a project, especially on such short notice. While appearing to yield to Gilliam's argument, he certainly knew that a web of contracts and deals anchored the film securely at Cinecitta.

The dream was finally shattered at a meeting between Schuhly, Gilliam, Cooper, Idle and Abbott. "Schuhly did a memo to us," Idle recalled, "about how much it would cost to close down in Rome. If we wanted to take it on, however, we could. He would just take his money — *like plus about $4 million*!! — and Prominent would take over this monster that had already swallowed $7 million. In view of how it turned out, it would still have been a smart move."

• • •

Meanwhile, Schuhly had what he termed a "very serious clash" with his partner on the set at Cinecitta. Gilliam was furious to discover that equestrian trainer Tony Smart remained unpaid after numerous requests. "Terry charged me in front of twelve people," said Schuhly, still incensed at the memory.

"This was more or less the start of the very end. I told him that I'd never *played* producer in my life. Either I'm the producer or I'm not, but I don't play at it. If he charged me with this shit, I told him I would send Smart home. I didn't even know who he was and I wasn't interested in knowing him; he was one of those *assholes* he brought over from England.

"Terry said he was used to a different style of producer. I told him *his* style didn't fit in this film. I'm not responsible for how many fucking elephants, or for overtime and salaries getting paid, or whether somebody's happy with their hotel. This was not my problem. He wanted the good old days of the sixties with collaboration, but this was the past and it didn't work today. It was bullshit. Dave Tomblin is the most expensive in the world and maybe the best, Dante Ferretti is the best, Peppino is the best, so why should I get involved? He wanted me to be responsible for nonsense — whether a television set was there, if a hotel room had been paid. I was interested in the screenplay, the cast, storyboards and design — *that* was my job."

"That was Schuhly all over," Gilliam said, shrugging. "Everyone from England was an 'asshole.' Anyone who expected to be paid was an 'asshole.'"

Now that filming was finally underway, a major part of Gilliam's frustration was the difficulty of on-set communications. Back in England, with familiar faces around him, a series of Neanderthal Gilliam-type grunts would send his team into immediate action; they knew him and they knew what he wanted. In contrast, everything had to be slowly spelled out in Rome, then carefully translated. A "them and us" feeling between the Italians and the various other nationalities rapidly developed.

Gilliam found that Peppino Rotunno's fractured English that had charmed him at their introduction lost its appeal when it left the realm of pleasantries and an understanding of nuances was called for — especially technical ones, since all his instructions had to be run through Rotunno to the camera crew. The first head-on confrontation with the cinematographer was over the viewing of the daily rushes. Rotunno was shocked when Gilliam proposed a general showing. He protested that he was used to watching them first with the director. Relations deteriorated further when Gilliam insisted that, in his democratic way, this was simply not possible.

As the situation with Rotunno worsened, Schuhly sought to reassure Gilliam by letter (the only current means of communication now possible between them):

"Dear Terry,

I talked with Mario (Di Biase) this morning about this 'Italian/English' issue; according to Mario (and this is my opinion, too) there are no problems at all! There is a certain 'irritation' on Peppino's side, but this has nothing to do with English or Italian. He is one of the last prima donnas of our business and he has to get used to your style to direct the film. I will talk to him in Spain.

"After all the nightmares we (all) had to get this film started — the very short preparation time, the delays with sets, props, costumes etc. — all of your crew have been on the edge of their physical capacities. Therefore there was an enormous nervosity, fear, anger and desperation in the atmosphere. And when people are weak, they have the tendency to become sort of aggressive 'racists'; this is not a question of different countries. I heard many times from the Italians, 'This fucking *Milanese* . . . the fucking *idiot* from Turino, etc.' Then I become, for some Italians, the *fucking Nazi*. That's the way it is!

"I'm sure that Spain will help a lot. Shooting abroad has always something to do with 'vacation'; husbands get rid of their ball-breaking wives (for Italians very important!) and for a period the film has something to do with an adventure. But you know this. This break will help to form our unit to *one* team which will carry on the film for the second period. You can be assured that I'm aware of the problems and of *your* problems. Part of the problems have exclusively to do with the nature of this film. The other part, and here you are right, has to do with the fact that you don't have your (own) crew. The both of us have to do our best to get the production in a better shape in order to get the film you wanted to make.

"For the coming weeks in Spain I wish you good luck, 'break a leg,' etc. Looking to our material, I know that we are on the right track and we have a very good chance to make a film which will leave traces in this business.

Thomas"

Gilliam was far from satisfied.

"I hear the sound of fingers pointing," he replied. "I can't do what I do without a backing organization. We've got several brilliant people, but that does not necessarily add up to a team that works well together, which is far more important on a film like this than any amount of bullshit. The reasons for slow shooting are as follows:

1) Sets not ready in advance.
2) Props not clearly acquired.
3) Organization (lack of).
4) Chain of command — all chiefs, no Indians.
5) Vast amount of extra people doing fuck all.
6) Coordination of elements (lack of).
7) Peppino still trying to contact labs.
8) Rushes not sorted out.

"Pumping money in is not necessarily the answer if it's going in the wrong direction. Like Don French, I am not about to get stuck for the shitty preparation of this film. I'm quite happy to take a break until things are properly clarified and prepared. If I see money being spent wisely and good people doing their best, I'm more than happy to compromise, otherwise . . ."

"I realized that it was a major error that Terry didn't know Italian," Schuhly briefly conceded as he looked through the correspondence file. A few seconds later he qualified that point: "*John Huston* never spoke Italian either and there was no problem on the many films *he* shot in Italy! Personally, I couldn't cope with this problem — it was a *people* problem, not a *nationality* problem. American mentality matches 100 percent with Italian mentality. I didn't know that English mentality didn't. It's complete nonsense to talk about language problems, pure stupidity. Terry was telling me all these problems, but I wouldn't listen. From the first day of shooting I had two parties, the English crew and the Italian crew, and it was too late. I *had* to save the film and *insisted* on continuing in Italy; it would cost far too much to move it all to another country. The *bullshit* about language is bullshit, it belongs to the world of my grandparents. I told Terry he had to lead the film; he always wanted me to lead it. I said that if I did, then after three weeks because of my ego, and my charisma in this country, they would listen only to me. The same thing happened to Fassbinder. Terry has problems leading because he is very shy. I said to him, 'If I come on the set, then after two weeks they will listen only to me. It's part of my chemistry. I don't want to do that.'"

When Gilliam was informed of Schuhly's charisma-overload theory, his response was short and sharp: "I can only laugh. Thomas is a *crazy* human being. The three or four times he came to a production meeting — *that's* what happened when he came on the set? Charisma? He was *shouted* at!"

Gilliam studied with dismay a late-September memo from Schuhly. "According to what Richard Soames had told me," the missive ran, "the following over-budget positions are *not* covered by the bonding contract . . ." Included in the list was one major item — the salaries of Cast, Stunt and Extras. "These will be charged to the director and producer personally," Schuhly warned. After studying the memo Gilliam scribbled across it, "Delay of two weeks in starting is responsible for these costs. I will *not* be charged for them!" Then he realized how ludicrous the whole thing was and angrily filed the epistle in the wastepaper basket.

With shooting on the Cinecitta theater set, originally planned for ten days, still far from complete, the unit had to depart for Almeria on October 1, leaving the set dressed, standing — and chargeable — until their return. In the hectic ten-day turmoil, Gilliam had shot precisely seventeen minutes of film. Surely, he thought, things can only get better once we're on location. One thing was certain: Film Finances would be closely monitoring progress in Spain.

CHAPTER TWELVE

We never knew how many of the delays were caused by Thomas saying, "Go slow, we don't have the money." We can only guess.
　　　　　　　　　　　　　　　—Terry Gilliam

Terry will in this lifetime only work like he did on Time Bandits *and* Brazil. *He has not the mental or psychological structure to work on a professional operation. He must work in his garage.*
　　　　　　　　　　　　　　　—Thomas Schuhly

With the possibility now long gone of Gilliam and Schuhly communicating directly in *any* known language, the separate camps of Britons and Italians were firmly entrenched. Many members found themselves being used as go-betweens. Schuhly recalls one particular situation that arose when Dante Ferretti arrived on Gilliam's behalf. "Terry says he's the co-producer," Ferretti declared. "He knows that you're the producer, but *he's* co-producer and he wants this problem solved right away."

"In this situation," Schuhly told me, "I would normally go home and say, 'OK, if you're the co-producer, let's cut out the 'co' and you're the *producer*, because either I do the job myself, or you become the producer and I become the director.' I could sue Terry easily for this, for it's unprofessional behavior. If you say things like this to people like Dante, it creates a gap. You have to remember these people are Italians. This is the land of Machiavelli; they get it with their mother's milk. This for Dante is paradise. The moment he knows this is my weakness, then I'm done. Dante came back to me and I could see in his face how much he was relishing it. He said, 'Thomas, I'm sorry, but your co-producer just told me —.' This was simply not professional."

Now that production was underway, Richard Conway was well placed to judge the "professionalism" of Schuhly's organization as he set about creating the many special effects involved. He had nothing but praise for the Italian artists themselves; he found Ferretti's sculptors, painters and property men second to none. The difficulty lay in coordinating the disparate elements of the mammoth production. Cinecitta's sets were invariably late, due, apart from anything else, to their distinctly archaic bureaucratic system that often left Ferretti with a scant 48 hours to get them together.

"The Italians aren't geared to physically putting together a film like this," Conway maintained. "For one thing, the setup at Cinecitta was so peculiar. There you 'buy' a set and when it's ready you have to employ your own production people to continue to make that set work. In England the production people provide the service right to the end of the film.

"Even the simple act of trying to get something heavy moved from one side of the set to the other was difficult. I often saw a poor guy struggling with one fork lift truck, which was the only way of pulling equipment around the studio. We spent a fortune on cranes. In England there are a lot of block and chain tackles which lift a quarter of a ton, but in Cinecitta the roof couldn't take the weight. Despite this lack of equipment, though, there'd be ten unit cars waiting downstairs to take you anywhere you wanted to go or pick up your wife at the airport. The priorities in Rome were just totally upside down!"

• • •

In Schuhly's office one day Gilliam spotted a wall chart with a list of salaries. Michele Soavi, the second-unit director, was shown as earning a very considerable amount — incredibly, more than David Tomblin. The discrepancy struck Gilliam at the time, but it wasn't until months later the subject came up again. "You must be a very good businessman," Gilliam declared to Soavi at dinner one night.

"What do you mean?" Soavi asked.

"Well, I noticed you made a very good deal on the film." When Gilliam quoted the figure on the wall chart, Soavi threw his head back and laughed. "You are mistaken, Terry. I got precisely *half* that," he assured him.

One English special effects assistant confided that he had never seen so many scams going on in one place. "Bit players, obviously friends of someone or other, were getting paid fortunes for little more than walk-on or even extra work. Italian drivers were getting more than $1,000 a week, a couple of Italian 'bully-boys' posing as production assistants were pulling down $2,000 a week. Nobody ever knew how to get hold of Schuhly. He was rumored to have three identical black Porsches parked outside Cinecitta's various entrances, so that you never knew whether he was in or not!

"Then there was the great hire-car scam; every time someone required a hire car we were supplied with something that had babies' bottles or toys in the back seat. Obviously they weren't regular rental cars at all: they were borrowed from someone's relatives. They would invariably have something wrong with them, so right away they had to get the brakes fixed or new tires or whatever, all at the unit's expense. I think there must have been a car pool organized where relatives phoned in when they needed their car repaired! They lost the use of the car for a few days, were paid for it, and got it back fixed!

"Anything and everything was corrupt. You couldn't just go in and claim your expenses, whether legitimate or not; you always had to go through a performance. I felt sorry for many people. I saw men walking out of the production office crying. I had never seen that on a production before.

"Then they have this horrible system with extras. Each man provides a crowd of ten, which he oversees. I was talking to a couple of the girls who said it was made quite clear to them that if they wanted to be in the film as extras they were expected to offer their services to their overseer. They were getting *laid* so they could earn a pittance! Their 'overseer' got a cut for every extra he produced *and* the perk of the girls' favors as well!"

• • •

Pierre Lechien and his lurchers waited in vain for the call to the studio. He had offered to go home and take the dogs with him. His offer refused, when he went to collect his fees he found that they had been calculated on the basis of a five-day week. After pointing out with great agitation that this left him ten days short, he was informed that *no one* was paid for Saturdays and Sundays. Lechien produced his contract, which clearly stated he was to be paid *per day* from the moment he left Paris to the moment he returned. "You're too expensive," Lechien now was told, "and you've done nothing for a month." "That isn't my fault," he protested.

He was summoned before production supervisor Mario Di Biase, who threatened to write the dogs out of the script completely unless his fee could be discussed. Lechien caught the distinct whiff of bluff in the air. He would consider a renegotiation only if he were first paid in full for the month in dispute. "We've not filmed with your dogs yet, and we don't need the animals until next week. So we are not committed to your lurchers," Di Biase insisted. "Fine," Lechien replied, "so you have the weekend to find other animals. *Bon chance!*" He found himself followed out of the building by an anxious Di Biase. "Have your dogs ready on Monday," he told Lechien.

"And the money?"

"Come inside and we'll settle everything we owe."

Once the dogs had begun filming the following week, Lechien knew he had the unit where he wanted it — paying $2,100 a week for his dogs. The question of renegotiation was never raised, except on one occasion by Thomas Schuhly: "Why don't I buy the dogs outright from you?" he asked. After several minutes a figure of $10,000 was reached. Lechien's eyes gleamed at the endless possibilities. "No," he told Schuhly. "If they are worth that much to you, I think I would rather stay with the present arrangement."

Lechien continued to collect his $2,100 a week, together with $120-a-day "per diems," for months to come. And all for two seriously mangy old dogs he had purchased from gypsies for the magnificent honorarium of $150!

CHAPTER THIRTEEN

*It wasn't that we went into the picture
naively, thinking everything would just
magically happen. We sat and planned it, but
nobody pressed the buttons to make it
happen. Schuhly was saying that we didn't
have to worry, that we could fake it, which
was true a lot of the time, but only when you
plan everything carefully and then fake it.
This gives you the ability to invent.*

—Terry Gilliam

*How can you tell when a Hollywood accoun-
tant is lying? His lips move!*

—Eric Idle

In Rome the cast and crew of seventy were only allowed one
piece of luggage each on the Saturday charter flight to Almeria. The
airline soon discovered the impracticality of the instruction,
especially as far as the Italians were concerned. Since they intended

turning up throughout the shoot in constantly changing wardrobe, the edict was treated as a joke.

With everyone on board, the captain explained in exasperation that because the hold was overloaded with excess luggage, passengers would have to rearrange themselves at the rear of the plane. All, that is, except Winston Dennis, whom he judged should remain at the front to provide balance. Everyone burst out laughing at this, and amidst much joviality the plane achieved lift-off. If they had known that Gabriella Pescucci's lovingly designed costumes had been left behind on the runway, their laughter would have been decidedly muted. And Eric Idle recalls looking around nervously before take-off and noting that the only key face missing was Schuhly's. "Oh, no!" he thought. "We're going to be part of the world's biggest insurance claim!"

When they arrived in Almeria they had to endure what Idle described as the "well-known international customs scam, No. 1 in the custom officers' manual," the first rule of which is for some fairly vital piece of equipment, like a camera, to be impounded. The "greased palm syndrome" followed.

Since the costumes left behind in Rome were needed for the Sultan's tent sequence, the first due to be shot in Almeria, there were frantic efforts to have these forwarded on the next available flight. Unfortunately, this was canceled due to bad weather. There was no other flight scheduled until the first day of shooting, Monday, October 5, and no cargo space was available. By the time this was discovered, it was too late to hire another charter.

• • •

The Andalusian province of Almeria is famous for being the hottest in Spain, with temperatures commonly reaching 100 degrees in the shade. It is also one of the most popular film locations in Europe. Lunar landscapes, sandstone cones and fields of esparto grass lie inland; the intense, luminous quality of the sunlight is normally guaranteed; and the golden beaches of the coast stretch for miles.

Hundreds of films have been shot in the area, including numerous spaghetti westerns in the wake of *A Fistful Of Dollars* and epics like *Lawrence of Arabia*. Almeria has changed significantly since those early days. The reclamation of much of the scrubland led to considerable building development, forcing, for instance, the unit's move to San Jose, fifteen miles further north along the coast. "Normally I think it's full of nude German windsurfers," Eric Idle informed his friends, "but it's the end of the season; we've missed them!"

When Idle checked into his hotel room, he found what he thought was the standard breakfast menu hung on the doorknob. Instead of bacon and eggs, however, were diagrams of pipes, pliers, lightbulbs, television sets, and something that looked like the original flatiron blueprint. "Would you please be so kind as to let us know your required repairs," ran the decidedly plaintive legend. "Christ," Idle thought, "this is bad news. I've only just arrived and haven't even touched anything yet!"

Liberal quantities of margaritas saw Gilliam, McKeown and Idle through the evening, while they discussed the revised schedule in the continuing absence of the vital costumes. Since all they had were uniforms for several hundred locally-recruited "Turkish soldiers," establishing battlement shots were planned.

An unexpected gale blew in the next day and threatened to whisk away anything inadequately pinned down. Oddly enough, the wind velocity did little to lower the sweltering temperatures. Shooting in Rome began to seem efficient by comparison. Twenty four seconds was put in the can on the first day, thirty-five seconds on day two.*

It was time to set the cannons in the sand and get the battle into full throttle. But the cannons, which had been transported from Rome, wouldn't budge. Although Gilliam had stipulated that only four needed to be fired, all twelve of the monsters, beautifully recreated at the studio of fiberglass with metal tubes inside to hold the explosives, proved impossible to move once they had been positioned in the sand.

Rome-based American Eugene Rizzo, the unit publicist, saw the cannon episode as symbolic of the studio's expense-no-object

---

* There was, however, the one tiny welcome discovery that all the stock footage logged in Rome had been erroneously recorded by the production department on the daily reports. Film Finances had been fed these erroneous figures, which exaggerated even the parlous state the production company was undoubtedly in. The "good news" was brushed contemptuously aside in Los Angeles.

attitude. "I wasn't expecting anything remotely as heavy and spectacular," Gilliam assured him. "My vision was rather along the lines of a Monty Python cut-out thing. OK, more sophisticated than that, but very theatrical, very phony. Suddenly I've got all these massive, hugely ornate props. And the bill for them, no doubt."

For a while Gilliam came close to the breaking point. "I can't do it," he told McKeown, when the missing costumes failed to arrive on the second evening. "I just can't go on." Tomblin found himself hastily summoned. "Have a word with Terry, otherwise he's gone," McKeown pleaded.

Tomblin took his director by the arm, walked him along the beach, past the gigantic battle towers scattered at strategic intervals. "You're right," he told the startled Gilliam, "you're not going to make it, you should just call the whole thing off. Stop now and pack it in."

His tactical "advice" turned out to be exactly the electro-convulsive therapy Gilliam's brain had been seeking. "Hello!" he thought. "*Stop*? We can't do that!" It had been fine for him to ponder the unthinkable, to yearn for it, to mentally succumb to it, but once it was objectively and coolly established that the mission was truly impossible — why, then, there was only one possible response: Back to Work.

• • •

Tomblin provided therapy for the rest of the unit as well, defusing many a potentially depressing development with odes he composed, including one on the cannon episode: The Case of the Carefully Constructed Cannons:

"We must put a ban on the number of cannons,
We'll have to settle for half,
Terry said, 'Fine, but let's make it nine,'
Then we took all twelve for a laugh!"

The missing costumes arrived late on the evening of Tuesday, October 6. With them came accountant Arthur Tarry, a freelance emissary Columbia had hired to keep an eye on the film's progress. A jovial man with a shock of white hair, he became what Gilliam described as a "Cheshire cat observer."

Determined to finally get on track, Gilliam called full costume rehearsals for the Sultan's tent sequence on Wednesday with filming set for Thursday. He had intended to have the elephants arrive early so they could be measured for the "towers" they were to carry and to familiarize the animals with the various stunts. Unless the animals arrived early, he would have 400 heavily costumed actors lounging around on the sand while the elephants were laboriously put through their paces. For reasons never determined, the animals, in fact, arrived at the last moment. Gilliam groaned at the sight.

• • •

As the Sultan, Peter Jeffrey heroically resisted the stifling heat which his black and white silk robes made even more excruciating. "Fatter," Gilliam declared, "I need you fatter. And I don't like the facial hair you've been given. Let's see how we can change it."

His makeup took two hours each day to apply. With his costume padded still further, Jeffrey bemusedly surveyed the enormous black spade beard and the little silver bells dangling from his mustache that Gilliam had dreamt up, as well as his voluminous white turban. The Italian assistants meticulously insisted on placing every last hair by hand, even for scenes where Jeffrey was in the background or in the middle of a sandstorm.

Jeffrey questioned Gilliam closely about the impending tiger scene. The beast, after all, was only supposed to lie at his feet. "Don't worry," Gilliam told him, "we're getting a very docile animal."

Looking decidedly travel sick after its seven-hour journey, a huge tiger emerged out of a dingy little van. "It is going to be OK, isn't it?" Gilliam asked the trainer. "Ees no problem," he was assured. "Esmerelda, she make many feelms."

The wind had dropped, pushing the temperature up even further and fully justifying Almeria's claim to be Europe's hottest corner. The beast paced nervously around, ignoring her keeper's commands. The Spanish unit's vet stepped forward. "Perhaps a leetle tranquilizer would help?" he suggested. After Esmerelda had taken the shot without a murmur, her eyes began to glaze. After a moment she flopped over and lay utterly still. The keeper quickly crouched down beside her and felt her heart. "Ees *dead!*" he screamed, arms widespread. My Esmerelda is *dead, dead, dead!*" Peter Jeffrey leapt into dynamic action. "Quick," he roared, "someone get the unit doctor!"

Anxious moments passed in surreal pandemonium before the doctor arrived. After listening to the vet's garbled story, which was almost drowned out by the wails of the keeper, he reached for his black bag. Measuring a shot of adrenaline, he pumped it into Esmerelda. Following the merest twitch of an eyelid, Esmerelda, looking extremely groggy, sat up on her front legs and blearily took in her surroundings.

Without the slightest warning, she leapt into the air, barely clearing Jeffrey's left shoulder before landing and speeding out of the tent like a being possessed, scattering the cast and crew amidst crashing equipment.

Next day, this time anchored by a chain on one of her hind legs, Esmerelda stubbornly refused to cooperate by sitting docilely at the rose-petalled feet of an increasingly agitated Sultan. Jeffrey was desperately trying to rise above it all in the stifling heat and tension. Jonathan Pryce eyed the beast suspiciously through his Horatio Jackson granny specs, anxiously fingering his cravat. "It's never going to happen, Terry," Tomblin offered. "Maybe it's just nervous at the thought of acting with Jonathan and Peter," Idle suggested in what he deemed to be a helpful tone.

Even as he spoke Esmerelda was slipping her chain. Free once more, she again bolted for the tent door. Jose Escolar gave a terrifying scream and leapt into Gilliam's arms as the tent collapsed around them. "That's *it*," Gilliam declared, after the unfortunate beast had been safely recaptured, and Escolar's palpitations had ceased. "We'll shoot the damn scene with a *stuffed* tiger. There's no way we're doing anything more to that poor animal."

"I want a note made of this," Idle told Jonathan Pryce. "This is one for the books! Terry was *worried* about the tiger. He *has* got a heart! It doesn't matter a bugger about Peter or Jonathan, or poor Jose. But he *was* worried about the tiger!"

• • •

Richard Soames flew from Rome to check on Gilliam's progress. When he tried to check into the plush Gran Hotel, he was informed that they held no booking for anyone named "Soames." Just as he was about to be turned away, an assistant suggested they check under "Soam-ez." "Ah — si, si," the receptionist declared, beaming from ear to ear. For the rest of his stay Film Finances' boss was known to one and all as "Soam-ez."

Usually dressed conservatively, the chubby Soames looked totally lost when he turned up on the beach location in a Hawaiian shirt barely covering his paunch and Bermuda shorts adorning his pale, hairless legs. Gilliam showed him around the Sultan's harem, desperately trying to exude enthusiasm and purposely overlooking the wretched tiger incident.

Soames seemed strangely unresponsive to Gilliam's PR tapdance. Unknown to him, Soames was up to his neck in an even more pressing crisis than the state of *Munchausen*. His company was in the midst of sale negotiations. *Munchausen's* problems wouldn't make the transaction any easier.

Pre-*Munchausen* the situation had been oh-so-simple. Soames had met Nigel Kayser, head of the rival Entertainment Completions, back in 1986, where he detected the first intimation of Kayser's desire to buy him out. Soames was able to view the prospect with equanimity. As it happened, one of his major shareholders wanted to retire, the merchant bank with whom the company was involved was happy to take a profit, and for Soames himself retirement was looming. At the right price, the chance for a sellout was enticing. The *Munchausen* overruns had thrown negotiations back into the melting pot.

Only weeks after they had begun, on October 19, billions of dollars were lost overnight on the U.S. stock exchange. The overseas value of the dollar plunged. It never rains but it pours, Soames must have reflected as the darkening storm over *Munchausen* was followed by Black Monday.

With Esmerelda safely dispatched, probably to another movie, it was now time for little Gustavus to blow away one of the elephants. The mammoth animal was expected to obediently lie on its back with paws in the air, then move rapidly backwards on a huge platform with rollers. The elephant was perfectly content to climb on to the contraption, but insisted on jumping off again the instant it began to move. After the umpteenth attempt, as one of the crew was whacking it back on to the rig, the enraged elephant suddenly swung its trunk around and caught its tormentor between his legs.

The unfortunate member was rushed off to the hospital. With that kind of cooperation from one elephant, it was clearly time to set up the elephant stampede. The elephants, in a spectacular scene involving hundreds of extras, and accompanied by the roar of the cannons, were to charge the Turkish tents and bring them crashing down. Disoriented by their first demonstration of cannon fire, the elephants turned in confusion and headed straight for the rolling cameras, sending cast, crew and equipment flying. "I don't think they liked the guns," one of the crew observed as their pachydermal rear ends were glimpsed disappearing around the coastline, hotly pusued by their anxious keepers.

The animals were at last pacified — but the director remained agitated. Out of the corner of his eye, Gilliam could see the Romany family who had brought the elephants to them in the distance against the background of a roseate sky, laughing together and hosing down the animals in the sea. He looked back at the incredible chaos he was trying to transform into a fluent scene, at the multitude of individuals hanging on his every word, at the sweat-stained pages of script in his trembling hands.

While Rotunno was demanding to know what he should do in the failing light, Gilliam decided that he had only one logical course of action left. The thought briefly occurred to him that if he headed out to sea there was the possibility of an escape to Africa. The cast and crew looked on astonished as, with a mad "Whoopee-e-e!" he flung his script in the air and made a lumbering dash towards the sea and the cavorting animals. Helped by the gypsies, he heaved himself up and sat on one of the elephant's backs. The unit in the distance might have been a million miles away as far as Gilliam was concerned. He was experiencing his first blissful, unadulterated moment of peace and contentment for many weeks.

CHAPTER FOURTEEN

I interviewed Thomas Schuhly the first week I started on the film and was struck by his frank admiration for the Rambo character, which is so at odds with Terry's world. Terry basically left the USA because of Rambo, it was a time when people were reacting strongly against Vietnam and militarism in general. Then he ends up in Europe making a movie with someone who thinks Stallone is great!
—Eugene Rizzo

A lot of Terry's films seem to follow the pattern that is set by the major theme. Brazil was about the basic struggle with authoritarianism, which is basically what happened to the movie in its history with Universal. In Munchausen the mixture of bluff and reality seems to be exactly how the film is progressing.
—Eric Idle

Soames' visit to Almeria was followed by a stinging memo alleging that shooting was being slowed down by the documentary crew covering the picture. The crew Soames witnessed was in fact Columbia's own Electronic Press Kit unit at work on trailer and promotional shots — yet his attitude seemed to sum up the completion guarantor's general view toward all publicity, as a complete waste of time and money. Gilliam was alarmed at the strident, almost frantic tone of Soames' message, as well as the naïveté it displayed of the process of filmmaking.

For Gene Rizzo the *Munchausen* publicity assignment was a potential dream come true, for he knew how rare it was to work on movies where both the producer and director were publicity-oriented. "Schuhly in particular," he noted, "*adores* being interviewed and is always available for 'photo-opportunities.' And for all the demons and problems on Terry's mind and the creative frenzy on the set, he's always marvelous with journalists. Terry seems to work best under chaotic circumstances. Many people need everything cut and dried, but Terry positively seems to gain inspiration from it. I think you always have to remember where Terry's coming from. He's an animator and he can probably divorce himself from all the chaos round him and cut through to what's going to be seen on the screen."

• • •

Never having actually met Schuhly, casting director Irene Lamb decided to take up David Tomblin's invitation to visit Almeria. "Come on out," Tomblin had suggested. "You'll have a wonderful holiday here."

There was, after all, a lot to be sorted out. Bill Paterson and Allison Steadman had both cooled their heels for weeks after their original contract date and Schuhly was saying he would only pay them for the period they had worked.

Lamb was met at the airport by a unit car in the middle of the night, driven miles up into the mountains and dropped off outside a hotel. Beautiful as it was in the lull before dawn, she sensed that something was wrong and refused to let the driver go until everything was checked out. Sure enough, the hotel was not expecting her; the driver was to have picked up a video crew instead. A call to the Gran Hotel, where the *Munchausen* unit was based, established her true destination.

Later the next day a car was provided to take her on location. After a lengthy drive she was dropped in what looked like the middle of the desert, with nothing in sight for miles. As the scorching sun beat mercilessly down, Lamb began walking. She innocently rounded a dune to unexpectedly behold a truly incredible sight.

On the beach were 360 Turkish soldiers, their cutlasses flashing in the sun, three elephants, sixty horses, and dozens of enormously fat women — the Sultan's odalisques — all charging about. In the distance she could see the resplendent figure of John Neville, unmistakable in his gold-braided scarlet jacket and tricorn hat. Overcome by the spectacle, she felt she might have wandered on camera. Gradually she began to edge forward. Just then Roy Button, sitting on top of a crane, spotted her. Lifting his megaphone to his lips he boomed, "Look out, everybody. English casting director approaching."

Lamb walked tentatively up to Gilliam, who was looking very much on edge. "He'll be glad to see a familiar face from back home," Tomblin had assured her. Instead Gilliam muttered "hello" and carried on as if she had been on the shoot all along. Spotting Jonathan Pryce at the entrance to a tent, she explained that she had arrived to wring some sense out of Schuhly. "Really?" he asked with a sly smile. "You plan to stay indefinitely, then?"

After chatting for a few moments inside the dark shelter of the tent, Pryce suggested that they move out. He explained that there was this drugged tiger, who had escaped, been recaptured, gone to sleep and was just starting to come around — at their feet! A horrified Lamb, watching the beast stir, was saying to herself, "Dear God, this is a madhouse I've walked into."

Schuhly made it crystal clear he was not in the least bit interested in seeing Lamb during her visit. Two days passed before she caught up with her quarry. After ten minutes of stating her case in what she thought was a down-to-earth, businesslike manner, she began to be irritated by what she perceived as Schuhly's mocking asides. "You seem to think I'm joking all the time," she accused. "Aren't you?" he countered. "No," she crisply replied. "I'm simply trying to put a case for my clients, who deserve to be paid for the ridiculous way you've buggered them about."

After another hour of difficult negotiation he offered, "I'll bet you didn't think I was like this." Staring at the muscle-bound creature across the table from her, Lamb did not have the faintest idea what he was talking about. "The reason I'm so intelligent," he clarified, "is because I was brought up by Jesuit priests and until I was nine years old I spoke only Latin or Greek. That's how I have the route to so many languages.

"You're probably wondering," he continued, "why Terry's not speaking to me. Can I be frank with you? Terry's jealous because I'm so much better looking and younger than he is. Did you know they call me the Bruce Springsteen of Rome?"

"I hadn't heard," Lamb managed.

"Oh, yes." Schuhly assured her. "It's because of my brilliance and dynamism, which the Italians recognize. Terry doesn't understand the love they have for me." Confronted with an ego she could not believe, Lamb decided to play along. "How does it feel," she asked, "to be absolutely perfect?"

"I do have some flaws," Schuhly conceded, "but I can't think what they are at the moment. Can I get back to you?"

It was several days before Schuhly would even agree to look at the artists' contracts. At their next meeting Lamb was completely taken aback as she surveyed the copy contracts Schuhly produced. He had whited out the starting dates. "You can't *do* that," she said, staring at him with her mouth open. "I've just done it," he replied, utterly triumphant, "and I'll fill in new dates later to suit myself."

"B... b... but everyone will know you've simply whitened through the original dates —"

"Ah," he replied, beaming from ear to ear, "but it will be undetectable once the contracts have been photocopied! Ya?"

"You'll never get away with it. I'll call Equity."

"You can't do that, Irene. You're working for me."

"No, I'm not. I'm independent."

Schuhly laughed. "Oh, Irene," he said, "you're very clever. And so *very* funny!"

"Look, Thomas, be serious. Bill and Allison have already gone back home and they're needed back here. Unless you agree to pay them the full amount, there's no way they'll return. What am I supposed to tell their agent?"

"Tell them I'm a shit," Schuhly suggested.

At a later meeting he openly bragged about his whiteout maneuver. "You should have seen her face!" he told everybody. The word came from London that Paterson and Steadman would not be returning unless they were paid from their original starting date. Lamb knew perfectly well that they would come back for Gilliam's sake, but kept this to herself. The bluff continued for a week while everyone waited to see if Schuhly would transfer the full amount of money to London. At the eleventh hour of 5 p.m. on Friday, the money came through.

CHAPTER FIFTEEN

There are certain elements missing that I don't think Schuhly's capable of fathoming, like the things that go on between the cogs that make people tick — things like loyalties and passions.
—Charles McKeown

Schuhly is either totally mad, which I don't think he is, or he took on more than he could cope with. And instead of admitting it, he literally pretended nothing *was going wrong!*
—Eric Idle

As they strolled along the beach in Almeria, Schuhly explained his "great scam" to McKeown: to spend as much money as possible as quickly as possible in order to commit Film Finances to the project. He also ruminated on the breakdown of his relationship with Gilliam. "What's a producer without a director?" he reflected. Schuhly seemed genuinely upset at the acrimonious turn of events. McKeown detected the first sacrificial rumblings to suggest that the producer might back out for the sake of the movie.

• • •

John Neville's old friend, hair and makeup artist Pam Meager, had received the fateful call from Gilliam's wife, Maggie Weston, another ex-BBC veteran, in June 1986. Seasoned trouper that she is, Meager was nonetheless over the moon at the thought of working with Gilliam in Italy. She fondly sees Gilliam as a genuine English eccentric who just happened to be born in America. "There's a bit of a madman in there somewhere," she suggests. "He might still have an American accent, but I actually think he's an English Munchausen! He cares what other people say, but you have to be prepared when you go to him and show him something you're terribly proud of, for him to say, 'Oh, no, that's not right.' But it isn't hurtful, it's simply that you haven't pressed the right button, and it takes you a while to realize he's talking to you as an equal."

Lee Cleary's advice to Meager was unequivocal. "Make sure you have at least half an English crew and half an Italian crew," he told her, "otherwise they'll *have* you. As soon as the Italian makeup people can do your work, there won't be any reason for you to stay around. And whatever you do, at least keep the Baron's makeup to yourself."

Meager chose to ignore Cleary's warning. Having modelled the Baron's huge hooked nose and chosen all the wigs, complete with side curls and saucy pony-tail, she proceeded to teach the Italians exactly how he should appear in all his incarnations. It was a fatal mistake. She was greeted by her Italian counterpart with a decidedly gleeful, but ominous, "Do you know 49 people have left or been fired from this production already?"

"I had what we'll politely call the Latin temperament to contend with," said Meager. "There was a wonderful local girl working with me as a hairdresser, who kept bursting into tears. When I asked what on earth it was all about, she told me that for 25 years she'd been mistress to one of the Italian assistants. He'd found a job for his new beloved in the costume department next door to us and every time she saw either one of them the waterworks started! Then there was this vast camera crew being assembled under Peppino, *all* of whom seemed to be related to him in some way or other!

"There was this tremendous sense that the film gave everyone opportunities for Oscars. Everyone was jealous of Terry's attention. With the makeup you could ask Terry to show you what he wanted, then you just refined it and gave it to him. With the costumes, it was different. They'd researched them at the Victoria and Albert Museum in London, taken endless photographs and obtained hundreds of fabric swatches. It was total indulgence and over-designing — and that attitude's contagious."

The Italians' notion of makeup duty allocations seemed a travesty to the British crew. Winston Dennis protested to Schuhly. "It's unbelieveable," he railed. "we've all got one guy each just to do our individual makeup. My guy works for an hour or so, then sits in his trailer the rest of the day doing sweet fuck all. Even if there's a hundred people waiting to get done for a crowd scene, he won't go near them and help out. Then when we have to get a quick touch-up later in the day because of the heat, that's done by a second, *junior* team!"

"Winston," said Schuhly, straining to put his arm around the giant, "it's the Italian way. And let's face it, it's worked for decades."

• • •

After the transition to Mario Di Biase, Bob Edwards became responsible for the installation of the much-heralded blue screen. Schuhly, the chief architect and godfather of the process, emphasized the residual advantages to Cinecitta, enabling foreground scenes to be shot indoors under controlled conditions. A multitude of special effects and backgrounds could be added later in state-of-the-art fashion. "The days of *Ben Hur* and *Cleopatra* are over," he declared, "because nobody can afford to pay for big sets like that anymore. If you want a film to look like that these days you have to go for effects, using models and blue screen."

Schuhly claimed to have recruited high caliber personnel to set up the blue screen stage, to work on the film, and at the same time teach the Italians to use the revolutionary technology. "I want this film to push the Italians into the 1990s," he maintained, "into the future of filmmaking."

Edwards was, however, grappling with the first of a series of monumental foul-ups in the installation. The 600 inverters that had been purchased from Philips Electrical to light the blue screen, at a cost of £12,000, failed to work when they were wire-mounted — despite having been successfully tested 24 hours a day for two solid weeks. It seemed that Philips' head office had changed the specification without bothering to inform either Cinecitta or Edwards. More costly Siemens inverters were obtained, 400 off the shelf and 200 on order. Edwards remained confident that the backing module for the screen could be delivered by early October, giving Cinecitta ample time to have it fitted for Gilliam's scheduled return at the end of November.

Four completed aluminum modular panels were air-freighted to Rome, enabling Cinecitta to work progressively on the erection of counterbalanced scaffolding to provide their support. A further 80 units were scheduled to follow before the end of October. Once the panels were installed, Edwards estimated that only a further three days would be required to rig the screen itself, and perhaps a few more days for testing.

The stage to support the blue screen naturally had to be ready for the arrival of the first modular panel. A complicated set-up procedure involved the placement and design of access doors, as well as the strategic hanging of catwalks. The stage would have to be spotlessly cleaned and then painted matte black, and the surrounding area asphalted. Edwards found little progress on any of these fronts during his visits to Cinecitta. A tentative dab of paint in one area was supposed to signal the start of work. Edwards was decidedly unimpressed.

"Given the likely bad weather conditions in Rome in November when the unit returns, it's possible," he warned everyone, "*even probable*, that the only stage on which the unit will be able to shoot on a regular daily basis will be the blue screen stage. If we don't have this in perfect working order, the production will be in an impossible position, faced with unrecoupable losses. Under the circumstances, I cannot emphasize enough the feeling of desperate uncertainty and anxiety that the current state of work, or lack of it, generates in my gut."

To Edwards' credit the stage was indeed ready in time for the installation. Unfortunately, a mistake had been made in the specifications of the screen itself. It was delivered ten meters too narrow, and had to be returned for modification. Upon its re-delivery, however, new problems had to be overcome. The ceiling from which it was to be suspended required considerable strengthening. And while the screen was now the correct size, there was no longer room to mount essential sidelights, necessitating the construction of twin cantilevered towers on which bulbs could be suspended.

One final miscalculation completed the picture. When the screen was finally and laboriously erected by Schuhly's experts it was hung back to front, rendering its unveiling by the heads of Cinecitta a distinct embarrassment.

• • •

As filming continued to run behind schedule in Almeria, the unit was dealt yet another major blow. Roy Button, Tomblin's trusty righthand man, announced he was leaving due to personal problems at home. Now the full burden of First Assistant Director would fall on Jose Escolar's shoulders. Although undoubtedly capable, he had no experience of films on *Munchausen*'s scale. Come to that, who did? And the communication problem was becoming ever more acute with Rotunno and his crew. Escolar's lack of Italian had him sorely disadvantaged. Gilliam's own requests often ran into an uncomprehending brick wall.

If the production was losing Indians, more chiefs seemed to arrive with every plane. From Columbia came Gareth Wigan, a tall, quiet, grey-haired Englishman in his early fifties. Together with Arthur Tarry, crisis meetings were held in a frantic attempt to arrive at a dependable expenditure figure to date, and a projected final budget. A different set of figures was produced each day, each of them allegedly based on the best information available. In the space of one week the eventual budget overage estimates ranged from $3 million to a truly alarming $10 million.

Deep down Gilliam now felt that the film would never be completed. "I'm saying one thing to the press," he told Eric Idle, "pretending to be confident we'll overcome all our problems, and all the time I know I'm talking balls."

"No, you've *got* to do it," Idle replied, "just to show John, the world's most reasonable, rational man, that a film like this can be done." Idle knew full well that Gilliam, like all Pythons, compared himself and his progress to the redoubtable John Cleese. His observation kept Gilliam going for several more weeks.

C H A P T E R
S I X T E E N

*Thomas was only around for a brief moment
in Almeria and ran. I would love one day to
discover where he was during the key battles
of this film, because I never saw him. When
there was a crisis, that's when he
disappeared, at all the key moments. He
would argue that his best defense was to
disappear. There were absolute panics, lost
weekends when he'd just vanish because he
didn't know what the fuck to do. Meantime,
the rest of us were taking heavy artillery fire.*

—Terry Gilliam

Winston Dennis, complete with an already painfully ulcerated
leg, found himself in sea water for eight hours in San Jose. As the
strongest man in the world, he was to swing several galleons at the
ends of the chains strung around his waist.

"Three of them weighing about a ton each," Dennis said as he
recalled the discomfort of the scene. "The background was meant to

be open sea, but these tankers kept sailing into view and ruining the shots. The only experienced stunt person there told me I could unclip myself if anything went wrong, which did nothing to make me feel better. I was standing on this "rock," a fiberglass platform in the water, which a motor underneath was supposed to turn. Every time it did it nearly broke up the platform. I had to be careful where I stepped when it was moving or I would have gone through it! In the end I had to rotate the chains myself.

"By this time it was 4 o'clock; we were losing the light and Schuhly had wandered onto the beach to watch the shooting. When he saw the lack of progress he began shouting and confusing everyone. The whole thing was a bloody great mess."

With Schuhly confined to his hotel room pleading food poisoning, Richard Soames dispatched Stratton Leopold to Almeria just two days before the end of the shoot there. A Greek-American in his late thirties, Leopold's dark eyes, curly hair and earnestly bewildered expression gives him the look of an overgrown Greek shepherd boy searching for a wayward flock. To him had fallen the unenviable task of bringing the runaway production to heel.

After the theater scene rushes were shown, Leopold was overheard murmuring enthusiastically to Gareth Wigan. Eric Idle, who had suggested the showing to boost morale, turned to Gilliam in the makeshift screening room that had been hastily put together. "The money should see this!" he whispered.

Just over thirteen minutes of film had been exposed in fourteen days of shooting in Almeria. The strange beachcombing trio of Leopold, Tarry and Wigan reminded Idle of nothing so much as the *Beat The Devil* villains — if John Huston were alive and planning a sequel, they would be perfect!

Among several dozen contact prints delivered to Gilliam of production stills processed in Rome were two pages of a familiar muscular character stripped to the waist and posing in boxing regalia and headband. Schuhly was playing out his role of Rambo, the fearless fighting producer. In the midst of the chaos, it was all Gilliam needed. "That *fucker*," he raged. "Talk about Nero fiddling while Rome burns!" McKeown could see the new tag line applied to the making of *Munchausen*: "The Production was in Chaos! . . . But the

Producer's Body was Perfect!"

"The pictures tell you a lot about the guy," Idle reflected. "One picture's worth a thousand assholes."

• • •

Back in Los Angeles after his brief trip to Spain, Soames tried desperately to coax extra money out of Columbia. As Schuhly before him had discovered, it was like chasing a chimera.

Paradoxically, the studio's inflexible attitude was to Gilliam's advantage. "We guaranteed to pick up a film, *The Adventures of Baron Munchausen*, directed by Terry Gilliam, for a total of $20.5 million," they kept repeating, "and not a penny more." If Film Finances chose to arbitrarily cut scenes from the script the studio had been shown, they would be potentially in breach of contract, automatically releasing Columbia from their obligation to accept the finished movie. If Gilliam were removed at this stage, *The Adventures of Baron Munchausen* would no longer, logically enough, be a Terry Gilliam movie.

Jake Eberts came up with a bright, if decidedly overly optimistic suggestion. If Columbia took over the whole show, $2 million in interest charges would be saved by paying off the Japanese bank loan. This, together with the $2 million contingency allowance saved by withdrawing from Film Finances, would release a total of $4 million. "We recognize your problems," was David Picker's flat response, "but they're not *our* problems. We have a deal, that deal is for a pick-up, and that's the deal we feel comfortable with."

• • •

With shooting finished at Almeria on October 20 Schuhly was left behind in his sickbed, while the *Munchausen* unit made the journey by charter plane to Zaragoza and then on to the ruined city of Belchite. There they were welcomed into an incredibly detailed city square complete with majestic cathedral as well as towering battlements and, on the outskirts, other magnificently constructed sets.

After taking an anxious stroll around, Stratton Leopold booked a call to Soames in Los Angeles. "Richard, I've never seen anything like this," he told him. "I'm overwhelmed. The sets here are huge; you'd have to come and see them for yourself to believe them. The point is,

Richard, everything is on such a scale, you must realize how expensive it will be if we continue . . ."

"Do I have a choice?"

"Well, you could cancel now . . ."

"Stratton, if we do that we're $15 million in the hole. It's out of the question."

The schedule mercifully allowed Idle to fly back to London for a week's break. "How they must be missing me at Belchite," he told his wife. "I've been on the film for four weeks already and only said about four lines!"

Refusing to fly, Valentina Cortese insisted on being driven all the way from Rome. "My thing with flying dates back to when I hurt my knees on stage many years ago," she explained. "I developed a wonderful idea of arriving at airports with a stick and putting on an act that I was unable to walk. I was given a wheelchair and allowed on the plane first, then they took wonderful care of me. You can even go through customs — because everyone feels so sorry for you! Once on an international trip I had to take about twenty planes, so I had twenty different wheelchairs! Then I arrived in some South American city and the wheelchair had already been taken. I went on with my act, and this handsome, wonderful young fireman carried me everywhere! I had to be careful, because I was laughing inside. I thought, what a pity wheelchairs weren't like him!"

Cortese checked in with Cleary from her every port of call on the journey — Naples, Monte Carlo, Nice, Cannes and San Tropez, eventually descending upon Zaragoza with her entourage of two Mercedes. One contained twelve pieces of luggage and the other herself, her maid Panucia, a striking young American couple, and her Yorkshire terrier in his own Gucci poochie.

After a withering glance she decided to have nothing to do with the Hotel Corona de Aragon, where the rest of the crew were quartered. "Too ugly and too modern," she scornfully declared, and promptly set off for the longer-established Gran Hotel.

Cleary watched, hypnotized, as she proceeded to take over the clerk at reception. Dripping mink, she leaned on the desk with one elbow, her tiny fist tucked under her chin. "Now, darling," she said with a dazzling smile, "I would like for me a very, very, *very* nice room! And for my maid," — a swish of the mink — "*not* such a very, very nice room."

She then proceeded to minutely inspect each and every one of the ten available rooms and suites, while two elderly, bewildered Spanish porters pushed her Gucci luggage everywhere behind her.

• • •

The ruined city of Belchite lies 25 miles southeast of Zaragoza, in the northeast corner of Spain. The site of one of the most ferocious battles of the Spanish Civil War, the town has been preserved since 1938 as a permanent reminder of the conflict. While the temperature was pleasant enough by day, the night brought freezing cold that immediately engendered a rash of colds, flu and bronchitis.

Stratton Leopold, beadily eyeing the "per diems" involved with the English side of the special effects crew, began decimating their ranks in favor of the Italians. The more Tomblin tried to point out the error of his ways — that *half* the people would simply take *twice* as long — the more hellbent Leopold became to prove him wrong.

Richard Conway took the full brunt of the cutbacks in the special effects department. From the beginning he had never been given the personnel support he had requested; these reductions further threatened the viability of his task. "From now on," he told Tomblin, "it's going to be like working on quicksand."

While Leopold had supervised smaller films in the past, Gilliam found him ill-equipped to deal with complexities on the scale of *Munchausen*. Lee Cleary watched from the desk he occupied in Gilliam's office as Film Finances struggled to assume control through him. "We'd already been cutting down the staff all the time," said Cleary. "We only had two assistant directors, which on the size of our film was unreal. Then Stratton arrived and immediately hired a secretary and a personal assistant! His function seemed to be waiting for us to be told the plug was pulled. Dave Tomblin forbade him to talk to any of the actors, because he always said the wrong thing through lack of experience and upset them."

With tempers frequently flaring on the set between the Italian and the English crew, Tomblin was required to step in on many occasions and mediate — when he got the chance, that is. After one particular confrontation between the wire riggers from England, Bob

Wiesinger and Kevin Mathews, and the Italian crew, Leopold decided to take the matter into his own hands. Despite the fact that the Englishmen had wired every set for the complicated special effects required, Leopold acted decisively. "You're fired," he told them. "I want you off the set."

"Right, fine," they replied, immediately pulling out their wire cutters. Lee Cleary saw what was going on and rushed in to stop them. "Hang on, you two," he yelled. "Hang on till I've found Dave Tomblin."

Leopold turned on Cleary. "What's it got to do with him? *I've* fired them."

"I know," Cleary replied, nodding furiously and shrugging his shoulders at the same time, "but hang on anyway until I've found Dave."

Within a few minutes Cleary put Tomblin in the picture. "Jesus, if Bob and Kevin cut the wires, we'll go three weeks behind —"

Leopold found himself summoned to Tomblin's office. "I presume you've got another team lined up to replace these men?" Tomblin asked, "Or how do you propose to get all the sets re-rigged?"

Leopold was defiance itself, and had what he considered an unbeatable trump card to play. "I'll get Bob Harman from England. He's a wire expert I've worked with before."

"Have you?" Tomblin asked. "Then you're bound to know he's also Bob Wiesinger's partner — one of the two guys you've just fired. Any other bright ideas?"

"W-well . . . no."

"Then I suggest you reinstate the two of them right now. Talk to them properly and they'll come round and apologize to the Italians. Be a *diplomat*, Stratton."

Later that same day Tomblin wondered out loud why Film Finances had held back from disbanding the entire unit. "It's the Gilliam factor," Charles McKeown explained. "Do you think they'll stick around for the entire remainder of the shoot?"

"Sure they will," Tomblin replied. "Like shit to a blanket."

CHAPTER
SEVENTEEN

Soames' lawyer, Steve Ransohoff, had this unerring habit of getting everybody's back up by writing the wrong letter when something diplomatic would have achieved a better end. He was abrasive and very, very slippery — in fact, a typical lawyer! He wrote the most godawful things to me and the next minute asked for my help in getting something he wanted!

Stratton spent the whole time sending memos back covering his ass. At this he was better than anybody I've ever seen! Dave Tomblin in particular tried to stop him before he did some outrageous act. Perhaps his arrival was a lucky thing for the film, because if they had sent someone really experienced, maybe the film really would have gone down.

—Terry Gilliam

It is impossible to overestimate Soames' anger at the quagmire in which he saw the company trapped. While rival completion guarantors who had fought for the *Munchausen* business were heaving "There but for the grace of God" sighs of relief, Soames was telling everyone who would listen of the stringent precautions he had taken before accepting the *Munchausen* challenge.

"We had one of our people from London vet it in Rome," he protested. "She was assured by Bob Edwards in July, together with Schuhly and Gilliam, that they could make it for $23.5 million. Yes, Schuhly discussed with us whether he should fire Edwards or not, since he wasn't getting results, and yes, it took Edwards a hell of a long time to get a finished budget. But our representative in Rome was particularly impressed by him. By the time we got to Spain, Edwards had gone, Gilliam was running the entire show, and was refusing even to acknowledge the things we were saying to him."

Stratton Leopold had been hired by Film Finances to troubleshoot on *Munchausen* as he had on previous occasions for the company. Because his powers would be unusually restricted, he accepted the *Munchausen* assignment with considerable reluctance. Three days of hard talking by Richard Soames were necessary before an agreement was reached, and even then it was under false pretenses. "It will only take a couple of weeks at the most," Soames promised.

Normally Leopold had the license to make whatever changes he deemed necessary on a production, then report back when the job was done. Because of *Munchausen*'s scale, however, he was empowered only to report back and await further instructions from Los Angeles. Soon a sense of utter frustration set in. While he appeared to the crew of *Munchausen* to be indecisive and arbitrary, he was in fact virtually powerless to act. For all the power he had, it was as if his balls were being checked in at the production office every morning, then collected again in time for his daily report to Los Angeles.

As far as the unit was concerned, Leopold was Film Finances' heavy, their hatchet-man, sent to do them in. While this strictly defined his role, no one realized the extent to which Leopold began to be seduced by the Baron as he cast his spell.

• • •

McKeown had long suspected that an informer inside the unit was leaking stories to the press. The suspicion was confirmed when

Charles Kipps, a *Variety* reporter, arrived from Los Angeles carrying a list of the most up-to-date bad news.

Publicist Gene Rizzo harbored similar feelings. "I never really figured out who, but there was definitely a looselips around, picking up the phone and calling somebody, who was in turn passing it around Los Angeles. Robert Osborne's column in *Hollywood Reporter* had it, correctly, that we were one week behind after one week of shooting. These early leaks of a purely negative nature influenced Columbia to such an extent that they gave me the command, early in the game, '*No* press in America,' which I think was a very tragic turn of events for the picture. If there was a mole out to sabotage the movie, he did his work, because there's a legion of journalists all over the world who adore Terry's work. All we had to do was bring them in; they would have done a nice story for the U.S., but Columbia imposed this absolute press blackout. We tried to protest, but we never knew who we were dealing with at Columbia in the aftermath of the Puttnam earthquake."

• • •

Schuhly's initial tacit acceptance of Film Finances' takeover soon turned into rebellion as the company leaned more heavily on him, finally attempting to dislodge him altogether from the production. Soames was calmly informed that if he continued to go for him, Schuhly would go down *blazing*. He refused to let Film Finances remove production files from his office, and prohibited their inspection on site — unless an "understanding" was reached. A rumor circulated that he even threatened to burn the negative of everything Gilliam had filmed to date.

So why *didn't* Film Finances fire Schuhly? At first the company would only admit to "good reasons." When asked if these reasons included black money payments, which if revealed would have had the Italian government pulling the plug on the whole show, Soames categorically denied this, but amplified: "Schuhly was just flailing about all over the place. He used all sorts of threats, like we wouldn't get Sean Connery if we got rid of him. For the sake of simply stopping him going on rampage, we decided to let him stay. And he was powerless anyway."

Film Finances and Soames had left themselves with only one

victim to gun for. Soames' interpretation of events was that Gilliam had *used* Schuhly to clinch the deal with both them and Columbia; as far as Gilliam was concerned, Schuhly's purpose had been purely catalytic. Once the director had his money he intended to make the movie his way, brooking no interference.

• • •

From the start the entire unit had been extremely impressed by the blonde youngster, Sarah Polley, aptly described by Eric Idle as a 10-year-old going on 30. When Susan Sarandon visited the set in Rome, Sarah raised eyebrows with her innocent, unaffected, but decidedly precocious suggestion, "Let's do lunch!" On the one hand her favorite daily reading seemed to be stock market reports, on the other she was a vegetarian because she "felt sorry for the animals."

She became terribly upset when her mother, who was also her agent, had to repeatedly beg Arthur Tarry for money to live on. "What can I do?" Sarah beseeched Idle, with an inherent sense of histrionics that would have done credit to a budding Bette Davis.

One of the crew was entertaining a local girl back in his hotel room one weekend afternoon in Belchite. Sarah was bouncing her ball in the corridor outside when another, rather louder bouncing — that of bed springs — began, accompanied by an apparently endless series of shrieks. Finally Sarah could stand it no longer and hammered loudly on the door. Only when the creaking and the shrieking had subsided did she let fly. "That's 37 times!" she scolded.

In Belchite, after the cast had spent an entire night shivering on an outside set, Sarah was once again at her most vulnerable and touching. As she snuggled up to Idle she sniffed miserably and confided, "I just want to go back to being a child again."

• • •

Even though the luscious Uma Thurman was 17, going on 35 — in Sarah Polley's terms — she was still classed as a minor, and strictly speaking only allowed on the set four hours a day. Like everyone else, she in fact worked 14-16 hours a day, her agent having made it clear that, provided she was paid overtime, she was willing to waive responsibility.

Since Uma had not been required in Almeria, she had returned to New York after shooting in Rome. Now she approached Lee Cleary on the set at Belchite. "How does overtime work?" she asked.

Cleary explained that it was quite straightforward. His timesheets were handed in daily to the accounts department for computation. "Well," Uma declared, "I've been off and on the production for six weeks and I've never seen a dime, either for basic time *or* overtime. If I'm not going to be paid, Lee, I don't think I can work anymore." Concerned, Cleary sought out Stratton Leopold. "OK, she'll get her money," he was assured.

A week later Uma went to Cleary just before the crucial Venus-on-the-half-shell scene. "I still haven't been paid," she told him, obviously close to tears, and in no fit state to act. "I thought you were going to do something for me," she accused.

Enraged, Cleary marched up to Leopold. "What's the rush?" Leopold wanted to know, belligerently brushing him aside. "No rush," Cleary replied, "except she's not going on the set until she gets her money. She's going to walk out."

Leopold glared at Cleary, then realized that a serious point had been reached. "Tell her to h-hold on," he stammered, "I'll be b-back in a few minutes." And so he was, hand in hand with Arthur Tarry, waving hundred dollar bills at the actress.

The undulating Uma embodied the one common cause shared by both the warring Italian and English crews — the matter of her deflowering. To the Italians the issue was one of nothing less than national pride, reaffirmation of their collective machismo. Frustrating as it must have been for them, the betting for a while was on one particular Englishman, who emerged as favorite for the prize in fairly short order. Ray Cooper perfectly summed up the beautiful, highly intelligent Uma when he declared, "This is a girl who has all the answers. But as yet she doesn't know what the questions are."

As the weeks went by, without any apparent, or claimed resolution of "Operation Thurman" word came down that an announcement, and a surprising one, was imminent. The question was who? Or was it *chi*? And — *quando, quando, quando*?

David Tomblin doubted it would be either and penned another lively limerick:

"Our lovely girl Uma
As lithe as a puma

Is close to the age of consent.
But this leggy young filly
Is sadly not silly
And will wait for a suitable gent."

• • •

Cleary watched as the real decision-making was made in Gilliam's office the first thing in the morning, around 7:30 a.m., long before Leopold or anyone else showed up. As for Schuhly, he never made an appearance in Belchite. "I'm sure he didn't know what we were doing most of the time," said Cleary. "I had two conversations with him throughout the entire shoot, which is ridiculous. He hated me because I was working for Terry and I had control of things I should never have been allowed to take control of — the actor's movements, their travel plans and such, only because no one else would take on anything to do with it."

John Neville had spent his entire life avoiding the movies only to be drawn into the ultimate movie to avoid. An extremely organized and efficient man, he was up to his neck in one of the worst organized films of all time, directed by a man who was often totally depressed. After four hours of makeup had been endured each day, half the time he was not even called. Once he was made up, his glasses wouldn't fit over his false nose, making reading impossible. Although Neville rarely complained, Gilliam felt constantly guilty.

On one occasion, however, Gilliam was totally responsible for causing a distinct, if brief, hiccup in his relations with Neville. The Baron's frequent modulations of age during the film led to a tremendous amount of logistical confusion for the makeup department. Maggie Weston had produced a master chart with the Baron's age defined for every scene, but for some unfathomable reason the makeup department often seemed to be working to a different schedule altogether. In the end the Italian makeup expert assigned to Neville would check with Lee Cleary, who had a copy of the master list. A typical exchange would be, "Today the Baron eez 50. No?"

"No, today he's 65."

With Cleary absent one morning, Gilliam was sought out. "Today eez 80. No?"

"Yeah, 80," Gilliam replied distractedly. Four hours later, when Neville emerged from the makeup department, the continuity girl rushed up to Gilliam and whispered the unthinkable. Aghast, Gilliam turned to the scarlet-bedecked Neville and apologized for his error: "John, I'm so embarrassed . . ." Even as he did, he could see the color draining under Neville's layers of makeup and latex. "You've given me the wrong age, haven't you?" the actor stormed. "Four bloody hours down the drain. This is the absolute giddy limit, Terry."

When the day's filming was finally in the can, Gilliam approached Neville once more, to be greeted with a regretful smile. "I should have checked it myself," he now told his director. "Never mind, it gave me a great opportunity to let off some much-needed steam at your expense."

Cleary witnessed much of the interplay between the fantasist director and the meticulous stage actor. "Basically he's a brilliant animator who uses actors to fill the screen. He wasn't really all that interested in dialogue. John is a *theatrical* actor, he was interested in *acting*, but he acted very little in the whole film. I mean, he was never *stretched*, as he'd like to have been.

"John used to say that he never found any of the Python material funny. When Terry was on his own he got on with him all right, but he didn't like when Terry was with Charles and Eric. Individually he liked them all, but when they got together he and Eric became the Pythons again. The other side of the coin, as John discovered, is that Terry's a truly remarkable man to work with. You can *get* to him, which is not all that usual in this business."

Neville did begin to resent Gilliam's reliance on the video monitor, watching it rather than looking directly at the set. Shapewise, framewise and composition-wise Neville could understand Gilliam's concentration, but not as a monitor for performances. His growing conviction was that he was being asked to play second fiddle to special effects.

• • •

The main difficulty on locations in Spain, as far as Peppino Rotunno was concerned, was the short working day. The late start in September pushed the shooting in Almeria, then Zaragoza, into the Spanish winter. One hour of sun would be followed by two hours of grey cloud, with the possible reward of an hour's watery sun before lunch. Only three or four hours of light might remain.

"There were so many people behind and in front of the camera," Rotunno maintained, "that to organize everything in such a short time each day was extremely difficult. I would say to Terry that we were waiting for him to tell us what to do. We all had to synchronize or the danger was it would become so many different films and we would lose the meaning of it. Two camps? I prefer not to comment, except to say that the problems were not between nationalities, but *personal*. I have worked with American, English and Swiss as well as Italian groups, and never had any problems. And I've worked with many directors. Terry is very bright, very intelligent, but he gets so many ideas, he needs more focus. In Italy we are quite used to directors who like to change things around. Terry himself has problems with communications, but not caused by the language."

"Of course it wasn't *only* the language problem," Gilliam admitted, "although the problem with Peppino was he didn't speak enough English, but thought he did and resented my eventual insistence on having an interpreter. I suppose the basic problem in working with the Italians is that they work in a different way, which always leads to recriminations. The English think the Italians are inefficient and the Italians find the English imperious."

CHAPTER EIGHTEEN

Film Finances could have fired everybody but me. Yes, we did reach an understanding. My presence was an enormous advantage for them. Otherwise, of course, it would have been their biggest pleasure to fire me. Soames is used to working in America or England and I'm certainly much better when it comes to dealing with the Italians. No Americans can deal with them, their language, their mentality. I had made all these deals with suppliers and crew, and they were intelligent enough to recognize that I had this know-how. They accepted the fact that I was better left to deal with the Italian money side.

—Thomas Schuhly

Charles McKeown had a revealing series of conversations with Arthur Tarry, the free-lance film accountant assigned by Columbia to keep an eye on the movie. Tarry chattily revealed that he was only on *Munchausen* until another picture started that Columbia was planning to shoot in Italy. He had thought *Munchausen* would cost $40 million as soon as he had accepted the assignment, he told McKeown, and was at a loss to understand how Film Finances had imagined it could be made for less. He also conceded that nobody could have shot it faster than Gilliam with all the problems that had arisen. Tarry remained quite sanguine and philosophical at this stage.

Just twenty-four hours after their last talk, the situation changed dramatically. The film Columbia had waiting in the wings for Tarry folded, and the accountant found himself swiftly dropped by the studio and taken on by Film Finances. McKeown wryly noted the instant personality change. While Tarry was with Columbia, McKeown had often asked, "How are the books?" eliciting a chuckle and the reply, "Cooking gently." Now that he had actually studied them, Tarry had undergone a complete transformation, aging, thought McKeown, twenty years overnight.

In his new role, Arthur Tarry now aimed to demonstrate the wild profligacy of the production by challenging Gilliam with a $100,000 bill for the transportation of the cannons from Rome to Almeria. Since he was not in a position to dispute the figure, all Gilliam could do was contact Schuhly in Rome and demand to know how he could justify the massive sum. Was this another scam? Whose pockets had been lined this time?

"I'm in enough shit without random, unjustifiable statistics like this being flung at me," Gilliam raged. Schuhly was as puzzled as anyone and promised to get back to Gilliam quickly. When he did, it was to confirm the true cost of the cannons' transportation: $12,000. It seemed Tarry had either inadvertently scrambled the figures — or Film Finances had decided to pile on further pressure.

• • •

"I was responsible for the film for exactly three weeks until Film Finances took over, under the impression they could do it better," Schuhly told his colleagues in Rome. His impotence was made official in a telex October 26 from Leopold claiming financial control for Film Finances from that date forward.

Gilliam was next to feel the cutting edge of the new regime.

Soames formally advised Gilliam's attorney, Eric Weissmann, at a Los Angeles meeting, that Film Finances was considering legal action against his client. Not only was Gilliam refusing to make cuts, Soames emphasized he was *enhancing* the approved script. The moon sequence had to be completely scrapped, he made clear, or Gilliam would be summarily fired. Weissmann tried to pour cold water over the enhancement accusation, the clearest possible signal of the dangerous, slippery route litigation might take. If Film Finances could prove that the original script *was* being enhanced, they could duck their responsibility for paying budget overages.

Gilliam was incredulous when Weissmann spoke to him after the meeting. "*Enhancement?*" he echoed. "Are they serious? I'm cutting stuff out every day and they think this is *enhancement?* Don't forget, Eric, I can't just arbitrarily agree to every cut they demand, there's Columbia to consider. If they don't get the picture they bought, they won't pay up."

Two days later Jake Eberts wrote to David Matalon, Victor Kaufman's second lieutenant in the new Columbia setup. He expressed dismay at the freshly raised dismissal threat from Soames but suggested an additional investment from the studio to protect the commercial integrity of the project. "Terry feels the moon sequence is crucial to both the story line and the commercial prospects of the film," his argument ran. "Richard wants the moon sequence cut because it will take four weeks to shoot and cost $3 million. The point we must discuss is whether Columbia is prepared to precipitate a confrontation with Richard Soames or whether for commercial reasons you are prepared to commit additional funds in order to keep the moon sequence and satisfy Richard." Eberts' letter was in vain; Columbia never for one moment budged from their position. They would give Gilliam their moral, but not their financial support.

• • •

Leopold and Tarry were due to travel from Belchite to Rome on October 28 to give Soames a progress report. At a meeting before their departure, both Gilliam and Tomblin confirmed that two extra days in Belchite were required to complete filming, extending their stay from November 6 to 8. "Don't fuck up, Stratton," Tomblin warned. "These two days are crucial, otherwise we'll return to Rome with the job half done."

In Spain Leopold seemed sympathetic to the problems, but the fear was that as soon as he was in Rome the Baron's spell would be broken and that dollars and cents would once again boil down to a matter of cuts. Tarry had a last word of encouragement for McKeown in their hotel lobby. "Your friend's in trouble," he confirmed, "but Terry should stick to his guns and state his case very clearly. And he should go ahead and make the film he wants to make."

Gareth Wigan had already formalized his concerns in a letter to Gilliam, where he suggested trimming scenes rather than cutting them. "I'm aware," he pointed out, "that the changes I suggested do not affect the current deficit. Only the cutting of a whole story sequence could do that, and the film would be seriously damaged, in Columbia's and my personal opinion. The only major alternative is a "re-conception" which, given the genesis of the film, no one but you could do. There may be other cuts and changes in addition to, or in place of, the ones proposed. As you consider them, please do so positively. I know how fiercely you care about the *Baron* and how very hard you are working on it, but I believe you could harm yourself very much in the future if you appear to be unwilling to cut or change anything with a view to reducing further overages."

The list of Wigan's proposed cuts included the chess game which Gilliam was prepared to consider. Wigan also suggested that the Baron and Venus might remain earthbound during the ballroom sequence instead of gravitating to the ceiling. Ultimately he conceded that the pair might rise off the ground, but only for two or three feet. "It scales down the joke a lot," Wigan agreed — ("Kills it," was Gilliam's reaction) — "but it would save shooting time and very complicated effects." ("And everyone's ass," thought Gilliam.) Still, there was no doubt that Wigan's suggestions were well-intentioned.

McKeown was left with the distinct impression that whatever was brewing would boil over during Leopold's de-briefing in Rome. It was a shock to everyone's central nervous system, however, when Soames dispatched a bald ultimatum to Gilliam after the meeting:

October 29th

Film Finances hereby instructs you to finish all shooting in Spain by Friday, the 6th of November, and to perform in accordance with the instructions we have given you, which you have failed to do to date.

Regards, Richard Soames

Gilliam was shattered. He had counted on Leopold's advocacy to Soames for the extra two days in Belchite.

Thoroughly alarmed, Jake Eberts flew to Zaragoza to get a firsthand picture of the Belchite predicament. "They think they're saving money, but it's just the reverse," Gilliam told him. "If we leave we're going to have to rebuild all these sets at Cinecitta — the town square, the battlements . . ."

"How long will it take?" Eberts asked. "How much longer are we talking about?"

"An extra day and night."

"Leave it to me, I'll see what I can get out of Soames. Maybe I can put together an offer that'll change his mind. It's worth a try. But if I do that, Terry, it'll be on two conditions." The battle-weary Gilliam braced himself. Even though it was Jake Eberts talking, he was so punch-drunk he could feel himself flinch. "What are those?" he asked. "Film Finances must agree that no one else replaces you on this picture. And you must do your next two films with me."

Gilliam swears he felt the tide turn at that moment. He had just been given his biggest vote of confidence in many, many months. "What can you say about a guy like that?" he asked. "There I was, getting attacked from all sides, a point at which your greatest supporter could be excused for opting out, and along comes Jake with these extraordinary 'conditions.' What he did was extraordinary."

"Are you aware," Eberts began his call to Soames, "that if you insist on finishing at Belchite on Thursday night, the quality and acceptability of the movie, as far as Columbia is concerned, will be seriously jeopardized?" Eberts then offered to pay the difference between one night's extra shooting in Belchite and the cost of leaving prematurely, rebuilding the sets in Rome and finishing the shoot there.

Soames wasted no time in formally rejecting the deal. "Your assertion that the quality of the picture will be jeopardized," he told Eberts, "can only be blamed on Terry Gilliam, and is but another example of his inability to follow our instructions and perform in accordance with our agreement."

Gilliam decided to make one last appeal to Soames. "I continue to be astounded by your unwillingness to help us find constructive solutions to our immediate problems," he faxed. "You have yet to acknowledge or to comment on all the cuts we have made to the script since the version you approved dated August 3. Having had a long talk with Stratton last night we set about cutting the crew in Belchite right down to the bone to allow for an extra night's shooting so that we can actually get on film the extraordinary sets that have been built here. We were to get a decision from Stratton first thing this morning if the exercise proved feasible, but typically you sent a fax within an hour of that discussion saying no.

"If you are going to behave like the producer of this film then you should start assuming the responsibilities that entails rather than just giving blanket 'no's.' Saving a day at Belchite may be in accordance with the schedule but my guess is that ultimately it will cost more money and then will be even less in accordance with the budget.

"Stratton clearly is not allowed to make any intelligent decisions on his own without calling you every few minutes. Your continuing inability to come to Europe only exacerbates a difficult situation. We can only sort this out face to face with all the facts in front of us."

Soames' faxed reply defined the hostilities to follow. "I am not unwilling to find constructive solutions," he claimed. "You were instructed to finish all shooting in Spain by Friday, 6 November. This does not mean bringing back material to Rome. The 'extraordinary sets' you have built there are precisely what has created the terrible situation you have put us in. I am coming to Rome at the weekend, and I expect to meet with you on Tuesday, 10th November for as long as it takes to explain to you your position and the steps that we intend to take to finish the film.

"You should not delude yourself over the cost situation, which may be much worse than already predicted. You only have to ask somebody to telephone the bank to find out how much money is left to finish the film. It is only with the greatest restraint that I refrain from commenting at this time on the other *outlandish assertions* made in your letter."

Within a day of the "everybody out of Spain by 6 November" edict, Steve Ransohoff wrote to Gilliam's lawyer. During the two-week hiatus planned for the unit's return to Rome, he warned that "changes in personnel" of *an unspecified nature* would be made.

The communiqué that Leopold issued to the beleaguered unit on his return to Rome was even more shocking. The entire crew and staff of the film were notified that their contracts were terminated as of Saturday, November 7, 1987. "I have taken this decision for economic reasons," Leopold asserted, "and to allow time to reorganize the future schedule of shooting. *Unfortunately I am unable to indicate any future start date of shooting or indicate the exact numbers of staff and crew that my new budget will allow.* I wish to thank everyone for their collaboration, and hope that everyone will understand the irrevocable nature of the necessity that forces me into this situation."

"Jesus Christ, they've fired the whole fucking lot of us," one seasoned trooper was heard to mutter.

CHAPTER NINETEEN

*When we were all given our notice, I said,
"That's it. The Baron's dead. It's all over now
bar the shouting."*
                                        —Winston Dennis

Gilliam had to face the prospect that the "temporary hiatus" might go on forever. And the equally bleak possibility that the Baron might complete his adventure without him. Relatively undaunted, Gilliam made a heartfelt plea to Soames on the same day Leopold's order was issued, asking him to appear in person in Zaragoza. "This long distance decision-making is crazy," he pointed out. "At this end we want very much to make the film work for *all* of us, and we have a number of ideas that hopefully will make that possible. As we have demonstrated time and time again we continue to cut and trim scenes, but without actually sitting down and discussing the situation, face to face, with accurate information in front of us, all that is happening is that the film is being put in greater and greater jeopardy."

Soames' immediate reply, although chilly and to the point, was less ominous than Leopold's indefinite shutdown notice. The two-week layoff, Soames insisted, was "in order to reorganize, re-examine the script and complete the set constructions." Unable to come to Europe himself, he was dispatching a co-director, David Korda, whom he described as "an experienced producer in his own right."

"I trust," Soames concluded, "you will supply him with the 'accurate' information you refer to. I also look forward to hearing your ideas, which I hope will be constructive and will mitigate the damage that has already been done."

As news of the "hiatus" rapidly leaked, reporters from the world press began to look up Zaragoza on their maps. "I am deeply concerned," John Neville told one newshound. "When I took on the role of the Baron I agreed to be back at Stratford by the end of January. And there is a stop-clause in my contract to that effect."

Steve Ransohoff immediately scrutinized Neville's contract. There was, in fact, no stop-date, the infuriated actor was hastily informed; while it had been mentioned in correspondence, it had never been formalized. Neville was left to ruminate on the chances of the picture being completed in time for his scheduled return to Canada.

Gilliam was not about to spare his tormentors. Diplomacy was left to the gunboats. "John has always been the key to this thing," he confirmed to another reporter, "and the longer Film Finances play around and delay decisions, the more difficult his position becomes. They are sitting in Los Angeles making panicky decisions based on questionable information, yet they've guaranteed they will finish the film. If they fire all these people and only then sit down and discuss what we should be doing, I don't see how that guarantees completion of the film. They're in a strange position, because the suggestions for change they're making won't result in the film Columbia agreed to buy. These people don't know anything about the making of a film, yet they're trying to become film producers who assume they can do it better than we're doing it. They're expecting a great magical solution, which I'm supposed to haul out of a hat."

• • •

Just prior to the shutdown, Dante Ferretti was asked for a detailed progress report on the status of sets required for the balance of shooting. First taking a deep breath, he dutifully ran through them all:

- The Treasure Room (still missing the floor; walls to be painted)
- South Seas (construction of metallic structure to be done)
- Vulcan's Ballroom (ceiling molding and floor to be finished)
- Vulcan's Workshop (bases of furnaces to be done)
- Vulcan's Dining Room (in production: shells, columns, wall decorations, mirrors, floor, pool)
- Sultan's Chess Board (design submitted in October; no budget yet allocated)
- Sultan's Harem (budget to be approved)
- Interior of Giant Fish (budget to be approved)

Still to be designed:
- Ship's Stern and Wrecked Ship, Interior of Ship (budget to be approved)
- Row Boat (in construction)
- Mouth of Giant Fish (budget to be approved)
- Turkish Fleet (to be constructed)
- Banquet Room of Moon (in construction: Giant Parts: Queen's Head, Breast, Finger, 2 Glasses, 2 Eating Utensils, 2 Plates, 1 Platter, Section of Scroll, Section of Giant Chair)
- Prison Cell on Moon (in construction; cages to be constructed also)
- Gates made of Cheese and Large Door on Moon (budget to be approved)
- Interior Moon King's Room (to be constructed)
- Interior Floor Section Room next to Banqueting Room (to be designed)
- Tree outside of Belgrade (to be designed)

Following the submission of his report, Ferretti received the following instructions from Film Finances: "Hold *everything* until further notice."

• • •

Pam Meager had already resigned and had begun packing her bags before Film Finances had a chance to serve their dismissal notice. As she had been warned from the beginning, the Italians had taken over completely, leaving her virtually stripped of her duties. "Coping with them was a truly frustrating experience," she claimed. "They were like children. Unless Terry greeted them all, they sulked. Even Peppino — and Terry might be surprised to hear this — could be a sweetheart. If he didn't think he was getting it right for Terry, he was in tears."

Despite everything Meager retains wonderful memories of the movie. "Like John Neville striding across the beach at Almeria, the very image of Terry's original drawings come alive. I once said to Terry, 'You're doing this for your kids, aren't you?' He said, 'Yes, I am, and hopefully for the rest of my family as well.'"

For the Italian makeup contingent Meager's departure occasioned an afternoon of lusty community singing in their trailer, chorus after chorus of *Volare* ringing out loud and clear. Another alien in their midst had gone.

• • •

Soames spelled out Film Finances' absolute determination to sacrifice Gilliam in a letter to David Picker at Columbia. "The only way in which we can protect our position in the picture and lessen the damage which Terry Gilliam has created is to replace him," Soames wrote. "To this end, we are attempting to engage the services of a replacement this week (seeing as you have failed to do so) and are planning to send him off to Rome by the beginning of next week. The effect of Mr. Gilliam's behavior, both in terms of his creating a picture that is not capable of being handled by the budget and his constant refusal to follow our instructions, has mandated us to shut the picture down to sort out the enormous problems which he has created and for which he must and will be held accountable.

"Given this *catalogue of horrors*, all of which you are aware of, it astounds us that you would take the position that we do not have the right to replace him at this time. The only direction you have given us is that you will agree to any changes agreed to by Terry Gilliam, *which is like giving the fox the responsibility of tending to the welfare of the hen house*."

Jake Eberts again rushed to the rescue. For someone "not a warrior" in Schuhly's book, he was performing valiantly. In a letter to Picker, he reiterated the view that Soames must be informed that

Columbia's contract was for a Terry Gilliam film, not one by any other director. Eberts insisted that while Columbia had agreed to accept cuts proposed by Gilliam and accepted by Film Finances, they specifically had *not* agreed to cuts proposed by Film Finances and imposed on Gilliam.

In a separate letter to Soames, Eberts challenged the allegation that Gilliam had refused to reduce the overall number of crew members, citing significant reductions of which Soames had been fully informed. Although Soames had instructed Gilliam to finish shooting in Spain by Friday evening, he had been repeatedly advised that this was not possible. "As we are under an obligation to deliver certain scenes in the screenplay to Columbia," Eberts averred, "merely instructing Terry to leave Spain on Friday night whether or not he has shot these scenes, does not relieve us of that obligation. If these scenes are not shot in Spain, then the set must be built in Rome so they can be shot there."

"It seems to us." Soames replied, "that you are so far removed from reality that it is useless to reply to you. *I would ask you to refrain from all further activities in relation to the film*, and if you continue to do so, we will hold you fully responsible for actions which we find counter-productive."

Like Schuhly before him, Soames underestimated Eberts' resilience. In the best tradition of Gilliam himself, Eberts' strongest suit is his ability to bounce back. When he did, he quite deliberately chose to go on record with his argument. "Film Finances have this ridiculous myopic view of Terry as the bad guy," he told Michael Cieply of the *Los Angeles Times*. "They see him as the one who's gone over budget, the one who's built all the sets, the one who's refusing to cut the picture — all of which is downright *nonsense*. It was clear early on that the production was in disarray. It was overstaffed, money was being spent needlessly and there never seemed to be a strong central control.

"My job's been trying to keep the thing on track and stop Film Finances from firing Terry, ever since I heard through a friend of mine in Los Angeles that the picture had been offered by Richard Soames to a number of directors. I think they felt they could frighten Columbia into putting up more money by raising this particular spectre. I know

Soames always complained that what drove him over the brink was his inability to get to Victor Kaufman, but in fairness to Kaufman it's clear he was advised not to get involved.

"There's no question that if they deliver a picture other than one directed by Terry Gilliam, Columbia will have the grounds to say that's not the picture they bought. At the other end of the scale, Film Finances are saying, 'Fine, but are you seriously saying *no one* else could finish it? Whether it's Spielberg or Lucas or Sydney Pollack, there must be some other director who could finish the picture.' This is the argument that Steve Ransohoff's putting up, I believe. Maybe he's right. But he's not talking to any of these people, so that falls flat. And in any case, no director worth his salt would take over in the middle of a Terry Gilliam picture.

"What I can't stand is the guarantor not paying up. That's his *job*, that's what guarantor *means*. When a ship goes down they ring a bell at Lloyd's. Everyone thinks it's tragic, but they put their hands in their pockets and pay up. My argument is simple: *You*, Richard Soames, came here *personally* to Rome in the first place, *personally* looked over the production schedule and *personally* signed the guarantee. Now, either your word is your word, or it's not. Maybe I'm still living in cloud cuckoo-land. Lord knows *I've* often made deals I wish I hadn't made. But Richard Soames signed a deal with us and that's what offends me so deeply. We've invested $17.6 million to date in the movie and we're relying on the Columbia pick-up to pay us back. If for any reason Film Finances let us down and don't finish the picture, *we'll* sue *them!*"

• • •

Soames' latest emissary could not have arrived in Belchite at a less propitious moment. Gilliam, in the middle of a night shoot, had just read a Canadian report that Film Finances intended to sue him for misrepresentation and fraud. The spectre of the seizure of all his personal assets, including his house, haunted the night. His wife Maggie, pregnant with their third child back home in Highgate, was frantic with worry. Enter David Korda, stepping boldly into the middle of this scenario, despite a nimbly coordinated attempt by Tomblin and Cleary to postpone the confrontation.

Gilliam was instantly offended by what he saw as Korda's

sardonic expression, icy calm and superior attitude. "We'd been having a great night's shoot despite everything when he arrived," he recalled, "and I just had so much adrenalin charging through me. All I needed was a jerk making wisecracks about our lack of progress. I went *crazy* at him, I could have killed him. I don't think he knew what was happening, I'm sure he thought I was a madman. He was just the wrong person to confront me at that particular moment."

With the rest of the crew looking on incredulously, Gilliam stormed away from the encounter, fists tightly clenched, shoulders hunched. As he passed a station wagon parked nearby, he jerked his right arm stiffly back and punched his fist through the rear window. Having exorcised the rage from his system, and with his hand miraculously only bruised, he went back to the night's shoot and worked through until dawn. Only then did he discover that he had wreaked his frustration and anger on his own car.

• • •

Gilliam and Tomblin now calculated the scaled-down schedule for Belchite: after eliminating everything from the main unit shooting that was not absolutely essential for telling the story and delivering a complete film, they were still left with more than could be shot by the Thursday night deadline. Monday would be taken up with the Baron's funeral, Tuesday with the parade to the city gates, Wednesday night with the theater exterior, leaving Thursday and Friday nights for the battlement sequences and the yet-to-be-attempted balloon launch.

Tomblin's strategy called for a return to Rome on the Sunday following the wrap. "They're bound to agree in the end," he assured Gilliam. "For the sake of an extra ha'penny worth of tar they're not going to be stupid about it." Gilliam was not so sure, particularly since there were already rumblings about the cost of the Spanish extras. Their daily rate had looked reasonable enough until they demanded triple overtime and threatened to walk out unless this was granted. A few extras even at that exorbitant rate would hardly have broken the bank, but no fewer than 235 were involved at Belchite — 15 (upper-class) men, 27 (middle-class) men, 50 (poor) men, 16 boys, 25 (upper-class) women, 25 (middle-class) women, 30 (poor) women, 15 girls, 10 European infantry, 10 European artillery, 12 townsmen —

every last one of them appropriately made up and costumed.

The scams in Spain continued their unabated orgiastic pace. One technician revealed: "Everyone ate beautifully in Almeria, but the catering bills were phenomenal, and I mean hundreds of thousands of dollars. In Belchite I watched cases upon cases of wine and beer being loaded out of the canteen into the backs of cars. It looked like whoever was doing the catering was screwing them right, left and center."

Tomblin was stunned with Leopold's reply. Leopold would indeed allow Thursday night and Saturday morning, but no Friday night — all so the unit was unable to travel back on Saturday instead of Sunday. Tomblin decided it was memo time. This was one for the books. "Your action will result in building a section of the battlements for later shooting," he wrote to Leopold, adding a request for acknowledgement of his missive.

The crucial balloon-floating-along-the-battlements sequence remained to be shot. On that final Saturday — after everything else had gone wrong with the movie — with hundreds of extras costumed, made up and praying for overtime, what were the chances of the balloon actually taking off on cue? "We'd never had a chance to try it out," Tomblin explained. "I'd worked it out with the wire men and the balloon expert, but it had never been actually put to the test.

"It doesn't bear thinking about what would have happened if it had failed to function, or if the weather had been bad and it had broken loose from its moorings. But no — up it went and it looked magnificent. It was a big moment in Terry's life and mine to see this bloody great thing sailing without any problems."

The *Munchausen* jinx seemed to lift along with the balloon's ascent. With an inspired Peppino Rotunno himself taking over the camera the crew raced to pan along the faces of the soldiers on the battlements as the sun began to disappear. The light miraculously held until the very last man had been reached, gloriously picked out in the sunshine, then faded mere seconds later. For one wonderful moment the *Munchausen* unit was utterly united.

CHAPTER TWENTY

Basically we destroyed the whole film so we could build it back up again. There's something exhilarating about killing something and having it reborn. We sat around laughing, and two hours later we'd broken the back of the problem.

—Terry Gilliam

Gilliam's Rome office in Cinecitta reminded him of a morgue. Despondency had descended like a thick black curtain. "Once they do that, they never re-start," was the cry heard from many an old soldier at news of the shutdown.

Hostilities opened in earnest with the initial meeting on Sunday, November 8, among Soames, Ransohoff, Gilliam, McKeown and Tomblin. Accusation and counter-accusation ricocheted around the room. "It's *our* money you've been squandering," Soames berated Gilliam.

"Look," Gilliam shot back, "*I'm* the director. I'm *supposed* to fantasize. *Thomas* is the producer, at least on paper, and he's *supposed* to con you. And *you're* the money guys. You're *supposed* to have checked out what was and wasn't possible. Why haven't you at least had someone countersigning all the checks that we've issued since you took charge? If you're looking to put all the blame on one person, you're looking at the wrong guy."

Soames barely flinched. "Whether we are or not," he pronounced, "it's hardly the point of this meeting. We just hope you have specific cuts in mind."

"Only one," Gilliam replied, "the chess board sequence — but we're not sure how we can lose it."

"That's a start," Soames conceded, "but the moon sequence has to go as well. Figure a way of doing it before your lawyer arrives for our final meeting on Tuesday."

Gilliam clung tenaciously to the original moon sequence through all the pressure that followed. It represented the most Gilliamesque concept in the entire movie. During a huge banquet scene, for instance, the heads of the eccentric monarchy detach from their bodies and land with a resounding splash in huge goblets of wine. The director was also particularly devoted to the role of the moon's Prime Minister, to be played by Michael Palin.

Determined that the Baron's lunar journey had to remain, the creative team re-examined the script minutely for ways in which other savings could be made. With virtually nothing to show for their day and a half sequestered in Gilliam's flat, Tomblin wearily returned to Cinecitta. "It'll *never* be restarted," was his parting shot to the disconsolate Gilliam and McKeown. Tomblin's odes neatly captured the mood:

> "Has fate chose to pair us,
> To make us pallbearers,
> To carry old 'Munch' to his grave.
> Will we match his sad ending,
> As slowly descending
> He's returned to the land of the brave?
>
> "Or will he be reincarnated,
> Have his life reinstated

And climb once again on his horse?
Will he race on his stallion
Or fly in his galleon
Will the moon in the sky be his course?

"I have a strange feeling
That soon we'll be kneeling
To say our farewells and last look —
He'll be trapped once again,
Going slowly insane,
In the pages of some dusty book.

"Is the flag at half mast,
Are his glories all past,
Has the figure of death had its way?
Is our friend still alive,
Will the Baron survive,
Or is it sackcloth and ashes this day?"

"Look, Terry, let's at least de-populate the bloody moon," McKeown suggested, "the lawyers are arriving and the shop's closing." "I *know*," Gilliam replied, "but Charles, can we make two people as funny as 2,000?"

"We can't let the whole thing die," McKeown argued. "It's just too pathetic." Gilliam had never known his friend so adamant about anything before. "OK," he agreed, "let's just tear the shit out of the whole thing. We'll shoot the entire episode *in my office*! Everyone can just sit around in their costumes and read the script. That'll make it *really* cheap."

When Tomblin was finally re-summoned, however, the lunar population had indeed been reduced to a royal couple, the King and Queen. The revised sequence would be achieved at a fraction of the original cost. The Baron had cleared a major hurdle in his journey.

The chess game sequence, to be played with life-sized figures on a gigantic board between the Sultan and the Baron was officially forfeited by Gilliam to budget constraints. A less opulent bridging sequence would have to be devised. A further trim related to the segment in the sea monster's belly, where the number of sets was drastically reduced, and Harry Andrew's sea captain character reluctantly dropped.

Tomblin was jubilant; now they had something concrete to offer Soames. Nonetheless angry exchanges did erupt at the meeting, attended by Steve Abbott and Gilliam's lawyer, flown over from Los Angeles at Jake Eberts' insistence. Soames brought up the question of the film's anticipated length even after the cuts. "It'll be close on $2^1/_2$ hours long. *Far* too long," he maintained.

"It won't run 90 minutes if I shoot the entire script!" Gilliam retorted. "Look, Richard, why don't you just cut my arms off?"

"It's *our* arms *you're* cutting off!" Soames shot back.

At one point in the proceedings Gilliam threatened to quit, ran out of the room, then came back as soon as he had calmed down. There was nonetheless a perceptible shift away from the brink. Litigation was out, a replacement director was out; Gilliam was back in.

Ransohoff and Gilliam's lawyer sat up the entire night drafting a new contract involving a further deferment of salary, to be paid only when the completed film was handed over. The epistle was duly signed on the hood of a car in the street before the party split up.

To this day Soames denies that he was forced by Columbia to keep Gilliam on, and that all the rest was posturing and bluff on his part. Although the two directors most frequently mentioned as replacements for Gilliam were Richard Fleischer and Gary Nelson, Lee Cleary had spread the rumor back in Belchite that Michael Winner had been asked to look at the script. The very idea reduced the participants to helpless laughter. John Neville took off Winner's inimitable style to devastating effect. "Hey, *you! Yes, you* with the big conk! Get your arse down here double quick!!"

As far as Gilliam was concerned, the hiatus was like any other episode of Munchausen's adventures. Over and over again the Baron wanted to die, but he always managed somehow to be revitalized. Notices were posted to all of the waiting cast and crew that the movie would definitely be re-starting on schedule.

There was still consternation when it was discovered that Tomblin's new schedule for the film's twelve-week completion failed to fit the revised budget Film Finances had laid down. A further

$1.5 million was required — either that, or a reduction of 3 weeks' shooting. The prospect of ending up with a vastly expensive, underweight turkey seemed ludicrous to all concerned, and in the end Soames agreed to accept the revised schedule in full. Everyone was again irrevocably locked together into the Rubik's Cube, with every person and part interdependent and with no possibility of escape until the completion of the endeavor.

The one exception, perhaps, at least in his own mind, turned out to be Thomas Schuhly. Bernd Eichinger discovered this for himself when he contacted his friend by phone to commiserate. "How is it going?" he asked.

"Great, great," Schuhly replied.

"But I hear you're having difficulty with the movie . . ."

"What movie?"

"What do you mean, *what movie*? *Baron Munchausen*, of course!"

"*Munchausen*? Bernd, that's ancient history already! I thought you were talking about my new project, the story of the greatest guy who ever lived — Alexander the Great."

After the call, Eichinger pondered the fact that his friend Schuhly was once more skiing down the Arctic slopes of hyper-reality.

• • •

Jake Eberts felt that the press was responsible for exacerbating the genuine difficulties of the project beyond their true proportions. Thomas Schuhly, according to Eberts, did little to keep matters in perspective. Eberts was revolted by the volume of distortion Schuhly regularly poured out to *Variety*'s Rome correspondent. According to his account, the "$25 million handshake deal" with David Puttnam had soon proved "as whimsical as the movie's subject, on one day and off the next." He blamed the budget overages on Columbia's "not signing the contract on time," the "triangular production and financial structure," Gilliam "going two weeks over schedule in Spain" and "the lawyers' establishment in Hollywood."

"Your ego appears to have gone wild," Eberts blasted Schuhly in an epistle. "You continuously take credit for having done much more than you have, at the same time disowning any responsibility for what are clearly production problems, for which no one can be blamed but you. Furthermore, at a time when we are trying our best to get further cooperation and money from Columbia, you blame them for the film's woes. This is simply a dumb thing to do at this stage.

"Your statements to the press imply that you not only initiated the *Baron Munchausen* project, but that you were solely responsible for getting the Columbia deal. As everyone knows, it was Terry's project from the outset, and, with the greatest humility I can muster, the Columbia negotiations were not only initiated by me but largely conducted and concluded by me.

"You fail to mention the one overriding reason — inept production on your part. The plain fact is that you have permitted production to go wildly out of control. You were too busy playing the role of the Hollywood producer; it is now apparent that you were simply too inexperienced to effectively supervise the production of the film.

"I am getting very bored reading what a terrific job you did on *The Name Of The Rose*, which seems to come up with dreary regularity in your conversations with the press. It is clear that someone else must have produced the film, as your performance on *Munchausen* certainly proves that you could not have done it.

"I think the time has come for someone to do some straight talking to you. You have managed to alienate everybody at Columbia Pictures, most people on the crew and me. *Enough is enough.*"

Eberts sent a copy of his letter to Gilliam, then changed his mind about sending Schuhly the original, reasoning that the written message might further sour relationships to the detriment of the movie's progress. Eberts opted to convey the main sentiments of the letter to Schuhly by phone.

• • •

Just when everyone thought it was safe to go out in public again, Allan Buckhantz surfaced once more, this time via Karl Woerner of Munich's Transit Film, the company that had sold Buckhantz the remake rights of the 1942 *Munchausen*. Woerner complained that Columbia's Ronald Jacobi had referred to their 1942 version, in a telephone conversation, as being one Columbia wished to separate itself from as much as possible, since it had been made as propaganda under the Nazi regime by Goebbels.

Buckhantz, a former concentration camp inmate, was reportedly outraged by Jacobi's observation and proceeded to file a lawsuit in Los Angeles Superior Court on November 18, 1987, seeking losses and damages from the studio. Slander, libel, intentional infliction of emotional distress and intentional interference with prospective economic advantage were listed. The defendants included Columbia Pictures, Columbia Pictures Industries and the Coca-Cola Company, as well as Jacobi personally. General damages, medical damages, loss of earnings and costs of suit for each individual cause were claimed, together with *punitive damages totalling $80 million.*

Ronald Jacobi now made another comment that would upset Buckhantz's ideological applecart. Although he was merely stating Columbia's position with regard to budget overages, the implication for the Buckhantz camp was dire. "Columbia Pictures has agreed to acquire certain distribution rights (in *Munchausen*) for a fixed price," his statement began, "payable on delivery. The price will not be affected by the final production costs and is not required to be paid unless the film is delivered in strict compliance with the terms of the original agreement." Although clearly aimed at Film Finances, Jacobi's concluding thrust held a sinister message for Buckhantz: "Columbia Pictures is not involved in any way with any aspect of the production of (*Munchausen*)."

Buckhantz's lawyer, Stanley Caidin, immediately protested what he saw as Columbia's original misrepresentation of the film's ownership. "Columbia has (always) referred to *Munchausen* as '*our*' (Columbia's) picture," he raged, "now it's *their* (Prominent/Laura's) picture." He asserted that the word "pick-up" had never been brought up by Columbia until this point. "On the contrary," he claimed, "in my discussions (with them) we were always working on the premise that it was a Columbia picture."

Buckhantz and his attorney may have been further misled by Thomas Schuhly's announcements to the German press: "I am the first German producer who has been entrusted by a major U.S. company with a $45 million project," he had boasted to *Abendzeitung* on August 10. "Columbia is putting in no less than $40 million," he told *Film Echo* a few days later.

The agonizing realization dawning on Buckhantz and his battery of lawyers was that in Columbia they had picked the wrong target for their lawsuit. In a stoic attempt to distract attention from their embarrassment and to keep the pot boiling, Buckhantz declared that he intended to produce a musical version of *Munchausen* in West Berlin, and also that he expected to see the UFA version of the Baron's adventures released on video in the U.S. "within the next month." Columbia may have felt that Buckhantz was performing a considerable service for them with his plans. They might, after all, raise a flicker of interest in the Baron and serve as a trailer for Gilliam's adventures to follow.

• • •

Having made the irrevocable decision to restart, on the basis that there was $15 million already spent and they were going to end up $10 or $12 million over the original budget, Film Finances was delivered a jolting blow.

"I don't know how to break this to you," was how Arthur Tarry approached Soames. "Every figure we've projected has been based on expenditure to date, and our best estimate on this basis of how much it would cost to complete the movie. Well, now at long last we've managed to extricate the books from Schuhly and his accountant. *And* $5 million worth of unpaid, undeclared bills which we found stuffed in a desk drawer! This changes the overrun estimate to between $15 and $17 million. Richard, the *entire budget of the film is spent. There's absolutely nothing left in the bank!*"

The Adventures of Baron Munchausen was once again running on empty.

CHAPTER
TWENTY-ONE

We could have got rid of Gilliam contractually. Columbia would have had to take the picture. There was a mechanism in the contract permitting us to get rid of him. All we had to do was give him instructions and if he failed to follow them we could have fired him. We had a director in the wings who could have taken over the film and finished it. The only way to deal with Terry at that time was to tell him either he made the cuts, or he went, and we were fully prepared to do that. But he did make the cuts, so we kept him on.

—Richard Soames

Soames had been aware that the Italian bank assigned to dispense funds to the production had been dishing out money at a faster rate than scheduled. Schuhly, when challenged by Soames, explained that while he was indeed drawing out money faster, it was not to *spend* it, but to put it into a German bank which paid much higher interest!

At Soames' request a breakdown of this transaction was sent out to Los Angeles for scrutiny. Since all the details were in German, however, nobody could make head nor tail of it. "It was a masterful job they did," Soames recalled, "a *brilliant* scheme to hide costs. If we'd known what the real costs were, we could have just paid the bank off and walked away, but the accounts were kept from us so they could draw the money."

Schuhly's accountant had created his own system whereby checks were deemed unissued until cashed by the bank. This had the effect of making expenditure figures an average of two weeks out of date. Soames had kept Lloyd's as fully informed of the worsening situation as he was able through their London broker. Now they would have to become *directly* involved. With the production point of no return well and truly past, all future bills were required to be met by Film Finances and Lloyd's, their re-insurers.

Two main factors dominated the speculation about Soames' ultimate financial position — recoupment and the exchange rate. First, the good news: if the film turned out to be a hit, Film Finances and Lloyd's were next equal in line to recoup after Columbia. A $75 million U.S. and Canadian box-office gross would see Columbia break even, returning $30 million net to the studio. With a one-third deduction for their distribution arm's expenses, the $20 million left over would cover the $12.5 million investment as well as $7.5 million for prints and advertising.

And was $75 million so ambitious? After all, Gilliam's *Time Bandits* had grossed close on $50 million in the U.S and Canada way back in 1981 when ticket prices were around half those of 1988-89. A *Time Bandits*-type success might reasonably translate into around $100 million. Then there was the rest of the world, excluding Germany and Italy, which might yield considerable revenue. A final financial reprieve for Film Finances was not out of the question.

If "recoupment" was the bright shining light at the end of the tunnel, the lire exchange rate, which had strengthened considerably against the dollar, was the flickering bulb. For the *budgeted* funds, Jake Eberts had ensured forward currency cover. All of the *excess*, however, would have to be shelled out by Film Finances and Lloyd's at the *new* rate. Back in October $100 would have bought 13,330 lire; by November this was down to 12,160 lire. Over the next few months this one item alone would cost an extra $1 million.

• • •

Film Finances decided in their wisdom that Mario Di Biase and his assistant should remain terminated after the shutdown. Lee Cleary was sorry to see Jose Escolar, having finished the stint in Spain, off the picture as well. The baton had been handed over to Briton, Bill Westley, during the last week in Belchite.

Back in Rome, Westley took another look, decided it was all too much, and left for home. Film Finances' David Korda was another defector. He refused point blank to continue with what he termed "the madness," despite several inducements offered by an increasingly desperate Soames. The list of the "fallen" was lengthening daily.

Mario Pisani found himself asked once more to join the production. Having turned the assignment down originally back in June, Pisani could see that the circumstances had genuinely changed. After scrutinizing Tomblin's new budget and schedule, his response was immediate: "No problem now."

In fact there was a serious problem built into the new equation, the burden of which fell almost entirely on the long-suffering shoulders of Dante Ferretti. "Deciding to restart the production after a break of only two weeks is disastrous," he advised everyone who would listen. Although set building had only been suspended for a few days, very little catching up had taken place during the layoff. No new sets were ready.

The actors had already been recalled, and were once more devouring salaries and expenses. Ferretti set about the recruitment of a huge number of "dailies" to augment the Cinecitta crew of carpenters, plasterers, sculptors and painters. Even with sixty of these craftsmen working full time he still knew it was insufficient to ensure a start on November 23. "We worked Saturday and Sunday overtime to get the sets ready," he recalled, "but it was *never* going to happen. It was such a terrible idea to leave Spain without the shooting being finished. As Tomblin had predicted we had to reconstruct part of the tower and the desert at Cinecitta, at *tremendous* cost."

On Mario Pisani's recommendation the new First Assistant Director hired to complete the picture was Gianni Cozzo. Tall, distinquished-looking, Cozzo was without question one of the most experienced "Firsts" in Italy who, as a tremendous bonus, also spoke beautiful English. Cozzo had turned down the project twice before, in February and September, each time with the same comment: "This is a 20-week picture with a 10-week budget!"

His decision to accept the assignment in November, despite his recent major heart bypass, was based on his friendship with Pisani and a favorable review of Tomblin's new schedule. Ominously, his first words of advice echoed Ferretti's: "Whatever you do, *don't* start on the 23rd. Nothing's ready, it'll be *suicide.*"

As forecast, no fresh sets were ready at Cinecitta. The first Monday's shooting centered on the original theater shell, left forlorn since September. Selected props and pieces of set equipment were nonetheless needed back from Belchite. When these failed to arrive, a furious Tomblin further revamped the schedule to accommodate their estimated mid-week arrival.

Tomblin was even more furious when he discovered the reason for the delay. Spanish handlers at Belchite had refused to touch the goods, since the unit had left without having their bill settled by Film Finances. Stratton Leopold tried to cover his embarrassment by claiming the dispute was not just about money, that a Spanish holiday had caused at least part of the delay. In his view "only" twelve hours of filming were lost; Tomblin gloweringly maintained it was several days.

The first day back Gilliam was only able to shoot below-stage scenes in the theater. In the continuing absence of props from Belchite the second day was planned around the Sultan's Treasury set. Painters were still working away furiously throughout the morning, leaving the crew with nothing to do but cool their heels. At lunch with Soames, and without having shot a single foot of film that day, Gilliam told him he had no answer but to plow ahead.

By evening, and still with nothing in the can, it was John Neville's turn to let off steam. "Another day wasted!" he exploded. "I don't care *what* my contract says, I'm leaving at the end of January and that's *that*." Later he calmed down. "But please," he pleaded, "let's see just one iota of progress." The sight of the unfinished sets together with the absence of measurable progress filled Neville with horror. Unless something fairly radical happened he could see no way he could ever escape from the picture, let alone by the end of January.

If there is humor in every predicament, Gene Rizzo saw it in Neville's: "There were so many oddities and curiosities on this film," he mused, "but none more than John in full Munchausen regalia working away nonstop on faxes to send back home to Stratford. He was desperately keen to continue conducting business, since he wasn't called half the time and otherwise would have had to sit doing nothing for hours. At the same time he was having trouble reading because of his makeup, since he had a latex nose that would be dented with spectacles. I went to Schuhly twice and brought this up. In the end we had a lorgnette made for him. *That* was one thing we can say Thomas achieved!"

Toward the end of the first week of the re-start, an almost unprecedented sighting was made of Schuhly on the set, wearing dark glasses and a long black leather coat. Gilliam did a double take when he saw him. "Hello, who are *you?*" he asked. It was as if a spectral figure from the past had reappeared for a token visit. It was also utterly ludicrous as far as Gilliam was concerned.

The re-emergence of Columbia's Gareth Wigan came as a major surprise. Everyone thought Wigan, a Puttnam appointee, would have been fired in the Night Of The Long Knives that followed his boss's departure. There was life after Puttnam, it seemed, at least for Wigan. David Picker, the early *Munchausen* champion, was now relegated to a non-executive consultancy role based in New York. When Jake Eberts broke that particular piece of news as "Our original ally has gone," the potentially dire implications were not lost on anyone, least of all Gilliam.

• • •

In the last few days of filming at Belchite, Pierre Lechien had found himself up against his mightiest negotiating challenge. His dogs were to be on call 24 hours a day, working both the main and second units. Pointing to his contract, which clearly specified *"daily* rate," he demanded double time for night shooting — on top of his $300 a day he wanted $600 a night, a total of $900 for the 24-hour stint! Mario Di Biase, at whom every finger was pointing as the originator of Lechien's deal, was close to tears. "Your weekly $2,100 is enough of an embarrassment," he protested. "Now you want more!"

"You agreed to my rate back in Rome. And it's a *daily* rate."

"Yes, but we thought you'd only be required for a couple of weeks."

"So did I," Lechien retorted. "Look, I sympathize with you, but my marriage is going to pieces, my business out the window. If I'm going to be here and on call 24 hours a day, I want to be paid for it." In the end his demands were modified, but only slightly. Originally scheduled to work on the picture for eight days, the gypsy lurchers had been lapping up the gravy for nine tasty weeks.

The first Lechien heard of Stratton Leopold was on his dismissal notice in Belchite. He sought Leopold out and demanded to know if his dogs would be required again. "Don't take them back to Paris," Leopold told him, "we hope to refinance the picture and they may be needed back in Italy." Lechien agreed to put the animals into kennels in Rome for two weeks; if he had no word of the restart by then he would take them back to Paris.

Lechien left the dogs safely hidden in Rome, but not before he had signed an agreement with the keepers that the lurchers would be released only to him under pain of legal action. Lechien arrived home in France surprised to find a registered letter from Film Finances awaiting him. Claiming they were Film Finances' property, Leopold threatened to sue if the dogs were not immediately handed over. Lechien's attorney, after studying his contract, advised that Film Finances didn't have a hind leg to stand on: it was clearly stated in black and white that the dogs were rented. Lechien phoned Leopold and told him the dogs could be re-rented, but only on the same terms as before.

Lechien began to receive a series of phone calls from "an Italian gentleman" in Rome — in no way, as far as he could see, even remotely connected with the production — who indicated there was a way in which he might collect a sizeable lump sum. The insurance company involved would be obliged to pay up for re-shooting if anything happened to the dogs, like the eventuality of their sudden deaths, or even if they just vanished. Lechien is not the type of individual who requires a picture painted for him, but as with Schuhly's offer, he quickly realized that he would be out of the picture if this course was pursued. And who knows what he might be sacrificing? Already his rejection of Schuhly's $10,000 cash offer had paid off handsomely. The dogs might still be worth more alive than dead, if he handled the situation adroitly.

On the first day of re-shooting Lechien turned up at Cinecitta and went straight to Leopold's office. "Do you want the dogs, yes or no? If you want them, for the last time pay me what you owe me for the lay-off, or say goodbye to the dogs forever. I'll have them destroyed." Leopold blanched, blustered — then buckled.

Lechien drove back to Rome by the most circuitous route he could devise. If anyone was following him, he thought, he would give them a run for their money. And if any notions were being harbored of a kidnap attempt on his canines, it would be over his dead body — and theirs too. As far as he was concerned, with his money for the lay-off and a new run-of-the-picture contract safely tucked in his pocket, the safety of the dogs was now top priority.

• • •

The tenuous cease-fire between Film Finances and Gilliam was soon abruptly called off. In place of the giant chess game, Gilliam and McKeown had come up with the idea of the Sultan serenading the Baron with a few songs. Since he considered Eric Idle a wizard at lyrics, Gilliam commissioned him to work with composer Michael Kamen.

The Sultan would accompany his opera *The Torturer's Apprentice* on the Torturetron, a devilishly ingenious Gilliamesque instrument that resembled a cage, with an organ-like instrument attached at the side. Every time the Sultan played a note, the prisoners inside were prodded and jabbed with connecting poles, pipes and knives, producing the sweet strains of orchestrated torment.

Film Finances was not amused when presented with the bill for Idle's lyrics. (Kamen's music was fine, since this would be included with his film score fee.) Even though abandonment of the chess scene was saving the company a fortune, they still felt they should have been consulted about the substitution of *The Torturer's Apprentice*.

Steve Ransohoff went so far as to question the veracity of Idle's authorship of the lyrics. Claiming that his professional integrity had been impugned by Ransohoff, major correspondence was entered into of a distinctly litigious nature.

"Filming was tough going at this stage," Idle recalled. "I was by no means overjoyed at the prospect of spending the entire weekend writing, but you know we Brits and our ridiculous sense of duty: I found myself in a small room at the Hotel DeVille with Michael Kamen and large amounts of rented electronic musical equipment. On the Friday night I wrote a sample lyric called *Life Is Rather Like A Game* and took it in on the Saturday. But the big breakthrough came when I had the idea that instead of singing just the one song which was constantly interrupted, the Sultan should be singing several arias from a terribly bad opera he had written. We got rather excited over this idea, which had several advantages, not the least of which was that it gave the Baron the far more dynamic attitude of being trapped in the last hour before his death with this dull maniac singing appalling arias. And of course it solved the problem with the time lapse, since each time they came back the Sultan would be on another part of the opera, and we would know at once that some time had passed. Then I came up with the title, *The Torturer's Apprentice*, and we were off and running. Michael and I spent the rest of the weekend mapping out the various beats and writing this cod opera, including my decidedly inspirational *A Eunuch's Life Is Hard (And Nothing Else)*!

"Then came the punch-up with Steve Ransohoff, and our exchange of memos. I remember being insulted by something he said and then he was insulted by my insult. I scribbled a note at the foot of my last memo challenging him to custard pies at dawn."

Ransohoff denied having ever received Idle's memo with its challenge: "If I had," he later related with a decidedly humorless smile, "I would have told him where and when." Herewith Eric Idle's letter in full:

Dear Mr. Ransohoff,

I strongly resent your suggestion relayed to me by

Stratton Leopold that I am "sand-bagging" the movie because my lawyer, Tom Hoberman has informed you that I wrote a scene including several songs. For your information I gave up my weekend to work on this with Michael Kamen at the express request of the director. If as I am now informed none of the producers knew anything about it almost a month later, even after the shooting of the scene, several conclusions might well be drawn about the producers, but I fail to see how I can be blamed for working overtime to help the picture.

I have spent five months of my life so far on this film, I have had my head shaved, and I am not prepared to be insulted at long distance by Los Angeles lawyers for putting in extra work to help the film be as good as I firmly believe it will be.

I demand an apology or I am afraid I shall have to challenge you to a duel. I propose custard pies at dawn.

Yours sincerely,
Eric Idle

Jack Purvis, Terry Gilliam, Eric Idle

David Tomblin

Terry Gilliam, Peter Jeffrey

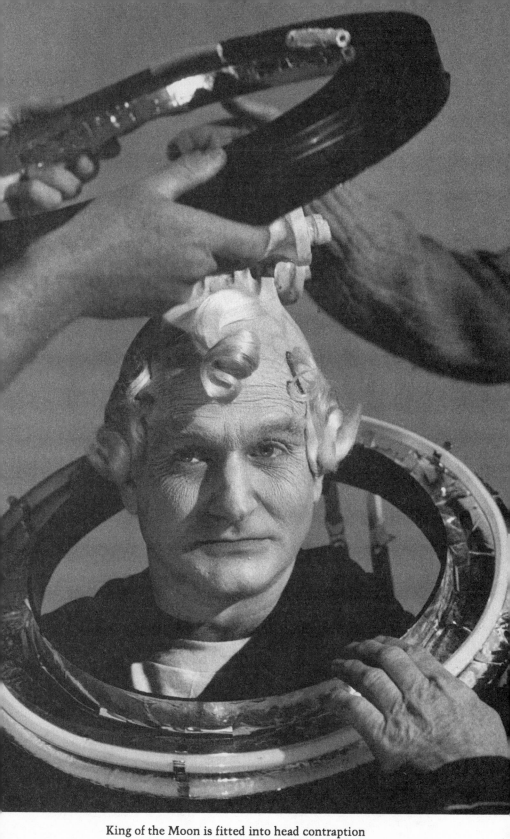

King of the Moon is fitted into head contraption

Richard Conway adjusts collar on dummy King of the Moon

Photo by F. Bellomo

King of the Moon's giant bed

Sally Salt (Sarah Polley) gently vandalizes her father's
theater poster, directed by Terry Gilliam

CHAPTER
TWENTY-TWO

Valentina was like royalty, she had visitors every day, Fellini, Zeffirelli, government ministers. When she had to do a scene she just kept them all waiting. She plays slightly eccentric, but she knows what's going on.

—Lee Cleary

Cleary was firmly established as Valentina Cortese's personal "minder" and court favorite on the set. "I love Lee," she declared, "a wonderful young man, but *very naughty*. He was always sending me up!"

"Valentina spent hours in makeup every day," said Cleary, "you could never judge how long. I had to play this game of walking past and saying casually, 'Ready when you are, Valentina.' 'Is everyone else on the set?' she'd ask. If the answer was yes, she'd be out like a flash, but she just had to be last to make an entrance. She would walk out in one of her wonderful outfits, always accompanied by Panucia."

A classic day for Cleary was conducting Cortese to the dressing room she was allocated at Cinecitta. "Persuade her it's wonderful,

Lee, you can do it," he was briefed. Cortese stopped dead at the few steps leading up to her proposed quarters. "Lee, this is not *possible*," she declared. "These stairs are too steep, my legs . . ." Two young Italian freshmen were duly summoned to lift the petite Cortese up the stairs. Although the room was beautifully furnished, with an elaborate bowl of freshly-cut flowers perched by the makeup mirror, the star looked around distainfully. "It's a bit small, Lee. Can I see the one next door?"

Jonathan Pryce's door was flung wide. "Mmm. Not bad. Can I see the others, darling?" When every dressing room had been inspected, she turned to Cleary, a quizzical expression on her face. "Lee, who has the trailer I saw on the lot this morning?"

"Oh, that. It's John Neville's. He need it for his fax machine and all that stuff."

"Really? It looks *very* nice."

"It's nothing special, Valentina."

"Lee?"

"Yes, Valentina?"

"Why can't *I* get a trailer, darling?"

• • •

After the various conceptions of who might play Vulcan had gone up in smoke, Gilliam turned to Bill Paterson in desperation. "You could do it easily," he told the startled actor, who was scheduled to leave that very day. "The four mechanics are all playing double roles, so are Valentina and Uma. You're the only one who's getting off lightly, Paterson! And it would only take a few more days . . ."

"I would have played Vulcan for Terry," Paterson claimed with an almost perfectly-straight face. Now he was safely back in London and busy on another set, he broke into a smile. "But I told him he'd be better getting a *good* actor to play him. I just *had* to get back!"

• • •

The imminent arrival of Lloyd's loss-adjuster and troubleshooter extraordinaire was an exasperating experience for everyone. "What fresh hell is this?" was the question on everyone's lips. Would he turn out to be another tormentor? David Taylor emerged as a dark-haired, fresh-faced individual of medium height who could be blunt both to and beyond the point of rudeness. Richard Soames would now take a back seat, relatively speaking, leaving Stratton Leopold to work with the man from Lloyd's.

With Gilliam pointedly excluded from their discussion, Taylor kicked off with a proposal that the sequence set in Vulcan's ballroom be chopped. That was one way, he maintained, of dispensing with the special effects and puppetry required. Then there was the matter of the beheading of the Sultan's treasurer. "Too bloody," Taylor decreed, "we'll never get the PG certification the film needs." A further conceit that struck Taylor as being in questionable taste was the suggestion that the Baron was a womanizer. Was this wise? At this rate, McKeown wryly noted, the movie was well on its way to becoming a Lloyd's of London production.

Taylor had, in fact, already contacted Schuhly, whom he intended to use as his conduit to the "impossible" Gilliam of Film Finances' legend. "Mr. Terry Gilliam," he decreed, "is to prepare a shot list each day for the following day's work following discussions with Stratton Leopold. This must be completed and discussed each night for the following day's work. I anticipate full cooperation from Gilliam and all concerned in this connection, and on any other instruction that either myself or Film Finances deliver."

With "Lloyd's Law" laid down, Schuhly himself was next to be tested. "With regard to our conversation of 8 December on the ballroom sequence," Taylor memoed him, "I would appreciate your phoning me today with regard to Mr. Gilliam's acceptance thereof."

The reminder left Taylor's proposed conduit in a quandary. Schuhly was unable to pass on Taylor's comments to Gilliam for the simple reason that the two were still incommunicado. In desperation, he summoned McKeown and explained that Taylor had to have his answer. "I'll discuss it with Terry," said McKeown, "but I can't see him giving in on any of these points. Surely we cut enough before the re-start. If we cut much more, there'll be nothing left."

"Look, I can handle Taylor," Schuhly assured him, "but if you can concoct a letter clearly stating your reasons for objecting to the changes it would strengthen my hand considerably. And please tell Terry I'm only acting to protect the script."

Gilliam and McKeown dutifully penned the letter Schuhly requested, starting with their considered opinions that the cuts would be detrimental to the picture. If chopping the Treasurer's head off were handled in a brutal and bloody way, they conceded that Taylor might have a point. The way Gilliam intended to film it, however, had the Treasurer's detached head winking at an Odalisque in a defiance of death, prefiguring the Baron's similar stance at the end of the picture. It was part of the continuing theme of reassurance, one of the keynotes of the entire movie.

As far as the Ballroom sequence was concerned, Taylor was advised that they considered the scene crucial. "This is one of the few musical sequences in the film," they asserted, "and we know it will be a remarkable visual sequence remembered when the plot and dialogue have long been forgotten."

With regard to the Baron's "womanizing," they saw this as a predictable foible that made for an amusing running gag, which would enable the audience to get a handle on the character. The Baron's own sexual energy was also a part of his gradual rejuvenation. "The only reason we can think of to cut either of these scenes would be to save money," they summed up, "but to do so would, we believe, be at a cost to the quality of the film."

McKeown and Tomblin were both summoned to Schuhly's Black Tower. "David Taylor is *insisting* that these scenes be cut," he told them. "The only way we can get around it is to offer some compromise position to save his face. Maybe if I suggest doing some blue screen work and saving time that way, that might be enough. But have another word with Terry tonight and see if he'll budge any more."

When their meeting reconvened the next day, Schuhly was told to make the position clear to Taylor — no cuts, no budge. This he decided to do by telephone immediately. The sentiments conveyed, McKeown was beckoned over. "He's not pleased," Schuhly whispered, "and wants to talk to you." McKeown dutifully picked up the receiver.

"Look, Charles, we've never met," Taylor began, "but I think it's fair to say that I'm known in this trade as a reasonable, open-minded man. When I think of some other loss adjuster you might have been given, with no experience in films, believe me, you're lucky to have me. I'm not a hatchet man, but my principals are leaning on me and

I've got to offer them something. So for God's sake talk to Terry and ask him to give me a ring."

A first face-to-face meeting was duly set up between Gilliam and Taylor for Saturday, December 12. Introductions over, the wary twosome quickly established an unexpected rapport. Instead of the obstreperous trouble-maker Film Finances had led him to expect, Taylor found Gilliam surprisingly level-headed, a "fantasist" with an admirable grasp of detail who seemed solely dedicated to achieving the best result for his movie.

"Lloyd's have now effectively taken over the picture," Gilliam was informed. "I want to help, but I need your cooperation. I'm prepared to *spend* money to save money in the long run. First, though, I have to compile a report and I need to know which cuts you're going to go with. The Ballroom sequence is surely the one we should all be looking at." Gilliam could hardly believe his ears. Taylor was going to *spend* money? After Film Finances' slash-everything approach this struck him as unbelievably good news.

By the following day, while still adamant that the Ballroom sequence must remain, Gilliam had conceded several minor, but still significant cuts. Suddenly the problems seemed to evaporate. Thoroughly impressed by Gilliam, Taylor returned to London confident that Lloyd's would be satisfied with his progress. Another chasm had been bridged. As far as Gilliam was concerned it now seemed that Taylor's arrival might herald an era of enlightenment. The hope immediately established common ground.

• • •

Taylor's physical arrival on the set was a galvanizing event. The ice with Gilliam having been broken, he saw the problem essentially as one of "man management." After talking to everyone involved in the production, he quickly came to the conclusion that the special effects team from England had been decimated to a dangerous extent. Richard Conway breathed a long sigh of relief and began to build back up to what he saw as a reasonable complement.

A growing intractibility at Cinecitta now reached hazardous levels. A general sense of annoyance that Gilliam had chosen to shoot half the film on location in Spain began to contaminate the critical relationship with the studio. The Cinecitta attitude ignored the fact that the move to Spain had been Schuhly's idea. The studio had turned its back on *Munchausen*.

David Taylor soon discovered that problems arose on the movie like a multi-headed hydra; as soon as one head was chopped off another grew back. Everyone constantly blamed everyone else — it was the director, the set designer, the cinematographer, the Italian element. The overriding problem, as far as he could see, was the deadly lethargic pace. Instead of the speedboat Taylor would have wished, Cinecitta's organization reminded him of a serene, stately ocean liner — but one with hundreds of leaks below deck.

Taylor quickly grasped Cinecitta's view of the movie as the golden chance of a lifetime. When Gilliam requested ten exotic birds for the Sultan's harem, a prop buyer reported that the owner wanted $10,000 for their hire." "I'll settle for five birds for half the money," was Gilliam's immediate response. When Taylor passed the request, the full ten birds were delivered for the modified price.

An initial skirmish with Schuhly ended their brief honeymoon period. "I was a little disappointed with Mr. Schuhly," Taylor recalled. "I shook hands with him over lunch on one specific item and the next day he reneged. That I did not find comforting. I knew that he had threatened Soames and yes, he made lots of threats to me too. The film world seems to live off threats and counterthreats, but I just play it straight down the middle. Allegations about who did what to whom don't get a film finished."

Taylor had to address the fairly tricky matter of extracting the negative from Cinecitta. Everything that had been filmed to date was under lock and key in the studio vaults, with the exception of some blue screen work that was being processed at Technicolor in England. An initial visit to the Cinecitta official concerned was abortive: they would only release the negative on receipt of signed letters of authority from both Lloyd's in London and Schuhly in Rome. Taylor telephoned Schuhly, who asked him to come to his office the following morning to obtain the release. He turned up, only to be told that Schuhly had left town "indefinitely." Infuriated, Taylor went to see the head of Cinecitta, who agreed to release 1,000 feet as a good-will gesture pending Schuhly's return. Something told Taylor it was going to be a long, hard winter. A thousand feet was by any standard only a token victory.

On one occasion, Taylor watched as Gilliam spent hours meticulously setting up an infinitely complicated scene in the Sultan's Treasury. As he sat on the camera crane ready to shout "Action!" an Italian lighting cameraman strolled across the set, casually picked up an arc lamp that had been fastidiously positioned after much careful discussion — and carried it away! Even as Gilliam put on a fairly accurate impression of an apoplectic fit, Taylor began to understand the "typing with gloves on" aspect of the movie's history.

"Sitting down with Gilliam is an anecdote in itself," Taylor testified. "You don't have to patronize him, but you sure as hell have to be in a position to keep up with his mind. He'll fight like a terrier for something he believes in. Often when I'd made suggestions to him he'd jump up and down and scream and shout, but I'd just wait until he'd finished and say, 'Fine, could we continue now?' and we'd get on like a house on fire thereafter. Film people are strange animals. They're like children. They expect you to know about films and how they work. They'll use buzzwords and if you ask what they mean, you're dead. Plus the fact that when you're looking at something that's costing £100,000 *a day*, you haven't got time to be taught. When film people are talking to you their favorite expression is, 'It's down to you.' The biggest criticism they'll make is if you never make a decision."

• • •

Lee Cleary first suggested Oliver Reed to play Vulcan, having worked with him on Nicolas Roeg's *Castaway*. Cleary found him a delightful, larger-than-life character. "But he's mad," Gilliam protested. "No, he's not," said Cleary, "that's the stuff you read in the papers. Whatever he does he'll always turn up on time, he'll give you the best performance he can give and he's no trouble."

"Can you handle him if he goes off?" Gilliam asked, still unsure. "Yes," Cleary firmly replied, whereupon he was urged to contact Reed's brother David, his agent and manager. Two days later Reed was on the set and presented to Gilliam in full leather-plated costume, complete with a fiery red wig and beard that looked as if it had been trimmed with a lawnmower. Gilliam surveyed him for a moment and to the actor's astonishment stuck a forefinger in each side of his mouth and pulled a grotesque face. "Too much ooo-eee-a-a-a-a-argh," he declared, then grinned broadly. "I see what you mean," Reed replied, rolling his eyes and wondering what the hell he'd wandered into. "Now let's talk about how Vulcan should be played," Gilliam suggested. "I have in mind a rich North of England accent, Ollie."

"Where there's muck, there's brass, lad," Reed immediately retorted, as to the manner born. Gilliam was then treated to the spectacle of the actor swaggering back and forth, yelling Vulcan-like epithets in a thick and fruity Lancashire accent that would have done credit to any 18th century Northern industrial baron.

"*Munchausen* was about the only time I've been allowed to do what I wanted with a part," Reed recalled with relish. "You can be over-directed by people, but Terry let me have my own way. There was a scene we rehearsed on Saturday where we really hit our stride. When we resumed, Terry said on the Sunday, 'You seemed to be having much more fun with the character yesterday. Could you take it a bit further?' I didn't need to be told twice! Once I realized I could get away with it, off I went!"

Reed's arrival totally upset the odds on the still-unresolved Uma Thurman contest. In Belchite the smart money had switched from England, but the wave of firings in Rome had removed a firm favorite.

"Oh, God, Oliver's asked her out," swept around the set in record time. And indeed he had. But it was only to a football match, and what could happen at a football match? Amid the sighs of relief, it was discovered that Reed had asked Thurman to the game under the impression that Rome was playing at home — or so he claimed. When it turned out to be an away match, their date became a weekend lunch that caused further anxious speculation.

Uma kept Reed waiting in the hotel bar for three quarters of an hour. Reed never waits that long for anybody, but so busy had he been telling all the waiters about this "fantastic-looking chick" he was meeting that he was obliged to sit it out just to show them. Their tongues were hanging out by the time Thurman appeared — then in she came, very blonde and very beautiful.

Reed recalls a few small gins being consumed with the lunch, and perhaps just a soupçon of wine, then it was off on a shopping expedition with Thurman to buy a present for his wife. On the way back to the hotel later in the afternoon, Reed spotted a group of Japanese tourists on the Spanish Steps. After inviting them back to the Grand Hotel for a small refreshment, he challenged each and every one to take part in a kung fu contest. As the inevitable climax approached, Thurman seemed to suddenly remember she was only 17 and burst out crying. "Stop behaving like a cunt!" Reed yelled, at the same time exhibiting a big sheepish grin. Her response was to run off in further floods of tears.

A sigh of relief swept through the unit as Reed's unashamed account of his kung fu climax was relayed. "It was all a bit too much for Uma," he conceded. "I know others who tried to date her as well, but I don't think in the end that *anyone* succeeded!"

Gilliam had declared the set closed to all but essential personnel during Thurman's scene as Venus emerging from the shell. Every available vantage point and peep-hole the length and breadth of the set, however, was fully utilized. "Jee-sus, these *tits*!" one worthy was heard to murmur, echoing the pent-up sentiments of other males present. "Take a good look, because it's all we'll see of them until the picture comes out," another summarized.

CHAPTER
TWENTY-THREE

*I wanted Schuhly removed completely, but
Soames said I had to learn to work with him,
that he could be "of help" to us. The
difficulty I had with him was that he'd hired
the crew originally and I wanted to make a
clean break in order to wrest control. That
clean break never happened. Film Finances
was in the process of being sold, Columbia's
structure had been completely altered, and
my impression was that nobody cared a shit
for us in Rome. Why wasn't I being told the
whole story — like, why Schuhly was still
around? Here we were, after all, spending a
million bucks a week — and nobody seemed
to care!*

—Stratton Leopold

*The Italians are all delightful people, but
slow, all after Oscars or awards or whatever.*

> *And they would only perform when Il*
> *Maestro, the director, was around. Terry*
> *would say, "Use your imagination," but they*
> *never would; it all had to go through the*
> *director, whether it was a new frock for*
> *Winston or a wig for Valentina. I know that*
> *got on Terry's wick.*
>
> —Lee Cleary

A herd of cows Gilliam wanted tethered in one corner of the cavernous Vulcan set was eventually argued down to a single, rather forlorn creature. Vulcan's men, the Cyclops, claiming imminent suffocation, refused to wear the masks that had been devised. The enormous chandelier that hung suspended over the massive set collapsed one day, causing extensive set damage. As far as Gilliam was concerned the filming of Vulcan was perfectly straightforward and simple — not so for ordinary folks like the wire riggers and special effects crew.

Stratton Leopold's position could scarcely be described as as having improved since the November break. Now he had to carry out David Taylor's instructions, as well as keeping in touch with Los Angeles. His pointed exclusion from November's "peace talks" had done nothing to help, despite Film Finances' logic that he could contunue to play "Mr. Nice Guy" more readily than if he attended.

While Leopold was at a loss to explain Schuhly's continuing presence, an ex-associate of the producer offered this off-the-record overview: "Schuhly knew all along the film would cost a lot more than what was down on paper," he confided. "So is it possible that Film Finances didn't look at it closely enough? There was a rumor that it was a sprat to catch a mackerel, with Schuhly implying he could get Film Finances lots of other Columbia business. If that's the case, it must be regarded as the most expensive sprat of all time. They went all over Schuhly's accounts with a fine-tooth comb, and found nothing wrong, apart from millions of dollars of unpaid bills, which Schuhly would doubtless maintain was perfectly normal procedure. It's true that most businesses defer paying bills as long as possible, although of course he should have at least declared their existence.

"You can say what you like about Thomas, but without him there's no question — the film would never have been made. He was perfect in his own peculiar way for the picture, disastrous in another. If only he could have combined the freewheeling spirit that bluffed the money men with nuts and bolts practicality. Once the abyss opened up between him and Terry, it just got too big. Maybe, deep down, Thomas is a bit of a lamb in wolf's clothing. He never denied Terry anything, maybe he was really too timid to confront that.

"Instead of helping Terry out, Thomas just stayed in his office and gave long interviews — not all that strange for a producer on a smooth-running film, but never on a troubled one. And we're talking *troubled*! The Italians stayed loyal to Thomas, all right, they are always loyal to someone who gives them work. And he was going to be around the following year — not Stratton Leopold, not David Taylor, not Richard Soames — and probably not Terry Gilliam."

• • •

Leopold's diminished authority was reflected in a memo he issued on the Vulcan set: "In a telephone conversation today with Mr. David Taylor, he directed that we must complete the Vulcan workshop today, a set which should have been completed yesterday. Mr. Taylor is allowing us two hours overtime to accomplish this."

He was promptly nabbed by an irate Tomblin. "What's this two-hour limit all about, Stratton?!" he demanded to know.

"I'm only passing on Mr. Taylor's instructions."

"So if we're not finished, you're going to strike the set?"

"That's right."

"Whether we're finished or not?"

"Yes."

"Bad move, Stratton. The whole Vulcan sequence will make no sense. How *can* you just lie down to someone in London imposing a limit of two extra hours when you *know* the problems we're up against in this scene. We've wires all over the place, a cow shitting and pissing away in the corner . . ."

"Do your best, David."

"Christ! Isn't that what we're doing already?"

Gianni Cozzo grew increasingly despondent over the film's economics and its politics. "It's *still* underbudgeted," he told Pisani.

"It's been wrong from the start and it's *still* wrong. If everyone were in harmony, it might not be so bad, but there's so much point-scoring going on. Mario, I'm too old and too rich, I don't need this — it's not my game."

The fifth in the line of first assistant directors that had begun with Don French and continued with Roy Button, Jose Escolar and, very briefly, Bill Westley, Cozzo would be gone by the Christmas break.

The holiday spirit never stood a chance. Peace and goodwill were in short supply between the director and his cinematographer. From Gilliam's prespective, Rotunno had plotted to control events from the start, going so far as to appoint his son-in-law as the cameraman on the second unit to establish his influence there.

Gilliam was accustomed to the English system where the camera operator, lighting cameraman, electricians and camera crew all reported to the cinematographer. The First Assistant Director controlled the standbys, stagehands, carpenters, painters and the rest of the floor. Not in Italy — where Rotunno's authority as cinematographer seemed boundless. Gilliam ultimately refused to tolerate Rotunno's apparent omnipotence on his film. "Visconti never had to rush, Fellini never had to rush, why should Gilliam rush?" seemed to sum up the Italian attitude.

David Taylor was upstairs in his office when a messenger appeared from the Vulcan set. "You'd better come quickly," he was told, "Terry has just stormed off the set." Gilliam had been unhappy with progress on a tracking shot with John Neville on a trolley, supposedly being carried on Oliver Reed's back, ready to be hurled into the vortex. Gilliam wanted the two trolleys to run at different speeds. One would run faster, almost catching up with the other, then fall back again, all to give the shot a certain density. Although this effect had been achieved in rehearsal to his satisfaction, numerous subsequent takes had all failed to work.

"I need five more minutes to reset the track," Rotunno had advised Gilliam, "so I can give the camera dolly more of a head start."

"No," was Gilliam's adamant response, "that shouldn't be necessary. It worked in rehearsal, it can be made to work now."

The confrontation roared into full throttle. Rotunno issued an indecipherable stream of Italian rebuttal, then clearly translated the gist of his remarks by pulling the plug and plunging the set into total darkness. "That's *it!*" Gilliam exploded, hurling his script to the ground. "Now you won't have me to kick around any more. I *quit!*"

Taylor surveyed the Gilliam-less set, where dozens of cast and crew awaited further instruction. "What did *you* think of the shot?" he asked Tomblin.

"I saw nothing wrong with it, but I'm not the director," Tomblin laconically replied, "that's Terry's job."

"What about you, Peppino?"

"For me, it was OK," said Rotunno gamely fighting back his emotions.

"So shoot it."

"But you can't — the director's not here — " Rotunno protested.

"*Shoot it,*" Taylor insisted.

Rotunno's answer was to set the scene up, then tactfully withdraw as the cameras were about to roll; his professionalism wouldn't allow him to remain in the director's absence. Having walked around the block and worked off his frustration, Gilliam reappeared, shrugged at Taylor, and took over once more.

In essence the blowup had been over the constitutional question of who was directing this movie — Gilliam or Rotunno. Gilliam later sat down with Taylor, Tomblin and Pisani to discuss the contest of wills. "I can't continue like this," Gilliam told them. "If Peppino's directing it, fair enough, let him get on with it. But from now on it's him or me."

In Italy the idea of getting rid of Rotunno was tantamount to regicide; to the locals Rotunno was God. His suggestion that if Gilliam would only allow him to talk matters over more thoroughly he could have whatever he wanted carried Godfather overtones that were unacceptable. Gilliam's Protestant direct approach was utterly at odds with Rotunno's perceived hierarchy where one only talked to God through the proscribed mediation of his priests and the Pope. The larger battleground would remain between the Italians' way of working and Gilliam's own ethic. "Peppino takes offense at me talking to people lower down the ladder than him," Gilliam protested. "I don't think he *means* it in a Godfather way, but there again —"

"Terry, Terry, *Terry*," said Pisani, shaking his head from side to side. "Surely you've heard of the expression, 'When in Rome —'" Gilliam swallowed heavily; he'd spent a career as an iconoclast — now he was being asked to pay deference to Rome. This was a battle he was clearly never going to win. A change of tack was required. With Gianni Cozzo's announced departure, reinforcements from the home front were underway.

Valuable as Tomblin was in his executive capacity, Gilliam persuaded him to take over as First Assistant Director, the job he had originally been offered. Tomblin proved invaluable as "the man in between"; on the one hand, Gilliam's appointed lieutenant, on the other, a clearly allied force to the production goals of the project. Gilliam could now rely on the tried and trusted approach he had used on several earlier movies. Responsibilities and power were evenly distributed between himself and his first assistant, which would ultimately allow Gilliam his accustomed creative space.

Idle watched as Tomblin manfully tried to reorganize the logistics of the film in his newly adopted role. "*Munchausen* could never have been finished without him," he maintained. "Somebody is always required on the set who's prepared to take control and say, 'Come on, why aren't we shooting?' Before Tomblin came down we'd often be on the set for 40 minutes with Italians, Spanish and English milling around, but nobody knew we were ready! All that stopped when Tomblin stepped in. Terry and Peppino? It wasn't a great love story. I liked Peppino, he was a nice uncle figure.

"I think Terry likes to create chaos and be the one in the middle, then control the chaos. He missed his team and without them he wasn't good at communicating. With Peppino he just needed one simple action, like sitting down with the man, but he's very stubborn, he wouldn't do that. A lot of things Terry does come out well instinctively. The right person comes along at the right time, like Olly Reed. He seems to have good fortune. I saw Terry at his lowest on this film. Although he hides it, you can tell he's glum. I tried to jog him along and make him laugh, although sometimes it's best to get him angry, because then he can let it all out."

Gilliam disarmingly confirms, then denies Idle's "chaos" theory. "It's true," he admits, "that changing my mind about something when everything is set up and the cameras are about to roll can create chaos, but it's *organized* chaos, in the service of creativity. And this you can only afford when everyone and everything around you is beautifully organized. On *Munchausen* I was *denied* that freedom most of the time, since I'd only have been adding to the chaos that existed around me."

Mario Pisani saw the clashes between Gilliam and Rotunno as almost inevitable. "Terry was suffering because the set was under Peppino's control, he was 'the King of the set,'" he told me. "In Italy, when a director calls Peppino in, they know his style and they know he will bring his own crew. Language-wise it's much easier for his crew to follow Peppino, not Terry. They're working for Terry for the first time and they don't know if they'll ever work with him again, but they know they'll work for years with Peppino. You can also say that Peppino has not the easiest of tempers in the world. Nor has Terry. I think also there was a generational gap between them.

"Terry was always talking to me about the problems with 'the crew,' so I asked him one day to tell me who is not working well and we will change these people. That was when I discovered it was not the crew at all, but Peppino. He had one of the best art directors, one of the best costumiers, people like plasterers, sculptors and painters that you've never known in England. The 'crew' he was referring to was basically Peppino and his camera crew; Terry just couldn't accept Peppino's way of working."

● ● ●

Dante Ferretti's buoyant sense of humor was tested to the limit on *Munchausen*, especially in the aftermath of the premature re-start. Surrounded in his office at Cinecitta by the original sketches that have beguiled millions of filmgoers in the works of Pasolini and Fellini, he held forth. "I'm not always a very funny man," he conceded, "because I can get nervous. And on this film there was plenty to get nervous about! I would go back home every day at two o'clock in the morning, Saturday and Sunday as well, trying to solve the problems of organization or buildings they never did, or the internal fights that went on all the time.

"The relationship with Cinecitta itself should have been through the production offices, but they never did that, they never got involved. There were many problems which I was left to deal with in person. Cinecitta were working in a very bureaucratic way and it was very slow. I worked with David Tomblin every day to make the puzzle work.

"Terry and I had a good relationship, because through all the problems he left me alone to work. He's the kind of man who knows what he wants on the screen. He reminds me of Fellini, but he leaves you to work more than Fellini. Fellini tries to represent a world of himself. When you work with him you have to understand his world. Terry involves you, he wants you to share *his* world with *him*."

• • •

Schuhly instructed an editor to assemble the footage shot so far so he could fly it out to Los Angeles to show Columbia. Gilliam was furious. "It's not a good idea to tout it around at this stage," he raged through McKeown. "It's too rough, it could rebound on everybody."

Anger was mixed with intrigue when the news leaked that David Taylor was Los Angeles-bound as well. McKeown's theory, which proved correct, was that Taylor was engaged in a final attempt to get more money from Columbia. There had, after all, been an encouraging fax to Gilliam from the studio's new head of production, Dawn Steel: "I am very excited about your movie," she had written. "I've been a fan of yours for a long time. Can't wait to meet you and see it."

Taylor flew from London to Los Angeles to keep his appointment at Columbia with Roger Faxon, one of Victor Kaufman's minions. The reasonable expectation that Taylor would view the rough cut with the Columbia brass was short lived; he was astonished when they insisted on screening the footage on their own, and very quickly gained the impression that he was addressing a series of closed minds. Their verdict confirmed his suspicion: "It *could* be a very good film," was the consensus, "but we don't think it will sell in America." The statement sent the recoupment hopes of both Lloyd's and Film Finances into a state of instant melt-down.

When Taylor went into his scheduled meeting, he noted that Faxon had two company lawyers present. "I represent Lloyd's," Taylor pointed out, "and I'm not legally represented here as you are." Aware that he was facing Faxon, a polite, blandly-smiling brick wall of preppiness — and a brick wall, furthermore, acting under strictest instruction — Taylor went straight to the purpose of the meeting. "You've bought a film which was going to cost $23.5 million, and you're getting one that's heading for $40 million. I believe in all equity Columbia should consider making a further financial commitment."

"Mr. Taylor," Faxon replied, "we have a contract."

"Aren't you prepared to change your mind?"

"No."

Taylor got up and snapped his briefcase shut. "Thank you, gentlemen," he said, and walked out of the office. The meeting had lasted precisely 6$^1/_2$ minutes.

CHAPTER
TWENTY-FOUR

Sean Connery can be very mean with directors and maybe Terry has never forgiven him for the slight of addressing him as "Boy" at one stage on **Time Bandits.** *Sean is the typical leader of the gang; when he is angry you can see death in his eyes. Only the law holds him back. He has an enormous presence and if you feel insecure as a director, he can become very ironical. I know how to handle him, you have to humor Sean. If you don't have the weight to withstand him, it can get nasty.*

—Thomas Schuhly

Maybe Thomas wanted Terry for the long run, to become his producer for the rest of his life. And maybe Terry was looking for that as well. Maybe they were both looking so intensely that they neglected the forest around the trees!

—Eugene Rizzo

It was hard for Schuhly to accept that his "dream ticket" of Sean Connery and Brando had broken up, but at least Connery was still in the bag. Or was he? The problem was that the actor had indicated his willingness to play the King of the Moon *as originally written.* Would he still be as keen with the cut down version? Schuhly wrote to him after the cuts Gilliam and McKeown made had been presented to Connery:

Dear Sean,

I am very, very happy that you did not turn down the revised 'King,' and that — assuming we can match your schedule — you will (still) be part of our film. As the material is already very exciting, beautiful and funny, I am delighted that we can crown it with your participation and wonderful acting. As this is my first big international film as sole producer and as I like and admire you very much . . . I am really happy and proud to have you on this movie. My very best thanks for all your goodwill, support and patience with our crazy production.

Cordially, Thomas Schuhly

Even as Schuhly was writing his upbeat letter of confirmation, Connery's attorneys were penning their own missives to Film Finances, listing their concerns with the "unfortunate press reports" that had leaked internationally regarding the state of the Baron's financial health. Steve Ransohoff at Film Finances wrote to Creative Artists Agency (CAA) , Connery's agents, assuring him that as far as they were concerned, the deal for Sean Connery to appear in the movie was in place, that the production of the picture would continue, that adequate financing was available, and that the producers were ready, willing and able to meet their obligation to Connery.

Since his letter of comfort was written during the film's November shutdown, Ransohoff's protestations may have rung a trifle hollow. And the question was — did Connery have any obligation to a skeletal version of what he had originally agreed to play? The answer came in a disconsolate letter Schuhly wrote to Gilliam a few weeks later:

Dear Terry,

Sean called me yesterday evening and turned his part down. I am still perplexed and I don't know what to say. We had a 'gentleman's agreement' . . . He had accepted the revised version (he even liked it) and he was showing us goodwill in order to match our schedule. Now — out of a sudden, he was complaining about our schedule and told me some major bullshit.

As he was mentioning several times his conversations with Michael Ovitz, I can only guess that he was given some negative advice by his agent.

Dear Terry, can you believe me that I'm awfully sorry for this situation, but I really relied on this guy and on his given word . . . and I didn't expect at all this end of the story. I was absolutely sure and convinced that Sean would do it . . . and there is no intelligent explanation I can give you for this change of mind.

Regards, Thomas.

Schuhly was down, but not yet out. During his December visit to Los Angeles, he secretly made up his mind to have one more crack at Connery. If it succeeded, everyone would hear of it. If it failed — well, at least he had tried.

• • •

During the Christmas break David Taylor's "good-guy" image slipped a notch when he made an oblique suggestion to Gilliam that he *still* could be fired if more cuts were not forthcoming. The shooting rate was languishing at one and a quarter minutes per day since the re-start. Taylor wanted to see the pace picked up. Gilliam was in no mood to be pushed. He had had enough. "Look," he said, "I *can't* go any faster and I *won't* cut the script any more. You'd better just fire me."

Even after Taylor backed off, Gilliam would still approach Charles McKeown a few days later. "Wouldn't it be faster and cheaper if we took the whole moon sequence back to England and shot it there on the blue screen?" he asked. For a dozen different reasons this turned out to be impractical, but at least every avenue had been thoroughly explored.

Schuhly continued to coax a further change of mind out of Connery. On December 17 he informed Gilliam that in principle the star was still prepared to fulfill his obligation, but only if his part was improved dramaturgically. That very day, he claimed, Connery had called him from Marbella and inquired if any further revisions had yet been made. "I feel the credit 'Sean Connery' will certainly be an asset to the different national distributors when they launch the picture," Schuhly concluded, "therefore, why should we not at least *try* to get him for the role?"

At Film Finances' behest, Gilliam wrote to Connery, setting out the facts as he saw them. While he still wanted the actor, there was no way he was going to pretend the King of the Moon was the great part it had been.

"FROM THE WOODEN BOX THAT TERRY GILLIAM SITS ON WHEN ON LOCATION:
Dear Sean,

Confused as I am about many things, I find that, as predicted, Thomas's return from his L.A. conversation with you has added to my predicament. I thought you were a definite 'No,' but Thomas claims you are a less definite 'If.' I'm not exactly sure what the 'If' is, but since Charles McKeown and I have just had some new thoughts concerning the Moon sequence, we thought you should see them straight away. As you will see, the King is quite a different animal. I'm not sure he will appeal to you, but I'll leave that to you.

It would be very useful to get your response quickly to ease my mounting confusion.

Thanks, Happy New Year, Bon Année, Terry."

The day after Gilliam dispatched his epistle, McKeown bumped into Schuhly at Cinecitta. The conversation quickly got around to the subject of Connery. McKeown expressed the hope that the matter would soon be resolved one way or the other; at least Connery would have taken on board Gilliam's patently honest no-bullshit approach. He was startled when Schuhly replied, "No, he won't."

"What do you mean, Thomas?" McKeown asked.

"I mean Sean will never see Terry's letter. Film Finances read it before it was sent and decided it should be suppressed."

McKeown's jaw dropped. "*Suppressed*? You can't mean —"

"Exactly. They told me not to send it. Their worry was that if Sean got the impression that he was being said 'no' to, CAA would have legal grounds to claim his money anyway."

"But Film Finances asked Terry to pen the letter in the first place."

"I think they expected a somewhat more heartfelt plea."

McKeown went into a huddle with Ray Cooper later. "I can't tell Terry," he told him, "he'll go absolutely bananas."

"I'll break it to him," said Cooper. "After all, he *should* know."

When Gilliam was informed, his reaction at first was one of utter outrage. "*Nothing*," he told them, "and I mean *nothing*, would surprise me now. I'm *drained*. All I want to do now is to get the picture finished and get the hell out of Rome."

Soon after the turn of the year, however, Schuhly had his brief moment of triumph. "In a long telephone conversation on January 9th," he trumpeted, "I finally succeeded in eliciting a clear 'Yes' from Sean Connery as to his revised part. He accepts the role as it now stands."

Only eleven days later his triumph had turned to dismay. "After everything seemed settled as to Sean," he now related, "he called me yesterday and *definitely* withdrew his acceptance of the part of the 'King of the Moon.' I am so thunderstruck by this sudden about-turn that I am at a loss for words. As to his reason for this decision, Sean stated that he cannot match the dates . . . but my impression is that Mike Ovitz, the head of CAA, is behind the decision. In our conversation, Sean referred several times to Ovitz, but I couldn't find out the real reason. I am very sorry that now, after all our efforts and endeavors, we are in this terrible situation. In order to find an acceptable and positive solution, we should close the file 'Sean Connery' and try to find an alternative that meets Terry's interests as well as those of the film. Sorry that we didn't succeed in having Sean in the picture."

Schuhly later offered what he regards as the *definitive* version behind Connery's defection. "Terry was quoted in the U.S. press saying that he didn't particularly want Sean for King of the Moon and that he had Michael Palin in mind. Once that was published, Sean phoned me immediately, and his agent at CAA explained that the article had been the topic at their 11 a.m. meeting. They decided then that Sean would *never* do a film for a director who was less than 100% keen on his participation. Sean called me and gave me two thousand excuses about preparation for the new Indiana Jones movie, all of that. Because he likes me a lot, he was willing to do me this favor. But he can't do it when he thinks the director doesn't want him."

Gilliam had always seen the special virtue of Connery in the film. "I tried to talk Sean into playing the King of the Moon before the film started. Even then I told him the part wasn't much, but it was a chance for him to play the big floating head that he didn't get to play in *Zardoz*. I needed an icon and he was that. It would have made the scene really work with somebody as majestic as him. Also the idea that the Baron could steal Sean Connery's woman is very important. That's what it was all about. When we rewrote the thing there wasn't any embarrassment, there was just no part for him anymore."

Gilliam claims to have been misquoted in the U.S. press, his mention of Michael Palin sandwiched between Connery's November "No" and December "Yes." "It never would have been a part where you would have read it and said *Sean Connery*," McKeown acknowledged. "But if he had played it, it would have been fantastic. I know Dave Tomblin once said, 'Somehow I just can't see Sean saying "Ticky, ticky, tick," but it would have been so surprising and so unlike him. That's what would have been so good about it.'"

Between misquotes, misunderstandings, gross misrepresentation, suppressed correspondence and a script that was twice completely revised, very few would take issue with the star's final decision.

• • •

With Schuhly's dream shattered, the race was on to find another King of the Moon. While Gilliam had only been thinking out loud back in December to the U.S. press, it was time now to check out his old friend and ex-Python, Michael Palin. He phoned Palin at home and spoke to his wife, Helen. Yes, Michael was unexpectedly free for the month of February. She would contact him and would get back to Gilliam, but was sure there would be no problem.

Steve Ransohoff was putting out his own feelers for King of the Moon, picking through a list of "suitable" actors he had compiled with Thomas Schuhly. Potentially available were Gene Hackman, Gene Wilder, Peter O'Toole, Jack Lemmon and Rodney Dangerfield. Walter Matthau was actually filming in Italy, and might be free for a few days' work. No, Bill Murray was *not* available. On January 27 Ransohoff framed an offer to Gene Wilder, which was turned down almost immediately.

The uncertainty over The Man Who Would Be King ended with Eric Idle's remarkable discovery that his friend Robin Williams was not only available, but positively keen to fill the breach. Congratulatory telegrams flowed from each set of warring participants to the other, united, if only for a moment, in the elation of this particular casting coup. That the actor had clearly taken the decision on his own was evident from the conditions his manager would lay down: There must be neither publicity photographs nor press releases attaching his name to the movie, otherwise the deal was off. Gilliam was told there was no way he would be allowed "to pimp Robin's ass."

Delighted as he was that Williams was on board, Gilliam had to explain the situation to Michael Palin, now ex-Prime Minister *and* ex-King of the Moon. "He's the one person who's never forgiven me," Gilliam lamented back at his home in Highgate Village. "After calling Helen, I had to call Michael to say it was off. It was awful. I know I hurt somebody that matters to me. That was *my* act of betrayal. Robin took a lot of pressure off my back with Columbia and Film Finances — everybody got a bit more relaxed with a big name in there again. But Michael — that's the one thing that still rankles most."

• • •

Gene Rizzo had further occasion to reflect on the continual leakage of information when he took a call at home one evening from a reporter in Los Angeles. "There's good news and bad news for you guys," he was told. "You got Robin Williams for the King and Film Finances have just filed for bankruptcy."

The news on Film Finances turned out to be inaccurate. What *had* taken place was the company's long-negotiated sale to Nigel Kayser's Entertainment Completions, carried out by Soames in the middle of potentially the most ruinous undertaking in his company's history. "Yes, *of course* the price was affected by the *Munchausen* debacle," he wearily admitted.

Speculation on the source of the leaks centered on the anti-Puttnam cabal, seen by some as headed by two of the producers he had spurned during his brief tenure at Columbia — Ray Stark and Marty Ransohoff. Or was Thomas Schuhly playing a double game? Was *he* the mole? "We always knew Thomas was paranoid," was one insider's view of this suggestion, "but is anybody *that* paranoid? Stark and Ransohoff might have been the mouthpieces for the leaks, but they weren't the source. For our money, and for whatever the reason, Film Finances was leaking all over the place — maybe to wear Terry down, maybe to play both ends against the middle, maybe for just sheer vindictiveness."

• • •

"Good morning, Lee darling."

"Good morning, Valentina. Have you heard who they've got to play King of the Moon?"

"No."

"Robin Williams."

"Really, darling? Oh, I know the name, but what's he like, is he very young —?"

"Pretty young."

"Younger than Sean Connery?"

"Yep."

"Are you *teasing* me? Summon the head of makeup immediately! I want to look like his *lover*, darling, not his *mother!*"

CHAPTER
TWENTY-FIVE

*I had my first meeting with Terry, which was
lunch at Cinecitta. One of the things that
came up was the Sultan's Palace and his 50
harem girls. I was really looking forward to
auditioning them! "How do you want them,
Terry?" I asked. Just at that moment one of
the waitresses passed our table — a 4'9" gypsy
girl who must have weighed all of 300
pounds. "Like her!" Terry said.*

—Lee Cleary

David Taylor's abbreviated powwow with the Columbia brass
was not the first time he had met face-to-face with shortsightedness
in the film industry. "It really goes beyond belief at times," he said,
shaking his head philosophically. "What they don't take into account
is that when they require guarantees there are a lot of people needed
to make that work. The banks won't lend the money unless they
know insurance cover is there. The film industry simply doesn't
realize how much they rely on insurance. People in this business
should occasionally just step back and take a long view, like Lloyd's.

Columbia'a attitude was shortsighted. You have to remember that when the Americans were negotiating the peace with Geronimo, Lloyd's were celebrating 200 years of history!"

The danger and menace lurking behind the scenes in Rome became clear to Taylor early one morning. Going down with him in the hotel elevator at 5:30 am for the early morning flight from Rome was a fully-uniformed soldier brandishing a submachine gun. When the elevator opened, there were more secret servicemen and armed soldiers than he had ever seen assembled in one place before. The police, it turned out, had cordoned off the whole area.

Mario, the unit driver sent to collect him, explained that the security precautions were to do with someone connected with the United Arab League. As they slowly drove off, Taylor remarked to his chauffeur: "God, the security here is incredible. I've never seen anything like it." Mario's reply was to pull back his jacket to reveal the gun that was nestling there. "It can't be that good," he muttered with a wry smile.

Taylor looked at the driver with new eyes. How much more than a "driver" was Mario, who had been allocated to escort him everywhere since his arrival in Rome? He had given little credence to an earlier rumor that Schuhly had drawn a gun on an unannounced visitor one night at Cinecitta. Now he was not so sure . . .

• • •

Taylor dealt with Gilliam's nagging sense of isolation by appointing industry veteran Joyce Herlihy to be his eyes and ears when he was away from Rome. Gilliam had worked in great harmony with Herlihy on *Jabberwocky*; her appointment was both a warmly inspired and shrewdly calculated move. "She was only there to hold Terry's hand," was how one observer saw it, missing the main point of the exercise. Herlihy's strengths as a freelance producer and her years of experience in every kind of difficult moviemaking situation would have proved a huge asset to anyone, let alone the beleaguered Gilliam.

• • •

"We can't go on spending money at the present rate," Schuhly was informed during one of Taylor's lightning visits to Rome. "We have to start making deals with people."

"What do you mean — deals?" Schuhly asked, somewhat distractedly.

"Deals. *New* deals. Whatever's been negotiated already we'll have to try to renegotiate."

"But I've already made these deals, it'll make me look stupid."

"Hard lines. We've got to try it."

Taylor managed to come up with some fairly spectacular renegotiations with all manner of suppliers — from Kodak all the way down to wardrobe and timber merchants. "If you look at the wonderful costumes," he pointed out, "there were thousands upon thousands of pounds spent on the materials alone. Schuhly says that he had worked out that it was best if they purchased these costumes at what he calls 'a really cheap price,' then *gave* them back to the hire company at the end. It was cheaper than hiring them, he said. *Work that one out!*"

One of the scenes left partly unshot in Belchite was Munchausen's assassination by Jackson from the perspective of the crowds in the street. Every other angle had been covered — the barrel locking on the Baron, Jackson firing — but no long shot of Jonathan Pryce skulking behind the gargoyles in the bell tower. With the set reconstructed at Cinecitta, there was only one problem — Jonathan Pryce was back in London and unavailable.

David Taylor gave the matter some thought and sought Gilliam out. "All you need," he suggested, "is after the rifle fires and the Baron falls to the ground, the camera cuts to somebody saying, 'Who did that?' Then this little old lady hobbles up, points upwards and says, 'It's that bastard, Jackson!'" Gilliam conceded the suggestion was novel, but decided to await Pryce's availability. One way or another, Taylor was still making quite an impression.

• • •

The punishing schedule of the last few months had caught up with almost everyone in different physical, medical and psycho-medical manifestations: flu for John Neville, gastroenteritis for Lee Cleary, arterial hypertension and respiratory arrhythmia for Sarah Polley, abdominal colic for Valentina Cortese, bronchitis for Giuseppe Rotunno, a twisted knee for Tony Smart, Bucephalus's minder, and countless cases of tonsillitis, low blood pressure, renal

colic, dizziness, allergic rhinitis, backache, earache, headache, fever
— and flu, followed by suspected asthenia (subsequently disproved)
for Terry Gilliam.

At several points the set looked more like a medical unit than a
film unit, with X rays and antitetanus injections looming larger with
each passing day. There were numerous accidents: rusty nails were
stepped on with great frequency, slivers of resin, deposits of lime,
sparks and other foreign bodies were lodged in eyes with grim
regularity, chests of both sexes suffered contusions and lacerations,
foreheads were scraped and hit by flying planks, backs and heads
bashed by falling reflector frames.

For Gilliam there was but one answer — get on with the job, keep
the head down, just *do* it. Through overcast skies and days of
torrential downpours, using weather cover or a retreat to the blue
screen, his only answer was to simply keep going. By the end of
January, however, the daily average "in the can" had fallen to just
over one minute of screen time per day.

Stratton Leopold tried desperately to talk Gilliam into dropping
the dancing puppets in Vulcan's ballroom sequence, convinced that
they would never work properly. A storm now ripped the roof off the
set and delayed filming by a further ten days until reconstruction was
complete. It seemed that Nature was also determined to see the
puppets vanish. "Let's cut it, let's not do it, or at least let's do it in a
different way," Leopold cajoled.

"When you see something that's expending so much money and
it's not working, it's time to cut back," Leopold argued. *"Terry's*
mistake was going ahead with the scene. *My* mistake was in not
ending it. My point was simply this — the puppets never *worked.*
Terry argued with that toward the end, and it was hugely costly,
because we had to hold the stage for a long, long time, hold the
dressing, hold the cranes. What I saw later in the final print is what
we shot the very first time, or only marginally better."

Richard Conway defended Gilliam's decision to persevere with
the puppets. "Terry was determined to get the best results he could,"
he maintained. "Many things were out of his control — the guy who
made the puppets delivered them looking absolutely fabulous, but he
clearly didn't dance himself, because he had them linked together

with Uma leading the Baron! Stratton's mistaken about the end result — the final shots are brilliant, and at least 10% better than what we started out with."

While the Baron and Venus were engaged in their dance, Eric Idle was called upon to do a few lighthearted steps of his own to divert the attention of the increasingly-jealous Vulcan. Leopold chose to demonstrate once again his peculiar sense of timing, choosing to inform Idle, minutes before the scene was to be shot, that he was being sued by Film Finances. With the scene completed, and Film Finances' memo handed over, Idle penned his reply to the company, behind which lay the full weight of the chairman of Prominent Features.

"I am upset and angry about the libelous allegations in Steve Ransohoff's memo," he wrote, "in which he accuses me of being on strike for a week and which libel is gravely compounded by his sending a copy to Columbia. I did *not* sit out the production for one week. The facts are as follows: along with several others, including the director, I did not catch the 27th December evening flight to Rome, as we were given the wrong flight times. On the morning of Monday, 28th December, Lee Cleary called me in London, apologized for the mix-up and asked me to stand by to fly to Rome. I indicated to him there was a problem with Film Finances not having fulfilled their contractual obligations to pay me by mid-December. Arthur Tarry then called me at 2 pm, informing me that I had now been paid and asking me if I was prepared to fly out. I said that I was, packed my bags and stood by to catch that afternoon's flight. Lee Cleary then informed me that I was not required for shooting on Tuesday, 29th December and that I should remain on standby in London. I did so, and per your schedule, I was not required for the rest of the week. I was eventually requested to fly on Sunday, 3rd January and report for work on Monday, 4th, which I did. As you can see from these facts I did *not* cause the production to slow down and it is a complete lie to say that I failed to report to work for the week."

Idle's missive ended with a truly spectacular legal flourish: "I hereby reserve my rights to take legal action over this slur to my professional reputation. The foregoing is not intended to be an all-inclusive statement of the facts in this matter. All rights and remedies are reserved, none of which are waived."

Clearly custard pies at dawn were inappropriate in this case; an apology from Film Finances was duly given. A lesser actor's performance would have had "I am being sued" all over his dance routine for Vulcan; not the indomitable Idle.

• • •

While shooting the harem sequence, and under the impression from the script that the Sultan was to deliver his speech from the side of his pool, Lee Cleary was approached by one of the wardrobe assistants. "How much cork do you think should be in the costume, so that it rises when the Sultan's in the water?" he was asked. "In the *water*?" Cleary replied, "What do you mean? *What water*?"

Since Peter Jeffrey was strolling past at that moment, resplendent once more in his Sultan's robes, Cleary grabbed him: "Peter, do you end up in the pool in this sequence?"

"Not as far as I know, dear boy," Jeffrey enunciated, nostrils flaring theatrically. Just to be sure, Cleary singled Gilliam out amidst the 70-odd people crowded on the set. "Terry, does Peter get knocked into the water or something?"

"No, Lee, he's *in* the water," Gilliam explained. "He gives his speech *standing in the water*." Now Cleary was totally baffled. "But — why?" he asked. Gilliam spread his arms and shrugged, grinning maniacally from ear to ear: "Why *not*?" he asked. "It might not be in the script, Lee, but you'll find it on the storyboards."

Cleary went back to the wardrobe girl and confirmed that the costume had to be waterproof, then informed Jeffrey he had to stand in the pool while making his speech. "If you took your eye off a combination of the script and the storyboards on this incredibly complicated film for one minute, you were lost," Cleary recalled. "There was just so much detail to be pieced together."

• • •

With Robin Williams' arrival on the film, the cast and crew were kept in constant merriment. "Ah, good morning, powder-puff," he might start, then throw his voice to the unsuspecting article: "Yeah, I've been selected, Robin, and it's a signal honor, to cover your entire visage this very day. *Ee-uugh*! Whooee, I'm so excited!" Williams shtick would start at dawn and continue nonstop until shooting finished.

David Taylor arrived in Rome two days after Williams and presented the star with a large brown envelope containing his air tickets. As soon as it was handed over, the comedian went into a five-minute monologue that reduced Taylor to helpless laughter. "Jee-*eez*, it's just what I've always wanted — *a brown envelope* I can call my own! Oh, you Lloyd's guys are smart, you know how to get to a fella!" Williams proceeded to give the envelope a squelching kiss. "From now on, baby, it's you and me. Ain't nobody gonna tear us apart. This is for *life!*"

"Your air tickets are inside, Robin," Taylor eventually managed, tears rolling down his face.

"Something *inside*? You mean there's something *inside* the brown envelope as well? This is too much, David!"

CHAPTER TWENTY-SIX

I think in many ways the making of the film is the story of people constantly forgetting that while they're wounding their opponents they're also wounding themselves. So many people were taking swipes at each other, vindictiveness was ruling the day. There was a horrible agency from London that was brought in by Columbia, they were like police dogs, snooping, trying to find out everything we were doing in Rome, since they had no one on the set. They actively opposed everything we were doing, vetoed everything they discovered. They kept saying Columbia had told them there must be no American journalists allowed near the set, that we mustn't do anything to upset their carefully laid plans. What plans? We hadn't seen any!
—Eugene Rizzo

No visitors were allowed on the set during the Robin Williams shoot to comply with his manager's "no publicity" ruling. Stratton

Leopold was all the more surprised one day to see three unfamiliar faces appear, and with camera equipment, no less. "Who are these guys?" he quizzed Gene Rizzo in short order.

"It's OK, Stratton, they're from Columbia's Electronic Press Kit."

"What are they going to do?"

"Don't worry, they're not going near Robin, they just want to get some shots of the set."

"No way. Get them out of here, they can't work while Robin's around."

"Stratton! They're from *Columbia*. They're *in-house*, whatever they do is for trailers, documentary stuff to help the film —"

"I want them out. Now!"

Rizzo, disconsolate, was left with no choice but to follow instructions. Further frustration followed day by day. "During the scene where Robin's body is trying to feed his face," he recalled, "the announcement came that he'd been nominated for an Academy Award for *Good Morning, Vietnam*. There was Robin being pelted with rotten tomatoes on our set and he was up for an Oscar! We turned out this little blurb, my friend Grady and I; then we were told we couldn't use it. It was a natural, but it was killed, typical of the missed publicity opportunities we had. I said to Film Finances, 'Look, where is it written on tablets of stone that we can't use Williams? Isn't it worth at least taking it up with somebody?' But they wouldn't."

● ● ●

As far as Eric Idle was concerned, Valentina Cortese raised upstaging to the level of an art form. "I've never seen a woman like that in my life," he told me, a mixture of glee and wonderment on his face. "In the middle of a scene you'd find an elbow in your back, then you were being pushed to the edge of the frame, gently but firmly pushed. Her style of acting is very straightforward — when somebody says 'Action' you walk to the center of the screen!! 'Valentina, you're actually not supposed to go right into the middle of the frame,' Terry would say. 'Darling, I think my character *would*,' she'd reply. She was great, but we just couldn't believe it. If she was standing alongside the other girls, she'd put her hands in front of their faces!"

Charles McKeown found himself exposed to the Cortese ethic

when she swanned in shortly after the Christmas break to read her part. She was still high from a singing engagement and looked very beautiful in an eau-de-nil ankle-length dress. "I gave her a couple of new lines," McKeown recalled, "but still she wasn't happy. 'You haven't given me enough!' she scolded me, pointing her finger and pulling an imaginary trigger. My standard reply to this diva of divas was to tell her she should speak to Terry about it. He would then say she should speak to Charles about it!"

By the third week of February Cortese had had enough. On set since the beginning of the month, she had not been called on one single day. Four times she had been put into makeup for no apparent reason. "She's leaving," Leopold was warned, "and she doesn't mind if we threaten her with legal action."

After a chat with Gilliam and Cleary, Cortese relented. She would stay until Friday, February 26, she declared, but not one second longer. "I will cook for you until then," Gilliam was told. "After that, darling, you're on your own."

When the fateful day arrived, a crucial scene remained to be shot. Leopold was assigned to do the honors. "Miss Cortese," he began, "you know how everyone here respects you?"

"Of *course.*"

"So we know you'll do this one thing for us. Stay just one extra day."

"I can't, darling, I have to pick up my poor husband at his clinic, I promised."

"But you *must* stay. Your scenes aren't complete . . ."

"Darling, I'm *going.*"

"Look, I hate to say this, but we'll *sue* you."

A tinkling laugh. "*Sue* me? Go ahead. Obviously you know nothing of our Italian legal system. It's so slow I'll be dead before it comes to court!"

Having exhausted the big guns in his armory, Leopold resorted to his Greek/American charm. Within an hour of the encounter a seemingly endless flow of flowers and chocolates were delivered to the star's trailer. When there was no room left, Leopold popped his head round the door. "Change your mind yet?"

Cortese looked beguiled and helpless. "What can I do?" she asked, eyes rolling heavenward. Graciously, she agreed to stay. As Leopold was leaving, Cleary arrived on the scene. "Who is that man, darling?" she whispered. "That's the producer," he replied.

"Oh," said Cortese. "*Another* one, darling?"

For all of her expertise with entrances, Cortese proved no slouch at exits either. On her last day on the picture a local hotel was contacted to cater for her farewell to the crew. Long linen-covered tables were erected on the set, on which fresh and smoked salmon, caviar and champagne were spread, the feast presided over by three waiters resplendent in white, gold-braided tunics, carefully supervised by the faithful Panucia. For each of the cast and crew, there were ties, clips or cuff links, all of them from the house of Gucci. An exchange of kisses and a few tears later, Cortese was gone in a decidedly poignant flourish of peach-colored organdy.

• • •

With five days of shooting left, the scene in which the survivors sail ashore in their ship-wrecked boat — fresh, if that is the word, from their adventures in the sea monster's belly — remained to be captured on film. An earlier attempt to achieve this had failed when the filter pump in Cinecitta's tank had broken down, leaving the water too murky for filming.

The boat, pre-rigged by the special effects crew with mild explosive devices to simulate the sound of Turkish cannons, was meant to emerge through early-morning mist with its crew of Purvis, McKeown, Idle, Dennis, Sarah Polley — and a decidedly edgy Bucephalus.

One of the problems with Cinecitta's tank was its position outdoors on the backlot, where filming was all too dependent on weather conditions. Sure enough, the unit was obliged to laboriously move to the blue screen by mid afternoon with the advent of a downpour. By the end of the day shooting amounted to just 21 seconds of useable film.

The weather had cleared by the following morning, although a further delay was caused by a change in wind direction which necessitated the smoke machine being moved. At last the scene was set to roll. "Action!" Gilliam shouted, whereupon the cameras began to perfectly capture the eerie beauty of the boat and its bedraggled crew emerging from the blanket of mist.

Bucephalus, however, immediately began backing up toward Polley, Idle and Purvis, trapping them behind his hooves at the rear of the boat. Tony Smart expertly manipulated the horse, secured by a harness at the end of a rope, over the side and into the pool. By the time the scene was set up again the wind had strengthened to the point where the boat, although guided by a wire, still drifted off-track. Unthinkable pandemonium was only seconds away.

As the first of the supposedly "mild" explosions went off with a deafening bang, Polley screamed in terror. The effect on Bucephalus was equally electrifying. Eyes blazing with fear, he roared and whinnied, rocking the boat and throwing its passengers off-balance. Just then an even louder second explosion detonated, blowing a gaping hole in the side of the boat and shooting it sideways. This was too much for Bucephalus, who promptly leapt on his own straight over the side and into the tank. As he swam for shore, he pulled the switches on the remaining string of explosives that had drifted away from the boat.

Miraculously they were spent. If they had gone off, the horse would have been blown to pieces. As it was, Bucephalus was quickly rescued from the tank and the trembling passengers from the boat. Two hours elapsed before young Sarah was able to stop crying. The 17 seconds recorded on film, all of which was used in the final print, could have cost the company dear.

• • •

David Taylor's overriding concern remained the extraction of the negative from Cinecitta. When Schuhly was eventually persuaded to sign the release, Taylor felt the glittering prize was within his grasp and elatedly went back to Cinecitta. "The negative's been moved," he was told. "Schuhly took it yesterday."

Taylor stormed into Schuhly's office. "What the hell do you mean by this? Where's the negative?"

"Calm down, my friend," Schuhly advised him. "I have good reasons for what I've done."

"I need to be persuaded of that," was Taylor's terse reply.

"Put yourself in my position. My accountant and secretary haven't been paid for months. Film Finances owe me money for my fee and expenses. When all this is settled, maybe then we can discuss the release of the negative."

Taylor agreed to pass on Schuhly's claims to Film Finances without comment, then next day began phoning his network of Lloyd's sources in a determined effort to locate the missing negative. Two days passed before the word came down: "It's at Victory labs."

"Yes, it's here," the laboratory confirmed, "but you can't take it. Thomas Schuhly has obtained a government order prohibiting its export."

"Look, I have authority from Lloyd's *and* a signed release from Schuhly," Taylor protested.

"Yes, but it's a release from *Cinecitta* you need. We're only holding the negative for the studio. We'd give it to you, clearly you have the authority, but we have to tell you it would not be too wise a move on your part."

"Just what exactly do you mean by that?"

"Think about it, it's nothing more than a friendly warning. You might get arrested at the airport if you try to take it out of the country. There is no export license for the material."

Many telephone calls later, Taylor tracked down the same government official Schuhly had persuaded to enforce the ban. "Mr. Schuhly told us that if the unit leaves and takes the negative with them, the Italian people who have worked on the production will not be paid," was his explanation. Taylor was ready with his unbeatable trump card. "Have you ever heard of Lloyd's of London failing to settle?" he asked. Armed with the export license, the negative was at last put into his hands.

"Do you plan to stay in Rome tonight?" Taylor was asked on the drive back to Cinecitta, the precious reels of film clutched in his arms. If he had ever heard a more ludicrous suggestion in his life, he was hard put to think of it. A ticket was booked on the first available flight for London.

As the plane sat on the runway awaiting takeoff, Taylor tried to put the day's events into some sort of perspective. Try as he might, he still had visions of Schuhly dashing toward the flight, Rambo-bandannaed, submachine gun in hand, yelling "Stop that plane!" Only when takeoff was achieved did he finally feel entitled to relax.

"Would you care for a brandy, sir?" the stewardess asked.

"Thank you," Taylor replied. As she began to pour he added, "Make that a double!"

• • •

The near-disaster in the water tank had left Gilliam shaken and demoralized. Fearless himself — he would shinny up the side of a building at the drop of a hat to demonstrate to a stuntman what he wanted — he had nevertheless been assured that the explosions would go off with the merest "pop." Still he felt the burden of responsibility.

With only a few days of production left, Gilliam was already running four days behind the revised schedule. Now he was faced with Film Finances' refusal to allow Rotunno, Tomblin and selected crew to stay on to do second-unit pickup shots that were considered vital. Tomblin more than eased the situation. "I've spoken to everyone," he told Gilliam, "including Peppino, and they've all agreed to stay on and do it for nothing. We'll shoot each day up to 10 am before Stratton gets in, he won't even know about it. Later, if Film Finances decides the material is required, you can say, 'Right, here it is, now pay for it' and reimburse everybody then. Other than that, Terry, you can just regard the whole thing as a token of their loyalty to you and the project."

Flushed with this support, Gilliam worked through the last couple of days with renewed vigor. That Film Finances relented in the end and sanctioned the second-unit work in no way diminished the validity of the gesture. For all the clanking of egos that had taken place throughout the shooting, it was a fine note to end on.

CHAPTER TWENTY-SEVEN

My team became the enemy *in post-production, especially in the frantic last few weeks. The final 48 hours I didn't sleep at all, just worked nonstop to get it finished. More "professional" people would have packed the job in. It was only my loyalty to Terry that made me stick with it.*

—Richard Conway

"As far as Film Finances is concerned," David Taylor points out, "*Munchausen* is their first insurance claim in 35 years; from an overage point of view they have been totally superb. People tend to lambast them because they come in when the going gets tough and have to make tough decisions. Lloyd's relations with them were always very good; I still count Stratton Leopold as a good friend. At the beginning he was wary of me and I of him, rather like Terry, but after we had sorted each other out we worked well together. Effectively, of course, all underwriters' decisions and guidelines and suggestions really go to Film Finances — they are the assured and must be protected."

Safely back in Stratford, Ontario, John Neville talked about Thomas Schuhly's involvement, or lack of it, from day one: "I don't buy his explanation that if he'd come on the set more the crew would have looked to him. Any producer has to override that and support his director! Instead, he stayed away in his ivory tower when he should have been helping Terry. He may want to be the greatest producer of all time, but he can't do it on that basis. If Thomas and Terry had stuck together, the whole thing would have been much smoother sailing. By splitting up, it allowed others to come in as mediators and produce a vacuum.

"Left to himself, Terry did an amazing job. There's no question that he's an incredible moviemaker. Look what's on the screen! *He* did that! He's also a very, very complicated man. In order to understand the making of the movie, you have to understand him, which isn't all that easy. Who gets close to him? I don't know. Charles, as close as any. I think it's the child in him that leads him to make movies. He can be very endearing."

At Cinecitta Giuseppe Rotunno was quietly and determinedly defensive. "*Of course* I can work fast," he pointed out. "I shot a whole mini series, *The Scarlet and The Black, in just six weeks*, with several cameras, two or three location changes every day — but with *perfect* organization and with a very satisfactory result. I like new experiences, working with new directors. For me, it's always the first picture. There is no room for ego in cinematography. The director *is* the film, the most important thing is the result. To get this we all have to be at one with him. The key is atmosphere, the atmosphere has to be right. It's not important to understand what the director *says*, all you have to do is understand the kind of *feeling* he wants. There must be intuitive rapport. Maybe we did not always have this on *Munchausen*. If Terry had problems in Italy, I'm sure he was happy with many parts of it, although I know there were many difficulties, financial problems, that fell on everybody. But Gabriella did a wonderful job with her costumes and I'm sure he was happy with Dante as well. I cannot talk about me. I would like to speak with Terry again, we could discuss things now with more distance."

Bill Paterson reflected on the after-hours camaraderie off the set: "Terry's a funny man. He'll come for meals and talk afterwards, so you get very fond of him. He doesn't hide away when the work's finished. He's not the most relaxed director on the set, though, and yes, he did lose his temper, but he was kind of lovable when he did. It was never taken seriously."

Safely restored to the opulence of her weekend pied-a-terre in Venice, Valentina Cortese looked back fondly on *Munchausen*'s filming. "I didn't get involved in the politics," she trilled, "mainly because I couldn't understand them, darling! All I could do was help Terry as much as I could. I even cooked for him sometimes to keep up his strength. Near the end I had a very long time in makeup as Queen of the Moon. It was so heavy it lasted no more than five hours before starting to slip. Poor Terry, he was feeling sorry for me because he knew I was suffering, such a *darling* man and such a *genius*! And wonderful Lee, always making fun of me! He would hold my hand when I was in makeup and if I said I was cold he'd disappear for a moment, then come back and surround me with not one, but *three* electric fires. 'Oh, you're sending me up again, you naughty boy!' I'd scold him. Little Sarah, too, she was the sweetest thing, I called her my little Duse after the greatest stage actress last century. She was so pale, so good, such a serious professional. I was amazed, I couldn't believe it from such a small child.

"Coming back from Zaragoza I wanted to be brave and take a plane, but at the last minute I said 'no' and caught a train from Barcelona to Paris when I discovered there was a sleeping car on it. Then I stopped for the day in Paris, did a little shopping and took another sleeping car to Rome. Very civilized, darling — I recommend it!"

David Tomblin counts *Munchausen* as the most difficult project in his forty years of moviemaking. "And I had the unpleasant job of making everyone's life a misery to keep it going, especially the art and special effects departments." He smiled and shrugged. "Perhaps when they get their awards they'll forgive me. Terry had his fantasies to put on film; I had to judge when to pull in the reins and when to let them out. Someone asked me if I'd work with an Italian crew again and I said yes, of course I would. The camera and sound crews were great, nothing wrong with them, just this general confusion. The whole problem was that a monster film had been scheduled and treated as a small film. David Taylor was good news when he arrived, because he was a very sensible man and not coming in to make a name for himself or make silly decisions to impress people in Los Angeles. We had a good relationship. That was a big factor in keeping the whole thing afloat until the end. Richard Soames I met on location and at meetings and found him calm and sensible, a man who listened to opinions. Of course it wasn't a good decision to stop shooting in Belchite, but in retrospect, from Film Finances point of view, they were getting deeper and deeper in the shit and in that situation one does make decisions that aren't necessarily for the best."

The workmanlike Mario Pisani saw no reason to alter the views he had expressed so eloquently before shooting began, when he first turned the project down. "The problem of this picture was that it was not really a picture with an *over* budget, it was a picture with a *wrong* budget. *It is very simple.* The wrong budget was convenient for making the deal and getting the picture started in the first place. There should have been a budget of $38 to 39 million, then the money that was spent would be seen to be perfectly justified, with the rest of the time for bad weather, late sets and the set reconstructions at Cinecitta. I'm sure Terry would still insist that costs in Italy are too high, but if you analyze this film, you will see that this is not entirely true. We wasted a huge amount of time with the special effects. There are a lot of mechanical effects as well which were difficult and laborious to achieve. And Terry likes to change things until he's happy.

"I've heard that Thomas has said it was Terry's fault that the costs went so high. That's not true either, although Terry certainly isn't one of the cheapest, for he wants the best result. Everyone gave the maximum, especially Dante, because it was needed on this picture. We all knew we were making a first-class picture, and in Italy everyone works with enthusiasm from the heart, knowing that Terry is the best."

Charles McKeown has no doubts as to the source of the pressure on Gilliam. "It originated with Schuhly," he declared. "The whole thing could have been achieved with much less pain and money, if it had been properly managed from the beginning. Schuhly truly believes there's no such thing as bad publicity and it's frightening to see that in action. When David Tomblin heard him telling the press how he'd solved the problems, he reckoned that Schuhly must conduct his meetings on the blue screen! I could feel very sorry for Schuhly, except he's such a twerp. He's bound to fall apart in the end, although perhaps he'll hold it together for a while. Eventually, though, I think he's in deep trouble psychologically."

Some of Schuhly's apparently preposterous actions were conducted with considerable forethought, and often with the astute aid of his lawyer. For every report that had him brandishing a gun at visitors after hours in Cinecitta — and there were several — he spent a lot of time and effort justifying in legal terms the various contortive positions in which he found himself. Only Schuhly could hold onto the the film's negative, still try to maintain relations — even distant ones — with Film Finances, *and* keep himself on the side of law and order. "The steps I have taken," he wrote the company while the negative was hidden away, "shall only serve to safeguard my contractual claims. David Taylor and I have agreed that all objections I raised will be discussed and that we will mutually try to come to an understanding. *Then afterwards the negative will be released.*"

Immediately after the production in Rome was over, Schuhly was in a conciliatory mood. "I think that Terry has enormous talent," he conceded, "and is a very, very good story teller. He has the problem that his generation of directors don't get the chance to make many films. Fassbinder, after 42 films, knew so much more about the making of movies and the chemistry of leading the crew and actors. With Terry there is a certain lack of practice that has nothing to do with talent. You have to know how people think, how actors respond . . . I took Terry to see Fellini — to watch the way he talked and the way he provoked his actors. *This* was directing, he was not *playing* the boss, he *was* the boss. I know Terry doesn't like being the boss, but it's part of the job; there has to be a captain, otherwise you make a film without human beings."

While he was rebuilding bridges, Schuhly composed a letter of reconciliation to David Puttnam. "Terry has proved to be a genius director," he rhapsodized, "and I'm convinced that the picture itself will prove to have been worth it all. This Terry and I fully owe to you.

"Thus I personally would once again like to thank you most cordially for the chance you have granted us. I know that in Hollywood you have been an 'exceptional personality' and that without someone like you 'adventures' like ours would never have been possible.

"With regard to some press articles I very much regret certain statements given by me and Terry and we thus have to ask for your 'generous and benevolent understanding' . . . but sometimes the difficulties we had to face nearly brought us to desperation and losing our minds . . . Sorry for that! Once again, thank you very much, for the chance *you* have granted us to produce the picture."

Puttnam's reply of May 5 suggests that Schuhly's obeisance had been accepted but not without some equivocation: "No one understands the stresses and strains of filmmaking better than I," he wrote, "but when one turns on one's friends and allies, then the strain really has become too much!"

• • •

When Allan Buckhantz finally dropped his $80 million action against Columbia, the studio now worried that this was only a temporary, tactical retreat. Columbia, aware that Buckhantz had roped in Transit Film, F.W. Murnau-Stiftung, Studio Hamburg and Conexco as partners, was concerned that he might be planning new action from a more favorable European base. Litigation might be escalated to a global scale which would see his partners joining Buckhantz in the U.S. suit, while the German quartet would handle his interest in any European-based claim. Columbia decided to take the offensive and file an action against Buckhantz for malicious prosecution, thus establishing jurisdiction in the United States.

Buckhantz's response was a swiftly-launched cross-complaint against Columbia, with the financial ante considerably raised. The copyright infringement aspect of the last claim was now dropped, together with the slander accusation. The new basis was Unfair Competition, Breach of Implied-In-Fact Contract, Intentional Interference With Prospective Economic Advantage and Injunctive Relief.

Buckhantz's main complaint was that the cross-defendants, which he had alarmingly — if prudently — widened from Columbia Pictures Industries and Ronald Jacobi to now include Terry Gilliam,

Jake Eberts, Charles McKeown and Thomas Schuhly individually, had "acted in a malicious, oppressive, despicable and fraudulent manner in willful and conscious disregard of (Buckhantz's) rights, and with a willful intent to vex, annoy, harass and otherwise injure (Buckhantz).

"Thus," the complaint concluded, "under California Civil Code Section 3294, cross-complaints are entitled to recover punitive and exemplary damages against defendants, *and each of them in the amount of $300 million.*"

• • •

As far as Film Finances was concerned the worst was finally over, with the bill hovering uncertainly somewhere between $35 and $40 million — depending upon whose figures you listened to. One remaining problem was the slim $2 million originally put forward by Schuhly to cover post-production. So much had been cut out in production, and so many compromises made, that it had become all the more essential not to stint on the model shooting, optical work, music and editing that would virtually make or break the finished movie. With Stratton Leopold's production assignment at an end, Soames persuaded David Korda, the *agent provocateur* of Gilliam's Belchite outburst, to supervise the critical post-production process in tandem with Lloyd's Joyce Herlihy, and Arthur Tarry continuing to hold the purse strings.

While the original plan had been to do all model shooting at Cinecitta immediately following the live action, this was quickly abandoned following a test shot with the second unit. Richard Conway dismissed the results as a "bloody disaster." "If we don't get back to England to shoot the models I don't want anything to do with it," he declared.

Steve Abbott at Prominent had raced to finish the studio's own post-production facilities in readiness for the unit's return from Rome. Their four small cutting rooms and 1,500 square foot stage would prove woefully inadequate. The unit took over G-stage at Pinewood instead, finally adding the mighty 007 H-stage as well. The move to England could be defended on other grounds. Everyone could go home at night, the studio was cheaper and the language barrier was reduced to English ambiguities.

Conway's original schedule of 45 model shots swiftly grew to

145. The 200% increase triggered another round of hostilities between Gilliam and Film Finances, the extended timetable stretching ominously from six to nine weeks on both Pinewood stages. The original schedule, argued Joyce Herlihy, had been prepared by an art department that had never worked with Gilliam before. In Herlihy's opinion anyone familiar with Gilliam's perfectionist disposition would recognize that the film had been ridiculously under-scheduled to begin with.

The elegant and assured Herlihy, one of the most respected women in the industry, readily concedes that Gilliam is an individual for whom nothing can be perfect enough. "'Let's try and do it again, it might be better this time,' is his constant cry," said Herlihy. "One specific instance was when Berthold goes whizzing over the hills; the sand dunes weren't the height Terry wanted when he saw the rushes. It wasn't dramatic enough, so we had to do it again with more sand blowing up. And the scene on the moon where the Baron and Sally land is written on my heart! Terry spent *hours* hand-combing all those sand-waves. When we saw it in rushes it looked absolutely lovely, but he did it again another ten times! He only perseveres because he thinks that perhaps there might be something more beautiful he can capture, then sometimes he'll get fed up and just say, 'Print it!' and go quickly to the next shot.

"And there was the whole drama of the sea monster, which had a big sort of iron jaw and was always stuck in special effects. This huge creature they devised never seemed to move properly, never got any nearer being a fish and was a monumental struggle to get ready in the water. Because it was delivered so late, Terry was disappointed with it and added all these funny bits. Its water spout was pathetic; it took us hours to get the velocity right, and it was freezing cold in the tank, with everyone sloshing about. The only good shot was when it turns around and its mouth wobbles!

"Often when Terry would insist he'd have to do a thing again, I'd reply, 'Fine, you can have until 11 o'clock'; then bet him £5 he wouldn't finish by then! On the other hand, how can you mind when he's got all that talent? I think it was quite amazing to get it done even in nine weeks. I've worked with some directors who are just as difficult to move on, but they haven't got Terry's talent. *That's* the difference."

Considering that Gilliam had loathed David Korda with such a deep passion at their first meeting, they wound up getting on extremely well. Gilliam acknowledged Korda was a decent, honest man who, not inconsequentially, was rapidly falling in love with the movie, following the honorable tradition set by Leopold, Tarry, Wigan, Taylor and Herlihy. "The Baron *seduced* them!" said Gilliam. "With David Korda you could see it happen almost on a daily basis, which was nice. He was just in an impossible position, trying to spend the smallest amount of money. We didn't have any major conflicts, which was remarkable when you consider how we started out. It wasn't in the interests of either one of us, and I did all I could to help him. I compromised on the moon sequence, which was originally going to be three-dimensional, very elaborate with all the buildings shifting and changing perspective. I think I was so knackered, and I saw it was going to be so much trouble, so we used the drawings that Dante had originally made for the moon, which were all part of the *original* budget — no *new* money involved! — then blew them up, stuck them on plyboard, colored them in, put some sequins on and moved them around. Although it saved a fortune, and I'm sure Korda appreciated it, Film Finances never even acknowledged it had been done."

• • •

Kent Houston of Peerless Camera had first become involved in the *Munchausen* saga way back in pre-production, when earnest discussions were held with Gilliam, Schuhly and Rotunno on possible optical techniques. Although Houston would only come into his own in post-production with the optical work on the film, it was clearly a good idea to find out before shooting what could and could not be achieved "after the event" — and, apart from anything else, to establish budgetary parameters.

The irony inherent in Houston's line of work is fairly simple, for by the very nature of what he does, much of it should neither be seen nor appreciated. On *Munchausen* there were matte paintings of castles and battlements to be superimposed on the real sets, while traveling mattes would enable the balloon's "flight" to be tracked, as well as the speeding bullets, the detachable heads on the moon that had to whiz convincingly about in space, and the giant asparagus spears — not to mention the ricocheting grains of sand. In addition to processing the blue screen work, there were endless frame-by-frame integrations of models and miniatures into live backgrounds, none of which could scream, "Fake!"

Houston submitted a detailed budget to Schuhly well before production was underway. He was astonished to be informed by Bob Edwards only weeks later that his provision had been reduced to a *quarter* of his original figure. No explanation was given.

Houston took up the cause in April, 1988 with David Korda. Korda adopted the stock Film Finances response: "We haven't got that kind of money." Since a completion date of August was the aim, Houston proposed an eminently practical solution: "It's four month's work. For four month's money, we'll take it on." A completion bonus on top was also agreed to if the targeted schedule was met. When the date was moved forward by two months because of the increased setups, Peerless ended up working for nothing during that period. Houston felt confident that at least the completion bonus would be secure; it wasn't. "You didn't finish on time," Korda pronounced, "so there's no bonus." A factor in Film Finances' decision was undoubtedly their "discovery" — which Gilliam never made any bones about — that he owned a 25% interest in Peerless. "We cannot make any financial arrangements that might benefit Terry Gilliam," was Korda's rationale.

"Without letting out any trade secrets," said Houston, "we should have been paid 40% more for what we did. Eight months later, as a company, we were just getting over *Munchausen* financially. Peerless in effect had to *pay* to do the film! David Korda was convinced I was in league with Terry, which is ridiculous. Terry's never taken a penny out of the company, he ploughs everything back in. He was hurting Peerless every bit as bad as Korda imagined he was hurting Film Finances!

"Terry's obsession with the figure of Death produced a cartoon from one of our technicians. He reckoned Terry as Death was fair enough, since he was working all of us into an early grave!"

CHAPTER
TWENTY-EIGHT

*There I was at Cinecitta editing this
wonderful footage, which only Terry came to
see. Schuhly was too busy giving interviews
and announcing his future plans, and the
money men were trying to make cuts and
score political points. My feeling was that the
film had become secondary. I was putting
together something wonderful, and nobody,
apart from the director, was giving a toss.*
—Peter Hollywood

Tall and imposing, Michael Kamen looks and acts the part both of
composer and conductor. One can imagine his bushy black hair
bobbing rhythmically in time with his music. Kamen joined the
Munchausen battalion before shooting began. It was an assignment
that would engage him for over fifteen months from Gilliam's first
casual request for "music to shoot to." Kamen was abetted in his
efforts by an ingenious computer-controlled keyboard machine
known as a Kurzweil, that virtually reproduces the equivalent of a
Polaroid snapshot of instrumental sounds. The sounds can then be

endlessly varied, both in pitch and tempo, and combined to give a stunning synthesis of orchestral sound.

All the main *Munchausen* themes had been composed, mixed and committed to the Kurzweil's incredible computer memory. *Munchausen* being *Munchausen*, however, the state-of-the-art apocalypse was not far behind. With nearly a thousand hours of work locked inside the omniscient instrument, the Kurzweil blew up! Kamen frantically dispatched the machine's steaming circuitry to the States for emergency computer surgery. Again being *Munchausen*, a team of experts finally managed to unlock and transcribe Kamen's precious themes. The music was recovered intact.

When a film director meets with Kamen to hear his suggestions on the Kurzweil, he normally sits beside him at the keyboard. "I think the tempo could be increased just a mite there, Michael"/"OK, let's try that" is the usual sort of polite interchange. Not with Gilliam, whom he'd worked with on *Brazil* as well.

"He stands behind you," Kamen explained, "hunched over and *pounding* you on the shoulder. 'No, no, that's not *right!*' he'll yell. 'You've gotta make it faster. And *heavier*. I said *heavier!!*'"

At one *Munchausen* session, Kamen turned around in exasperation to face his friend. "Look, I know what works and what doesn't work," he tersely explained. "When you make a brilliant suggestion I'll be the first to take you up on it. But not *this* one."

Gilliam glared at Kamen. "You've changed!" he accused. Kamen hastened to agree. "Terry, *Brazil* was around 20 movies ago," he pointed out. "If I *haven't* changed, it doesn't say a hell of a lot for me!"

Kamen visited Rome a few weeks after the November shutdown. "Would you like to see 45 minutes of the movie?" editor Peter Hollywood asked. "I'm *dying* to," Kamen replied. After the showing the normally locquacious musician was temporarily at a loss for words. "I'm just overwhelmed," he told Hollywood. "It's simply staggering."

"Isn't it, though? What's even *more* staggering is that you're one of the first to even bother to see it, outside of Terry. No one from Columbia's been, nor Film Finances."

Once the shooting was complete, fresh contractual problems

began for the company. Kamen had been working throughout for Gilliam unpaid and without a contract. A verbal deal discussed with Schuhly had somehow never been confirmed: paperwork was promised, but never arrived, and when "confirmatory" telexes did appear, they were meaningless. Kamen had to urgently sort out the matter of his fee, together with the recording budget — but with whom? Was *Schuhly* still the producer? Was *Columbia*? Did he have to talk to *David Korda*? Was *Gilliam* able to authorize action on his own? Kamen soon discovered a void at the center of power.

Korda ultimately informed Kamen that while Film Finances had "reserved" $200,000 for the music, only $100,000 of that was "left."

"When Schuhly put even the $200,000 budget together," said Kamen, "he must have been asleep or dreaming, or had a theory that Columbia would come in at the end of the day and help — which I guess, under normal circumstances, would not be an unfair assumption. Films go over budget all the time, though whereas Terry is terribly bad about time he doesn't have a reputation for going over budget.

"I had given them 30 minutes of music at that point and nobody wanted to admit it. And just $100,000 for the entire budget was going to make the orchestration paltry. It's less than you'd allocate to a "B" movie! What I'd seen of the film at this stage had just knocked me out, and I was determined to get more money to do it right, to do Terry's work justice."

At the end of February, 1988, one year after he'd commenced work, Columbia officially approved Kamen's appointment as soundtrack composer. He swung into action, contacting his friend John Beug at Warner Brothers Records, who was also an avid film enthusiast. "John, *Munchausen* is going to be extraordinary," he told him. "Nothing like it has been done for years. It'll make a great record, provided we get the money up for the recording sessions. Would you be interested in acquiring the soundtrack rights?"

"You mean the Michael Kamen score of a Terry Gilliam movie? *Of course* I would. How much extra do you need? I'd go to $250,000."

Elated, Kamen sought out David Korda. "Now we've got a proper budget," he told him. "An extra $250,000 in the coffers. For $450,000 we can achieve the superb results the film deserves, as long as you bump your contribution back up to the original $200,000 budgeted."

"I don't know about that," Korda replied, "and in any case you'll need to confirm Warners' contribution with Columbia."

"What's it got to do with them? It's *my* services Warners are paying for."

"Still, you'd better check it with the studio."

In a Los Angeles meeting at Columbia a week later, Roger Faxon calmly explained "that we regard the Warners deal as *our* doing."

Kamen was shaken. "What do you *mean*?" he asked. "It was all done through John Beug, *I* called him . . ."

"Sure, sure. But, Michael, we've been shopping the soundtrack deal around major labels ourselves. And I'm positive we contacted Warner Brothers . . ."

"So what are you saying?"

"I'm saying that we're entitled to keep half the money for the soundtrack deal. Or, to be more specific, $130,000 to your $120,000,since we prefer the balance of power to be in our favor."

"You can't *do* that," Kamen flung at Faxon. "How can you say *you* got the deal? I'm a Warners recording artist, dammit! It's *Munchausen's* money, it's *my* money!"

"Don't talk about *your* money, half belongs to us."

"Oh, we're partners, is it? So if I go wildly over, you'll give me half of that too?"

Faxon curtly dismissed Kamen's suggestion. "If you saw the size of our payrolls, you'd understand our position." Kamen reached into his pocket and flung a few dollar bills and some change on the desk. "Pardon me," he said, turning to leave. "I didn't know things were that bad."

A protest from Jake Eberts to Faxon proved fruitless. "By not having the $130,000, we won't be able to deliver the album to you, merely the score of the film," he pointed out. "It will be Columbia's responsibility to deliver the album to Warners, and at Columbia's expense." Faxon was unmoved. Film Finances, however, reluctantly agreed to increase its contribution to the original $200,000 budgeted, making a total of $320,000 available. Part of the economy imposed on Kamen required him to record the soundtrack in Germany, which offered the cheapest deal.

The move to Germany, quite apart from the obvious inconvenience, turned out to be a totally false economy. The studio and recording techniques required that everything be remixed in London. On top of the actual week of recordings and the two weeks of electronic re-recording, a seemingly endless period of mixing and remixing ensued — all to approximate the sound Kamen felt he could have got in England in the first place. "The German orchestra had its points," he conceded. "They played with a great deal of expression, really attacked the music, there were some fabulous players, but they weren't as experienced as a London orchestra, nor as precise."

The acid test was in playing the score for Gilliam. "I love it," he declared, as Kamen's solar plexus relaxed. Gilliam's expression changed as the final battle scene music began. "It's not right, is it?" Gilliam asked. "A certain lack of coherence?"

Kamen had to agree. "The only alternative," he pointed out, "is to re-record the passage, and do it here in England. Which brings us back to money — we've spent every cent."

"No, we haven't."

"But . . ."

"We haven't spent the $130,000 Columbia held back," Gilliam pointed out, a devilish gleam in his eye. "True," Kamen conceded.

While Kamen sat there, Gilliam put a call through to Gareth Wigan at Columbia. "Gareth? We've been listening to the music that Michael's brought back from Germany. It's *brilliant*, but it's simply not sustained through the battle scene. Sure, I know, we were still cutting it while Michael was recording. Some of it is *great*, all the rest of the music is *fantastic*. And the ending has to be *great* too!"

Shortly after, Kamen phoned his pal Bones Howe, Columbia's head of music. "Bones? Terry's not happy with the music in the battle scenes, which means Warners are not going to be happy either. It'll be unreleasable. I guess I just fucked up there somewhere. Look, you owe Warners a record. If they don't get it, they're going to want their $250,000 back. What would you like to do?"

After a series of hastily convened meetings at Columbia, agreement was eventually reached that two additional sessions could be booked in England, at the studio's expense. With uncanny, positively metronomical precision, the bill for the two extra sessions came to precisely $130,000!

Even for a Michael Kamen, inspiration can from time to time reach a low ebb. The movie's score included musical motifs for each of the characters which would interact with the others in a *Peter and the Wolf* manner. Halfway through the writing, he was still without a theme for the Baron himself. The Baron was therefore stranded with the "What will become of the Baron?" refrain sung during the opening theater scene.

"Why don't you take the same basic tune, play it in a major key and up the tempo? Then you've got your Baron theme," Ray Cooper suggested. "And for the balloon sequence, take the same theme and this time make it a waltz," said Cooper, "and throw in a bit of Can-Can for the frilly knickers."

Cooper had come to the rescue. "Quite simply, Ray's the best there is," Kamen enthused. "You work and work away with the basic themes, you get bogged down, then Ray comes in.

"For Death's leitmotif I worked a little device I borrowed from Rachmaninoff, then my daughter Sasha translated 'What will become of the Baron?' into Latin for the chorus. And both my kids started singing Eric's *Torturer's Apprentice* lyrics all the time! Terry finally got the result he wanted, Warners got their record, and I was able to get on with the rest of my life!"

Photo by S. Strizzi

The Torturetron

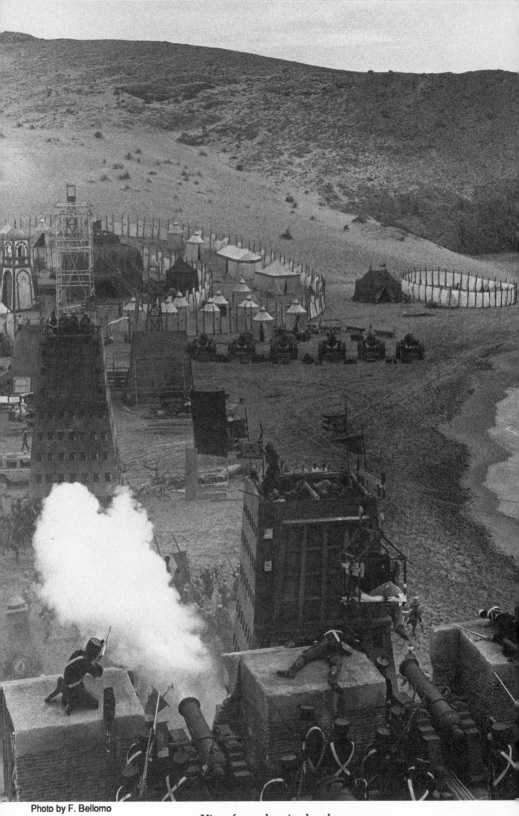

Photo by F. Bellomo

View from the city battlements

John Neville in Cinecitta's tank

Cranes for the ship, camera and crew at Cinecitta

Jack Purvis and his mannequin double

Oliver Reed (left, Terry Gilliam (right) watching the video monitor

Unnamed actor on the griffin

John Neville rides the cannonball

Sarah Polley and one of Lechien's dogs

oto by S. Strizzi

Uma Thurman

Terry Gilliam walking the rails

CHAPTER
TWENTY-NINE

The truth is Terry is not capable of being handled, that was the key problem. Terry didn't get along with anybody at all. He will in this lifetime only work like he did on Monty Python and Brazil. He does not have the mental or psychological structure to work on a professional operation. He must work in his garage! With Terry's Protestant philosophy, there are only two aspects that concern him — first, his career, second, who is guilty?

—Thomas Schuhly

With the special effects completed by early June, but with the bulk of the optical work at Peerless still to be added, Gilliam and the editorial team headed by Peter Hollywood began to assemble a "rough cut," albeit without Kamen's music, to see how the movie held together. This ran for two hours and forty minutes. "Too long," Jake Eberts maintained. "You need to get quicker into the film and quicker out."

Gilliam clung tenaciously to the assembled footage. When everyone he consulted echoed Eberts' feeling, Gilliam allowed a full twenty minutes to be snipped out of the cut to be taken to Columbia.

After a screening for 40 executives at Columbia, the reception for Gilliam was cordial. He sensed the studio's feeling of relief that the film "played"; although he knew even at that stage that much more work remained to be done. Since Victor Kaufman was unable to attend the Los Angeles presentation, a print was flown to New York for his perusal.

"Columbia seemed to like it," Gilliam reflected on his return, "although I'm not sure they understand it. It seems that if it's not a courtroom drama, a broad comedy, or Rambo, then it represents a marketing problem. They seem to assume that the rest of the world is a sophisticated place and Americans know nothing. My point is that occasionally you've got to go out and test the water, lift the level."

Gilliam had hoped that Columbia would proceed with their originally scheduled Christmas, 1988 opening. Bernd Eichinger at Neue Constantin still wanted the movie for December. But as far as Columbia was concerned, 1989 was now the plan for America. Officially, at this juncture, the delay would permit their sales side more time to familiarize the public with the character and myth of the Baron. Later the studio would claim that the film had been delivered too late — a rather hollow claim since the dubbed version was ready for pre-Christmas release in Germany.

The next aim was to prepare a public-preview print, complete with post-synching, Michael Kamen's provisional Kurzweil score and the bulk of Peerless's finished optical work. Previews were set for the end of October in New Jersey and Long Island, with the audiences recruited from the shopping malls in which the cinemas were situated.

Soames and Ransohoff reviewed their tumultuous relationship with Gilliam on the afternoon of the first preview in New Jersey. "Why did we go after Terry for enhancement?" Soames pondered. "Because it's not the movie either he or Schuhly represented to us. *That* was a $23.5 million movie. Everything else aside, they clearly had no intentions of honoring their commitments at the time of signing. Had the script not been cut, the film would have run $35 or

$40 million over at least, into the $60-70 million bracket for sure. Thirty pages were taken out, stuff that was really complicated. If Terry hadn't shot so much in the first place, we'd probably have saved $7 or $8 million. There wasn't a great deal of mercy shown to us. He did make cuts, but there should have been more. *That's* what it boils down to.

"The trouble with Terry is he won't listen to anyone. Just to give you one example in the finished movie: There's a joke about the townfolk refusing to return the Turks' fire because it's half-day closing on Wednesday. That's bound to fall flat here, since nobody knows about this European custom."

Ransohoff chimed in: "And how about young Sally altering the posters at the beginning of the movie to read, 'Henry Salt and Daughter' instead of 'and Son.' Meaningless in the States!" Sally's impulse, one might have thought, would be greeted by a chorus of "right on" in the country that made women's liberation more than a gesture. But Sally's instinct seemed foreign to Ransohoff.

Gilliam bumped into Dustin Hoffman as he was about to leave his New York hotel for the first preview. Hoffman was about to start work on Arnon Milchan's new production of *Family Business* co-starring, coincidentally, Sean Connery. "You're previewing *Munchausen* in *New Jersey*?" Hoffman asked incredulously. "That's *crazy*. Terry, I've had some real disasters there. Take it from me, they'll kill you!"

Just then the elevator opened and out walked Dawn Steel, David Puttnam's successor at Columbia, complete with her new baby. "Dawn, you've set us up!" Gilliam greeted her. "Dustin here tells me we're going to be killed!"

The screening went badly, with groups walking out as each new episode commenced. There were cheers at different points, from separate pockets, but there was never a united feeling of joy. Victor Kaufman turned up at the showing clutching his own personal pillow. He claimed to like the movie — "but I thought the dance between the Baron and Venus went on too long." The overall downbeat sentiment was confirmed by the below-average preview cards made out by those who stayed to the end. The same disappointing pattern was repeated the following evening. A focus meeting was held after the Long Island preview, with members of the audience invited to be film critics for a day. Gilliam watched the gargoyle-like reaction from Soames, Korda and Ransohoff as every negative comment stretched their corporate facades out of shape.

The next morning, Gilliam woke up with a certain clarity about the mission before him: "OK, the film's not working. Now we know the scale of the problem and we have to do something about it."

After breakfast he walked straight into his first head-on confrontation with Korda since Belchite. Film Finances, Korda declared, had no intention of paying for Rotunno's visit to London to color-grade the final print of the movie. "What do you mean, you won't pay?" Gilliam fumed. "You flew me out here first class, put me up on fucking Park Avenue and you won't pay one of the best photographers in the world to finish his job? I'll move out of this hotel, I'll go back steerage. With the extra money you can then afford to bring him over."

Korda was unmoved. "The reason you were brought out first class," he explained, "was because Richard Soames was on the same flight. I'm sure you wouldn't have cared to be seen in a lower class than him."

"Wrong!" Gilliam shot back. "I'd have *enjoyed* that. Richard would have been there *spending* money and I'd have been there *saving* it!"

The result of the closely-guarded previews was swiftly disseminated. "Research screenings last week," the *Los Angeles Herald-Examiner* reported on November 4th, "were a *washout*. And a walkout." Quoting "a source near Columbia," the report continued: "at least 100 people, out of an audience of 650, didn't even stay the full two hours. And the ones that did, gave the picture a very poor rating. We hear it got a 60 plus — on a rating scale that calls a plus 70 a dubious success. Columbia has reportedly shelved, for the time being, most of its advertising and marketing plans. Too bad. Gilliam, whose difficult but remarkable *Brazil* probably got weird numbers too, deserves better."

Gilliam began to feel the exalted aims of *Munchausen* slipping away from him. "There were these damaging leaks. And Columbia just seemed to be jerking Film Finances around," he recalled. "The interest on their money was going up because Columbia wouldn't part with anything. Although Soames kept claiming that Roger Faxon was a close friend of his, all I could see was Columbia enjoying the moment. Each time we got a good screening, and they got better and better, a week later they were scared again, because it didn't 'fit' neatly. The merchandising people seemed to be doing nothing — it was just crazy. Time kept drifting by with nothing happening on the promotion side. What had happened to the campaign to familiarize the great American public with Baron Munchausen?"

• • •

An astonished Irene Lamb had taken a call from Thomas Schuhly in August of 1988. "I'm working on *Alexander the Great*," he told her. "Would you be interested in helping me to cast it?"

"Thomas, I don't believe this," she replied, "I couldn't go through all that again. Dealing with you is a nightmare."

"Irene, you're more amusing than ever. Seriously, can you think of a really bright new director who might be interested in the project, maybe someone from television?"

"I can think of a few, but none that I would burden with you."

"You haven't changed a bit, Irene; you still have this amazing sense of humor. Tell me, do you think Terry would be interested in directing the movie?"

Lamb nearly dropped the phone. "Terry *Gilliam*?" she asked somewhat hoarsely.

"Of course. Who else?"

"You must be insane, Thomas. You and Terry didn't even talk to each other all through *Munchausen*. You nearly gave him a nervous breakdown."

"Oh, I know, we were both a bit childish, but we've both grown up since then."

"Thomas," she told him, "*you* might have done, but Terry hasn't, *thank God!*"

Schuhly's conciliatory attitude to Gilliam seemed to have undergone a dramatic shift a few weeks later in Rome. "Where did I go wrong?" he quizzed rhetorically. "In *not* insisting that Terry cut the opening scene down, in *not* insisting on Sean Connery for the Baron, in going to *Spain* — and in *not firing the director*.

"I saw Spain providing a scene like the arrival at Akaba in *Lawrence of Arabia*, something that would get the film out of Gilliam's weird fantasy world for a moment. This was my *producer's* concept. I took this decision, but everything went wrong and all we got on the screen is a piece of shit, something even under first-class TV level. Even the elephants aren't shot very well!

"I know that the film is not worth $40 million or whatever they say it's ended up costing. It's ridiculous. Going back in the same situation today, I would fire Terry. I would play a different chess game today. He based our relationship on all this shit like honor and friendship and confidence. And that's all it was — *shit*.

"My idea was to produce an excellent product and later on nobody would be interested in the cost of the film. Otherwise I would be nuts and dumb! If Dino saw the film, he would immediately ask me how many millions I had in my pocket! Lloyd's, Film Finances and the bank checked me 17 times — they were convinced I had taken $5 million. They are not professional enough to understand the chemistry of this, that in order to put $10,000 on the screen, it costs $25,000! Unless you're a Spielberg, who can make $4 million look like $10 million. On *our* film you see $10 million on the screen and it cost $25 million!

"Yes, I've heard Jake Eberts is making Terry's next two movies. He must be a *very* rich man! I know Jake blamed me for production delays, but this doesn't give me even ten minutes problem in the night. Neither Jake nor Terry have the expertise or knowledge to judge what my production capacity is, because I am 100 times better than they know! My hobby is to read history. If you know a battle is lost, then you want to win the war. Even if the war is lost, there's always the future!"

"Schuhly's right in one respect," Gilliam admits, "I *did* base our relationship on what he calls 'all this shit,' like honor, friendship and confidence. I *trusted* Schuhly, and kept on trusting him despite all the broken promises until I was in too deep and it was too late."

CHAPTER THIRTY

> *No one can say that we cheap-shotted it and made it look like a piece of crap. No one can say that it's not, technically and artistically, a brilliant film. That was all our money. We let Terry finish the movie. It represents his vision and his work. Life's got to go on. It's a disaster, but there are others.*
> —Richard Soames

One of the most prestigious groups of filmmakers in the world, Europa Cinema, conferred its Producer of the Year award for 1988 on Thomas Schuhly. First presented to David Puttnam in 1986, then Franco Cristaldi in 1987, Europa's board of directors — Fellini, Bertolucci, Wenders, Resnais and Costa-Gavras, established Schuhly as a major figure to be reckoned with in the art and industry of making movies. Regardless of his level of regard in the Munchausen camp, the award undoubtedly boosted his stature in the world at large.

• • •

Responding to Allan Buckhantz's representations, a California Superior Court ordered Columbia to attach a disclaimer to the movie and all advertising materials. "This is a new motion picture," the legend was to run in all countries outside the U.S., "not to be confused with the UFA/Transit/Murnau 1942/3 motion picture bearing the title, 'The Adventures of Baron Munchausen'." The confusion may have ironically been compounded since the wartime movie had in fact simply been entitled *Munchausen*, but the news must at least have served as a "get well card" to Buckhantz, hospitalized following a heart attack outside of Germany.

• • •

The pressure was now on Gilliam to hand over the final print of *Munchausen* to Bernd Eichinger. "Don't part with it till Film Finances pays your deferred salary," was the cogent advice from his colleagues. Thomas Schuhly had leveraged Film Finances into settling his account simply by witholding the negative. By witholding permission for his *Torturer's Apprentice* lyrics, Eric Idle forced the company to acknowledge his authorship and pay up.

"I can't hold it back, it'll fuck up the German release," Gilliam replied. "*Munchausen*'s got to open — they've booked all those cinemas." Renewed assurances were sought from the company, who declared themselves "honorable men who honor our commitments." Within days of the film being delivered to Neue Constantin, Gilliam received a missive from Steve Ransohoff, detailing the reasons Film Finances now felt they had no obligation whatsoever to pay the deferred sum. The subtext of the message was, "We have suffered enough."

• • •

Considering that Germany had been deemed the ideal territory in which to open, Neue Constantin's release of the movie proved a major disappointment. Dismal initial figures were faxed across to Burbank. "Jesus, if they're not buying it in Munchausen country, what chance have *we* got?" was a common lament. The movie's supporters could still muster some optimism secure in the knowledge that many successful U.S. films fail to take off in the German market; while German-based hits such as *Never Ending Story* and *The Name of the Rose*, regularly fail to find a commercial American audience.

The German experience did discredit, once and for all, the much-touted Baron recognition factor. Familiarity with the character was obviously not enough; quite the reverse, in fact. In a poll conducted in Munich during the opening week, two questions had been posed; the first, "Have you heard of Baron Munchausen?" producing a 90% "yes" response; the second, "Would you pay to see a new movie based on his adventures?" eliciting an 85% "No."

• • •

Just how dedicated, committed and determined was Columbia's new regime to making *The Adventures of Baron Munchausen* a hit? After all, the key executives who had coaxed David Puttnam into giving the movie the green light had all been ousted in the subsequent purge. Puttnam's successors, Victor Kaufman and Dawn Steel, might well take refuge behind the incontrovertible fact that no other production he had greenlighted had taken any significant money. Publicly, Dawn Steel remained adamant in her support. "Columbia Pictures and David Puttnam have one thing in common," Steel claimed, "a need, desire and obligation for the pictures made during his administration to succeed." Kaufman, however, had written off the previous regime's output financially only weeks after taking office. Would *The Adventures of Baron Munchausen*, one of the last throws of the Puttnam dice, be permitted to singlehandedly validate Puttnam's entire slate?

• • •

By February, 1989, Soames and Ransohoff remained livid that the post-production budget had escalated from $2 million to $9 million, escalating the final cost of the movie — per Film Finances — to $41 million, plus $5 million in "legal and financial charges." "And Gilliam's *still* tinkering with it!" Soames fumed. With Gilliam surrounded by David Korda, Joyce Herlihy and Arthur Tarry, all there to exercise control on behalf of Film Finances and Lloyd's, Soames continued to point the finger at Gilliam. He grudgingly conceded that "perhaps" the $2 million post-production budget had been tight. "At the end of the day," he mused, "what we're proud of is that the whole system worked. We met all our obligations. We did what we said we'd do.

"What's kept us going all through the horrors was the fact that we were going to get an incredibly good movie that was going to break all records. But I'm afraid that doesn't look too hopeful now after Germany."

Soames relaxed into his avuncular mode. "If anyone's interested, they can buy our share!"

CHAPTER
THIRTY-ONE

I think my priorities are right. I will sacrifice
myself or anyone else for the movie. It will
last. We'll all be dust.

—Terry Gilliam

In the run-up to *Munchausen*'s Easter release in the U.S., Gilliam
worked ceaselessly, giving nonstop interviews both on television and
in the press. The unfortunate aspect of the resulting articles and
appearances was the emphasis on production problems, rather than
the finished movie. Perhaps this was inevitable in view of the
nightmare stories that had been leaked from the set. Gilliam was only
telling the truth, but would these grisly revelations prove a turn-on to
see the film? Was "Step right up and see the worst-organized film of
all time" a really convincing ad-line?

"There were huge problems of language and communication,"
Gilliam told London's *Time Out*. To *City Limits*, he discussed "the
language problem, Cinecitta being useless to work in, the
non-cooperation of the studio bureaucracy, the Spanish location being
a logistical nightmare and the fact that we became the most popular

rip-off in the city. The whole agonizing experience can be summed up by saying that the sole memory I'll cling to will be how beautiful the sunset was over the palm trees on the Cinecitta entrance gate!"

The making of *Munchausen* had convinced Gilliam that God did not exist, he told London's *Mail on Sunday*: "If he did, he would have told me not to do it. Making this movie was like taking part in Napoleon's retreat from Moscow. It was a question of whether we'd get back alive or die in the attempt. It's the first time in my life I've ever been on a film set and looked at my watch to see if the day was almost over. It was like a lot of cripples carrying each other, the blind leading the blind. But somehow we stumbled through this nightmare and produced The Greatest Film of the Twentieth Century. Whoops! An editorial comment!

The last thing we should have told them was that we were following in the footsteps of *Cleopatra*, because that was the film that gave them the new house and the new car. Time and time again money disappeared in the wrong direction. Italy is number four in the league of industrial nations, thanks to us. We put them back on their feet. We should be proud of that!"

While Gilliam's every criticism of Italy was tempered with quotes like, "They have artists like nowhere in the world" (to London's *Sunday Times*) and, "When it comes to anything visual, the Italians are hard to beat. The three sculptors we had were Michelangelos. The cinematographer and the art director are artists" (to the *Observer*), the reaction from Rome was a foregone conclusion.

Said to be "beside himself with anger" and "speaking on behalf of Cinecitta," Thomas Schuhly leapt to the studio's — and Italy's — defense in the columns of *Il Messagero*, into whose offices he stormed. Facts were thrown out the window. He began by disputing that the movie's final cost was 55 billion lire ($43 million), asserting that it was *half* that sum.

"Sure," he conceded, "if you choose to throw in *insurance costs, overtime and other figures*, but that just demonstrates an *inability to be reasonable*. Not only that, Gilliam pipes up and has all kinds of nasty things to say about the costs when he himself pocketed $1.2 million and then *imposed* David Tomblin as production organizer, the most expensive in the business, $7,500 a week." (Schuhly to this author in October, 1988: "Tomblin was *my* relationship. He came on the show because *I* wanted him.")

"Gilliam was always the one behind everything that sent the budget up," he continued, "starting off with his insistence that all the cannons be able to fire. This man comes along and speaks about language problems. The plain fact of the matter is that the best part of the film, the look of it, is not his doing at all, but that of the Italians.

"Like the *colonial racist* he is," Schuhly raged on, "he treated the Italians as if they were members of the Third World. He was like one of these Englishmen who believe blindly in their little island and nothing else, one who's never grown up, just remained a child, one who had to learn that all the little toys and mechanical devices that the others made for him didn't always work. One who every blessed day was concerned solely with whether he would get a real tiger, only to have it killed by an overdose of sedatives administered by the special effects team. In any case, I'm still convinced that the work of the Italians, and the film itself, will find proper recognition in the long run."

The squabbling continued on BBC-TV's *Film '89*, when Schuhly and Gilliam appeared together through the miracle of the media — Gilliam in London, Schuhly in Rome. This time Schuhly's target was Film Finances. "When they took over," he declared, sitting in front of the tastefully-chosen background of the Coliseum, "we were over budget $5 million. Ya? So I feel responsible for the $5 million — but $5 million and $21 million, there is a big difference. And the responsibility for the other $16 or $17 million, this responsibility is *exclusively up to Film Finances*. As Film Finances contractually is acting on behalf of and as agent for the producer, and I find myself today in front of a budget of $42 or $43 million, maybe I have to raise the question as to *whether they did a good job?*"

Having warned the BBC that they would sue if anything defamatory was said about them by any participant, and after themselves refusing to take part in the program, Film Finances' response to Schuhly's statement was terse: "We have fulfilled our job, as have our re-insurers, the bank and Columbia. The people who have not fulfilled their obligations are Terry Gilliam and Thomas Schuhly."

• • •

Any summary of notices is bound to be selective. *Variety*'s listing of New York critics' reactions, however, speaks for itself: out of 19 reviews, 3 were *ambivalent* — Brown of 7 *Days*, Haller of *People*, Salamon of *The Wall Street Journal*; 3 *unfavorable*, Richard Freedman of Newhouse Newspapers, Hoberman of *The Village Voice* and Sterritt of *The Christian Science Monitor*. And no fewer than 13 *favorable*: Canby of *The New York Times*, Richard Corliss of *Time*, Roger Ebert of New York *Daily News*, Edelstein of *New York Post*, Jack Garner of Gannett News Service, Susan Granger of WMCA Radio, Joanna Langfield of ABC Radio Network, Mauceri of WBAI Radio, McGrady of *Newsday*, Pally of *Penthouse*, Joel Siegel of "Good Morning America", Williamson of *Playboy* and Wunder of WBAI Radio.

Noted author Harlan Ellison contributed an unqualified rave in *Fantasy and Science Fiction* magazine. "Gilliam's new film," he wrote, "will make you roar with laughter, disbelieve what you're seeing and have you clapping your hands in childlike delight. It is: A carnival! A wonderland! A weekend with nine Friday nights! Terry Gilliam's lavish dreams are beyond those of mere mortals. *Munchausen* is everything you secretly hope a movie will be.

"In this column, three years ago, I urged you not to miss *Brazil*, one of the exceptional fantasies of all time. Compound that enthusiasm by an order of ten and you may begin to approach my delight in alerting you to *Munchausen*. Every frame is filled to trembling surface tension with visual astonishments so rich, so lush, so audacious, that you will beg for mercy. It keeps coming at you, image upon image, ferocious in its fecundity of imagination, wonder after wonder, relentless in its desire to knock your block off! It is a great and original artist's latest masterwok of joy . . . It is one of the most wonderful times I've ever seen. And I ain't lying!"

At the other extreme, and vivid proof that Dustin Hoffman had predicted the New Jersey reaction with deadly accuracy back at preview time, came a review from Richard Freedman in *The Newark Star Ledger*. "The only wonder arising from *The Adventures of Baron Munchausen*," he wrote, "is how much money could have been spent by a presumably sober movie company on a fantasy so singularly lacking in charm (kids will hate it), wit or even common sense."

CHAPTER
THIRTY-TWO

We have no comment to make on the company's marketing of The Adventures of Baron Munchausen. *Respectfully. But we have no comment nonetheless.*
—Mark Gill (Columbia Pictures' spokesman)

A memo from Dan Michelle, Columbia's outgoing president of marketing, had vividly portrayed his conclusions as to *Munchausen*'s prospects in December, 1988:

    1. The finished picture's playability will achieve normative levels at best.

    2. The picture has limited appeal based on pre-interest in title and stars, genre, period setting and lack of marketable stars.

3. Based on Terry Gilliam's track record with *Brazil* and *Time Bandits*, the picture will receive mixed reviews.

4. The picture is not likely to generate a strong, positive word-of-mouth from mass audiences.

He conceded that if the final picture, by any remote chance, exhibited "significantly improved playability" when screened for recruited audiences that month, release plans could be modified. Dismayed field workers got the message loud and clear: It's going to play *horribly* and get *terrible* reviews.

Hopes were raised a little as Michelle passed his baton on to Buffy Shutt when she, together with her deputy Kathy Jones, actually expressed enthusiasm for the movie — as had Susan Pile months earlier when hired as *Munchausen's* Independent Project Manager. All three women had worked at Paramount with Dawn Steel, who, as late as January, 1989, still claimed that *Munchausen* was an extraordinary movie. "And," she claimed, "we are *supporting* it."

Following a top level marketing meeting, however, the limit of Columbia's intentions was graphically spelled out: "Initial discussions," a top-secret memo ran, "have focused on prints and advertising break-even, rather than expecting we can break even on Publicity and Advertising *and* Columbia's $20.5 million investment in the project." Kaufman having written off Columbia's $102 million investment in Puttnam's slate within months of taking over, their $12.5 million investment in *Munchausen* was clearly regarded as a prior year loss. Only the $8 million RCA/Columbia video deal was regarded as current.

The Publicity and Advertising expenditure was pegged at just over $3.5 million — the minimum the studio was committed to as stipulated in RCA/Columbia's video deal — since theatrical success is naturally regarded as a considerable boost for subsequent video release. Columbia's parameters were set. Claiming to have already spent upwards of $1 million in pre-release, only $2.5 million remained in the kitty for the actual release period, a pittance compared to the norm of $15-25 million for a major release.

Susan Pile recommended that Columbia open the movie in 30 key markets and up to 200 cinemas across North America. If this were successful the release could then spread out to 1,000-plus cinemas (750-2,300 being regarded as the boundaries for a "mass release"). Pile's release strategy seemed at first to have been accepted. Until just 8 days before the scheduled March 10th opening, that is, when the studio decided to scale the release down to 8 cities and 46 cinemas. Columbia's Roger Faxon, pushed to the forefront yet again by his masters, denied that the studio was attempting to cut its losses, while admitting that 22 markets had been dropped. "We're trying to concentrate our efforts in *major* markets," he explained.

In response to one exhibitor who complained, "When you get out of Los Angeles the awareness factor on *Munchausen* is almost *nil*," Faxon pointed out that a massive advertising blitz *the week before the March 10th opening* was imminent. "You won't be able to sit in your living room and not know it's there. It's always been planned as a two-phase release," Faxon maintained. "The question was which phase different cities would fall in."

Columbia's retreat caused dismay in the abandoned cities. "We had planned a Sunday story on Gilliam on the 12th and David Elliott's review was going to run on the 10th, both with big color spreads," said Mary Hellman, arts and entertainment editor for the *San Diego Union*. "We will still use it when the film opens, but it is very annoying to be treated like a second-rate market."

In Milwaukee the story was the same. "I'm going ahead with the story," said an angry Dominick Noth, the *Milwaukee Journal*'s entertainment editor, who had committed color coverage in his March 12th Sunday edition before the postponement. "We've been shuffling color furiously to accommodate changes. Now I'm calling 'cease and desist' to it. This is costing us production time and money." One baffled exhibitor told *The Los Angeles Times* that Columbia was badly misreading the film's appeal." They're going to be very surprised by this film," he claimed. "At our theaters, people have been applauding the *trailer*."

Columbia declared themselves "ecstatic" over *Munchausen's* opening weekend figures of $597,000, allegedly at 50 cinemas, $11,948 per theater. (In fact, the average should have been shown as $12,978, since only 46 cinemas were showing the movie. "An accounting error," said Columbia.)

The studio defended its decision to include several out-of-town sites on the initial 46-theater opening, by arguing that it was essential to know the movie's reception "in the sticks." Reasonable enough — but out of the twelve "New York" venues in which the *Baron* debuted, only one was a Manhattan cinema: the East Side Coronet, traditionally regarded as an "art house." Of the $170,000 taken at its twelve "New York" sites, the Coronet accounted for $75,000 *on its own* (a "fantastic" figure by *Variety's* reckoning), leaving just $95,000 to be split over the remaining 11 out of town theaters, or $8,636 per booking. With Manhattan as a well-known enclave of Gilliam's audience, one has to wonder whether Columbia was testing the film in the eleven sites in the sticks, or relegating it there. The resulting figures still were good, but clearly indicated that continued advertising support was crucial.

And support seemed to be on its way. A studio source jubilantly declared that plans would now be drawn up for a "further expansion" nationwide at a meeting scheduled for Tuesday afternoon, March 14. Jack Mathews of *The Los Angeles Times* phoned Buffy Shutt to confirm this. Yes, the meeting was going ahead, she confirmed, they were all very excited, and she would phone Mathews back with the details after the meeting. There was no call, and neither Mathews' further calls nor those of his colleague, Nina J. Easton, were returned.

Columbia refused to release the results of its exit polls. Ed Mintz, from the poll firm, *Cinemascore*, was more forthcoming. *Munchausen*, he declared, received an overall A-rating from customers leaving the Cineplex-Odeon Theater in Century City, Los Angeles. This was probably atypically high, he added, since 71% of the viewers were Terry Gilliam fans.

Columbia eagerly seized upon the implication that Gilliam's fans would come to see the movie anyway, TV ads or not, so there was no point in allocating more dollars to television or any other media. By March 17, Columbia's *Los Angeles Herald-Examiner* ad space had shrunk to 2.5 inches of a single column.

Instead of even the modest 200 screens originally discussed for the initial launch, the number finally edged up to only 88 for the third weekend, 92 by the fourth and 106 by the fifth. Easter, and the vital holiday momentum, was now gone, with just over $4 million tallied at the box office.

With his frustration at boiling point back in London, Gilliam telephoned Columbia and demanded to talk to Dawn Steel.

"Great to talk to you," was her opening remark. "I wish it was great to talk to you," Gilliam replied. "What the hell's going on with my movie? You've refused to spread it out as you promised, you've refused to make 70mm prints available, you've even 'forgotten' to order Dolby SR prints . . ."

"Terry, don't yell at me. I don't get yelled at."

"Well, you are now. What do you intend —" The line went dead.

A few weeks later, with prints up to 120, it was all but over with a cumulative take of just under $8 million.

• • •

One exhibitor, adamant that he speak only under a cloak of anonymity for fear of reprisals, bitterly condemned Columbia's approach to the movie, and pinpointed one area the experts appear to have overlooked. "Columbia reckoned they had no stars in the movie? Then they don't know their business. Both my kids sat up immediately when Sarah Polley came on. 'Dad, that's *Ramona*,' they cried. 'Oh, she's *great!*' They should have pushed little Sarah, she's a huge TV favorite, but I bet nobody at Columbia even knew she was in it. My impression was that the people on the ground were working hard on the movie and that the brakes were applied higher up. A lot of projects are killed by one man's bigotry or prejudice."

Around the world *Munchausen* scored a few isolated goals, reaching No. 1 in Paris and enjoying a respectable run in Britain, where Columbia's local office supported the movie to the best of its ability with the limited funds available to them. Nowhere, however, was the movie's massive budget reflected in either the promotion or the takings. Where a worldwide gross of $200 million would have represented breakeven, less than one tenth of this was achieved.

Was it prudence with shareholder's funds that made Columbia draw back from a major launch for *Munchausen*? The evidence, as supplied by their own release schedule for the six months prior to *Munchausen's* release, strongly refutes that theory. Of the dozen movies in this Columbia/Tri-Star list, not a single winner emerged. Yet no matter how dim the prospects, an average of 923 prints were struck, by the same executives who limited *Munchausen's* launch to

46 prints. (For a full list of Columbia/Tri-Star's releases six months prior to *Munchausen*, together with the box office results, see Appendix B.)

In contrast to the $9,524 average print return achieved by the other movies in the studio's release slate, *Munchausen* produced an astonishing $66,666 per print. The figures provide a tantalizing clue to the *Baron*'s possible fate had Columbia applied the resources it had managed to dedicate to their twelve earlier releases.

One veteran Hollywood hack came up with a compelling scenario. "Sure," he agreed, "it was always going to be a tough sell. It's not *Rambo*, it's not *Indiana Jones*, it's not *Ghostbusters*. But instead of all the chopping and changing and agonizing, all Columbia had to do was to duplicate Avco Embassy's $5 million campaign for *Time Bandits*. You have to believe they didn't even have that much faith in it — although $5 million at today's prices would come to considerably more change.

"United Artists spent $21.5 million on *Rain Man*'s launch — what would *it* have taken with *Munchausen*'s measly $3 million? Warners nursed *Dangerous Liaisons* along right the way through, supporting it with millions. Somebody simply decided not to press those buttons on *Munchausen*. As soon as it was bumped out of Christmas prime time, and the potential Oscar nominations, its fate was sealed. I mean, let's face it, what else did Columbia have in their hopper pre-Christmas? *My Stepmother is an Alien*, for Chrissakes!?

"I've heard about all that stuff from the *Munchausen* supporters — Columbia choosing inappropriate theaters, refusing to make it available on 70mm, neglecting to order Dolby SR prints, playing it big in the sticks from the beginning, even fucking up the opening averages. *Look! Someone had decided it wouldn't play. The rest is just detail.*"

A second veteran journalist put it differently. "You have to understand about Columbia Pictures. My impression is of a company in a holding pattern. They haven't started production on a single new movie in 1989. They're waiting for a takeover or for *Ghostbusters II* to open, whichever comes first. My guess is that *Ghostbusters II* won't be the panacea they think it will. And the same goes for the new *Karate Kid*. Yet they've built up such huge losses on the theatrical side in the last few years that the new management's got to be seen to be wiping the slate clean with a smash.

"If they had decided to back *Munchausen* with a huge campaign, say $15-20 million, and it had gone down the tubes, fingers would have been pointed, possible investors turned off. Far better for them to pass and just keep things steady, go for their prints and ads in the movie and not upset the graph. Why take a chance on something that isn't your own kin? Who do you think Victor Kaufman is — Baron Munchausen himself, off on a great adventure? Do you really see Dawn Steel as Sally Salt? Think in terms of Horatio Jackson and his functionary in the movie, and you're getting closer."

The same observer considered the Ray Stark conspiracy theory. "Well, there's no doubt that Stark's still a power in the land at Columbia, both as a shareholder and as one of their leading independent producers. And there's no question about his abhorrence of Puttnam, or 'that little prick' as he calls him — and with all things Puttnam, a feeling he shares with Victor Kaufman. Puttnam's rejection of Stark's *Sweet Libby* and *Revenge* during his brief spell as Columbia's honcho must have been devastating blows to Stark's self-esteem. Never before in his career has there been such a gap between his releases. But with Puttnam cold in the grave would Stark's thirst for revenge extend to Puttnam's stepchildren, like *Munchausen*? You know, now that you *mention* it, maybe Stark's capable of saying 'That could have been *Sweet Libby* or *Revenge*.' If that's the way he was thinking, then anything is possible."

When Victor Kaufman's office was called in May, 1989, to explain Columbia's marketing philosophy on *Munchausen*, there was no response. A few weeks later, Mark Gill of Dawn Steel's office finally issued his "No comment."

• • •

At the same time as Harlan Ellison was praising *Munchausen*, he noted that Universal's cut-for-TV version of Gilliam's *Brazil* had just been aired. All the changes and cuts Sid Sheinberg had threatened to make in the theatrical version, including a happy ending, had now been accomplished in a version trimmed from 131 to 93 minutes.

"It's wonderful," was Gilliam's comment, "because it gives Sid a chance to break into TV. The only sad thing is, the world doesn't get to appreciate that Sid made this film." On a more serious note he added, "They're selling it as *Brazil*, the film that won Best Picture, and that's nonsense."

Ellison's response was on a more visceral level. "There is a special sea of boiling hyena vomit in the deepest and darkest level of hell," he declared, "tenanted thus far only by those who burned the Great Library of Alexandria, by the dolt who bowdlerized *Lady Chatterly's Lover*, and by those who have torn down elegant art deco buildings to erect mini-malls. It is my certain belief that Sid Sheinberg will sizzle there throughout eternity. Standing on Ted Turner's shoulders."

On March 15, 1989, Columbia was staggered to receive a communiqué from the Saginaw, Michigan law firm of Peacock, Fordney, Cady, Ingleson and Prine, representing their client — none other than the current holder of the title Baron Munchausen.

The studio was informed that the law firm viewed the use of Munchausen's name as an invasion of the Baron's privacy, as well as a misappropriation of his valued and good name. Furthermore, they pointed out, one of the most disturbing aspects of the movie's distribution was the fact that Baron Munchausen's young son was also named Baron Munchausen — and as a direct result of the movie he was currently being ostracized and had undergone considerable ridicule in his schoolyard. What did the studio intend to do about this? Columbia's lawyers may be excused for feeling they now had faced every imaginable challenge.

• • •

In the end Lloyd's long view might well prevail, as future generations of investors begin enjoying a return from the movie. And revenue might well flow in this lifetime, thanks to Jake Eberts' dogged insistence on removing its video rights from the theatrical equation. Whatever happens, *The Adventures of Baron Munchausen* will remain eloquent testimony to the multitude of hybrid artistic, financial and technical elements that fused together during its creation.

POSTSCRIPT

Arnon Milchan's name continues to crop up on a number of movies, including *War of the Roses*, *Family Business* and *Pretty Woman*. Ray Stark's *Revenge*, starring Kevin Costner, eventually went ahead as a Columbia-New World co-venture and proved a dismal failure at the box office. On the other hand, Stark's *Steel Magnolias*, also released in 1990, was a significant U.S. hit, with a more modest international performance. Following *A Fish Called Wanda* and *Munchausen*, Steve Abbott at Prominent Features was behind Terry Jones' disappointingly lame *Erikthe Viking* and the Michael Palin vehicle, *American Friend*.

Back in England after his sojourn in Hollywood, David Puttnam released his first post-Columbia independent production in 1990, the lamentable *Memphis Belle*, to strong box office in the UK and lackluster U.S. response. His second production, *Meeting Venus*, starring Glenn Close and directed by Istvan Szabo, looks distinctly more promising.

Soon after *Munchausen's* release in New York, Gilliam bumped into David Picker, who told him that he'd loved *Munchausen* and what a great shame it was how it had been handled. "David —

Puttnam, that is — let so many people down in the way he behaved at Columbia," says Gilliam today. "A whole team of hundreds of people. He was playing as if it were just David Puttnam. I've never talked to him about *Munchausen*, either the movie or the way it was released, so I've no idea what he thinks of it."

Following *Munchausen's* box office failure, and despite the favorable critical notices, there were two schools of thought about Gilliam's future: a) "He'll never work again" and/or b) "He'll certainly never work at Columbia/Tri-Star again."

With Sony's multi-billion-dollar takeover of Columbia, and the ousting of Victor Kaufman and Dawn Steel, the equation changed. One of the first movies to be given the green light under the new regime was *The Fisher King*, starring Robin Williams and Jeff Bridges, to be directed by none other than Terry Gilliam!

"My theory," says Gilliam now, "is that Victor Kaufman was just trying to tidy up Columbia's books to increase the price of the Sony sale and the last thing he wanted to succeed was something Puttnam had initiated.

"On *The Fisher King*, which we shot in New York and Los Angeles, there was nobody in the unit who'd been involved in any way in *Munchausen*. I couldn't face it again; that's how deep the scars are." Here he is overlooking someone he describes as a particularly excellent video cameraman assigned to the *Fisher King* unit, who made himself known at the end of the shoot as — Allan Buckhantz's son!! (As to his father's litigation — no one seems certain of its current status.) *The Fisher King* was completed, incidentally, within its originally budgeted $25 million limit.

Early in 1990 *The Adventures of Baron Munchausen* was nominated for four technical Academy Awards: Best Achievement in Art Direction (Dante Ferretti, together with his set designer Francesco Lo Schiavo), Best Achievement in Visual Effects (Richard Conway and Kent Houston), Best Achievement in Makeup (Maggie Weston and Fabrizio Sforza) and Best Achievement in Costume Design (Gabriella Pescucci). At the ceremony Gilliam walked into Thomas Schuhly, leading the Italian contingent with a big grin on his face. The two men exchanged brief "hellos," with Gilliam feeling embarrassed for the Italians caught in the middle. "The worst part," he recalls, "came at dinner afterwards. I was at the top table with the head of Columbia and all the technical people were at the side table with Schuhly. It took the glow off the entire proceedings. To me it was proof that the only God that exists is the God of Irony."

Although *Munchausen* itself failed to win any actual awards, Jake Eberts had an exhilarating evening at the ceremony. *Driving Miss Daisy*, a movie for which Eberts had put up half the money, earned four Oscars, including Best Picture. In 1991 Kevin Costner's *Dances with Wolves*, also backed by Eberts, enjoyed an even wider Oscar sweep, claiming seven Awards, again including Best Picture.

Gilliam and Dawn Steel met at a party thrown after the Awards ceremony at Malibu by Disney's Jeff Katzenberg. Gilliam was at the foot of a set of spiral stairs that led to the beach when, out of the corner of his eye, he saw a woman stumble and fall. Dawn Steel virtually landed at his feet. After the token embrace Gilliam muttered, "Dawn, just because I'm kissing you doesn't mean I like you."

"But I've *forgiven* you . . ." Steel replied.

"You've forgiven *me*? What for?"

"Why, for yelling at me over the phone."

The remark stopped Gilliam temporarily in his tracks. "You equate my yelling at you with your strangling my movie?" he finally managed.

"That wasn't up to me, Terry. I didn't have the power."

"Really, Dawn? Well, you certainly acted like you did. And it was your name on the door, baby."

Is Hollywood, Gilliam asked himself, really about making movies at all? Or is it merely about phone protocol, games with friends, rubbing each others' backs, cutting partners in on the action? Are movies themselves simply the necessary byproducts of the system?

He wasn't the first to pose the question. And he won't be the last.

APPENDIX A

THE ADVENTURES OF BARON MUNCHAUSEN:
Balance of Critics' Reviews

Richard Corliss in *Time* was an early enthusiast and one who clearly sensed Columbia's jitters. "Everything about *Munchausen* deserves exclamation points," he declared, "and not just to clear the air of the odor of corporate flop sweat. So here it is! A lavish fairy tale for bright children of all ages! Proof that eccentric films can survive in today's off-the-rack Hollywood! The most inventive fantasy since — well, *Brazil*!"

On ABC-TV's Eyewitness News, Joel Siegel suggested imagining "our favorite storybook pictures from when you were a kid, where each picture turns into a dream . . . Like *Time Bandits*, like *Brazil*, this picture is about imagination and the power of imagination to conquer that dull, drab place we know as reality . . . As Baron Munchausen and his crew hang off the edge of the moon, and as the constellations float by, Gilliam teaches us we don't have to believe things for them to be absolutely true. You see Pisces and Sirius the dog start floating by. State of the art special effects. This is *magic — movie magic*! It's either the best kids' film ever made for grownups, or the best grownup film ever made for kids."

Jack Kroll in *Newsweek* pondered on the negative vibes produced by the film's budget — and neatly emphasized how the film could stand or fall on the studio's support. "Just because a film costs so much," he argued, "doesn't mean it will be a bomb — or that it deserves to be. A lot depends on how a studio — Columbia in this case — distributes and promotes it. And of course, how good is it? *Munchausen* is flawed but fascinating, a Pythonesque fantasy with awesome special effects. And win or lose, Terry Gilliam is a talent to reckon with. Much of the movie is truly astonishing."

Mike Clark in *USA Today* was won over by the movie, with a few reservations. "Hard as it is to believe," he wrote, "Terry Gilliam has come up with a more anti-'80s box-office prospect than *Brazil*.

Also a film three-quarters as wonderful. Also one that any kid in the 8-14 range should relish, assuming he, she or their folks ever make it to the theater. It's the long or, at least, curiously awaited *The Adventures of Baron Munchausen*, an alleged $40 million adventure epic whose flaw (can you imagine?) is an overdose of high points . . . This is a movie that bludgeons you with dazzle . . . Excesses or not, I'm rabid to see this again."

Jack Garner's syndicated review continued the theme, comparing Gilliam to a brilliant chef overseeing a great buffet — and sometimes offering too much. "But when so many filmmakers are content with too little," he concluded, "it's refreshing to find a guy who gives viewers more than enough to contemplate, and to enjoy."

Vincent Canby in *The New York Times* found *Munchausen* "full of moments that dazzle, just for the fun of seeing the impossible come to life on the screen. What the Folies Bergère once was for the foot-weary tourist, *Baron Munchausen* is for the television-exhausted child."

Roger Ebert in the New York *Daily News* was another supporter, though he found the film slow to get off the ground. "However," he declared, "the wit and spectacle of *Baron Munchausen* are considerable achievements . . . The special effects are astonishing, but so is the humor with which they are employed . . ."

Sheila Benson in the *Los Angeles Times* led the West Coast contingent with a stunning notice headed "The Magical Treasure Of Baron Munchausen." "We wouldn't want to be children again," she led off. "Mumps. Chicken pox. First day of school. Big dogs. But to find the world an adventure, an astonishment. *Believable* again. Who wouldn't want that?

"That is Terry Gilliam's gift . . . Children won't know that *The Adventures of Baron Munchausen* is the most sophisticated vision imaginable. That a treasure chest of references from movies old and new, animated and otherwise, from the history of art and from music and mythology, is being spelled out for them. That their imaginations as well as their funny bones are being tickled and that, actually, they are being taught to prefer the beautiful to the gaudy, the perfect to the shoddy . . .

"Children will simply accept the movie's magic matter-of-factly, the way they do a book by Maurice Sendak or a movie as effortlessly fine as *The Black Stallion*. They don't know yet how great a present it is, and that's probably best . . . The rest of us have no such stake in keeping our cool and from its very first minutes, *Munchausen's* witty splendor is reason enough to lose ours . . . *However* much this extravaganza cost, it is, as they say, all up there on the screen — a *thousand-fold!*"

John H. Richardson at the Los Angeles *Daily News* was in accord with both Sheila Benson's and Joel Siegel's imagery. "Picture an old-fashioned illustrated children's book," he suggested. "It has a creamy leather binding just old and cracked enough to hint of distant places and strange tales. It is big, something to hold in your lap, something to cuddle up with and make you want to turn the pages full of wonder. It's something to return to again and again.

"That's *Baron Munchausen*, the *best children's movie* to come along in many years, and one of the rare ones that is equally entertaining for adults. It's as if the makers of *Wizard of Oz* or *Ali Baba and The Forty Thieves* had access to the most modern special effects and the visual imagination to use them to the fullest. For *Baron Munchausen* Terry Gilliam deserves great praise . . . Magic and dreams *do* win in the end, in the story and on the screen."

Less beguiled was Peter Rainer in the *Los Angeles Herald Examiner*. "It's an astounding, throttling experience," he complained, "bracing, yet scary, and not really pleasurable in the way we've come to expect from movie fairy tales . . . Gilliam doesn't know when to let up. His inventiveness is a form of monomania, and he left me behind after a while."

"Something is missing," Dann Gare wrote in Chicago's *Daily Herald*, "that special connection between the characters and their audience that's so essential in delivering the emotional payoff a movie like this wants."

"Fantasy achieves nobility in *Munchausen*," Jim Emerson countered in the Los Angeles *Register*, "an elegantly shaped but boisterously busy movie that explodes with abundant, exuberant invention, outlandish visual puns and inspired cross-cultural references." Emerson's only worry was that the movie might be too rich for digestion at a single sitting. Repeat viewings, he felt, would "only enrich your appreciation of this bountiful, colorful and profusely illustrated spectacle."

Peter Goddard in *The Toronto Star* was another enthusiast. "Terry Gilliam doesn't make movies," he asserted. "He makes celluloid magic boxes, whirligigs, gimcracks, thingamagigs, eyeball-popping gee-gaws, elaborate devices which bemuse (*Time Bandits*) or creak and groan (*Brazil*), all to dazzle the blissed-out viewer numb. And his latest invention, *The Adventures of Baron Munchausen*, is by far his most costly, elaborate and overwhelming. It's his *most successful*, too . . ."

From the *Boston Herald*: "Gilliam's filmmaking technique is so polished it's quite *dazzling*. Gilliam also reminds us that the ideal response to art — from the paintings of Botticelli to a great film like *The Adventures of Baron Munchausen*, is a delighted gasp of joy and wonder. The film's a *visually stunning* celebration of the rejuvenating power of the imagination." From *People*: "With its Fellini-esque palaces to its Dickensian streetscapes, the film is a visual wonderland." From Stephen Schiff at *Vanity Fair*: "A *brilliant* and ravishing film," From *The Bergen Record*: "Epic entertainment for children of all ages. In a way, it doesn't matter whether *Munchausen* earns back its tremendous cost, Gilliam has triumphed over his foes by putting his version on the screen. It's a *stunner*!

"Forget the title," Robert Denerstein in the *Rocky Mountain News* advised: "*The Adventures of Baron Munchausen* is really the adventures of Terry Gilliam. Like his other movies, this one is immoderate and beautiful — an intoxicating visual feast." Dixie Whatley "At The Movies": "Once the Baron's adventures begin, you'll be afraid to blink for fear of missing a single fantastic second of fantasy. Just when you can't imagine a vision more monumental or magical, your eyes are filled with something even more riveting. See The *Adventures of Munchausen* on the big screen — that's a must — and take *everybody*." From Michael Medved in "Sneak Previews": "*The Adventures of Baron Munchausen* is a dazzling, *hugely enjoyable* film that's not only full of magnificent sets, costumes and special effects, but above all is shaped by a wonderfully inventive sense of humor — for anyone over the age of ten, this is a movie that can restore your sense of wonder."

Full acknowledgement was given to the technical wizards behind the movie, (as well as to Michael Kamen's "Superb score in the grand tradition of the Masters"): "Major credit to Giuseppe Rotunno, Dante Ferretti, Richard Conway and Peerless Movie Company." /"Sensuously photographed by Giuseppe Rotunno, all the film's technical aspects are on the same high plane — impeccable special effects, eye-popping miniatures and production design that quotes Gustav Doré, Bosch, Brueghel and other masters, as Gilliam creates a world of his own."/"Dante Ferretti has concocted Turkish harems with pajama-striped walls, lunar cities based on false Renaissance perspective, and a perpetual battlefield populated by ruined statues, dragon-mouthed cannons, actual elephants."/"Working with Italian designers and craftsmen including production designer Dante Ferretti and cinematographer Giuseppe Rotunno, the director has supplemented his eye-bending compositions with an airy, filigreed grace of line and mass that contrasts pleasingly with the blocked and heavy forms of *Brazil*. It is not surprising to see the Baron fly off into the sky on the handles of a cannon ball because all of the beautifully-scaled sets look like they might suddenly leap into the heavens anyway."

In Britain there were a few doubters, led by Victoria Mather in the London *Daily Telegraph*, her article headlined "The Adventures of Boring Munchausen." "Relentlessly clever," she felt. At least, she conceded, "one can see every penny of the $50 million on the screen."

Overall, however, praises were highly sung by the UK press: "Is Baron a great night out?" William Russell asked in the Glasgow Herald. "No," he replied, "it is a *marvelous* night out. A *fabulous* night out." Geoff Andrews in *Time Out* agreed, declaring the film "thoroughly entertaining and often all that one might possibly hope for — spectacular, affectionate, intelligent and funny."As far as Roger Lewis in the *Observer* magazine was concerned, "To watch this film is like dreaming wide-awake. It teases us into conceding that each shot is beautiful, that you can have an epic that's neither stagnant nor camp . . . *Munchausen* lasts two hours, it feels like two minutes."

Derek Malcolm in the *Guardian* heralded the movie as "one of the great fantasy films of all time", before the doyen of British film critics, Alexander Walker in the *London Evening Standard* capped them all, describing "Terry's Tallest Tale" as "A fabulous film that for once, adds up to the sum of its special effects — wonderful though these are. I haven't seen a magical universe so meticulously and lavishly created since Gilliam's last Pythonesque phantasmagoria, *Brazil* . . . There is not a half-minute that isn't packed with sly jokes and striking images, with breathtaking architectural concepts that conjure up the fantasies of Gustav Doré."

A P P E N D I X B

List of Columbia/Tri-Star's Movie Releases
Six Months Prior To Munchausen

	No. Cinemas Opening/ Prints Struck	Total US Box Office Gross	$ Return per print
Fresh Horses (Columbia/WEG)	1,276	$7.0 million	$5,486
Iron Eagle 2 (Tri-Star)	874	10.0	11,441
High Spirits (Tri-Star)	825	8.5	10, 303
DeepStar Six (Tri-Star)	610	8.0	13,114
My Stepmother Is An Alien (Columbia/AEG)	1,106	10.2	9,222
Physical Evidence (Columbia)	695	3.6	5,180
Who's Harry Crumb? (Tri-Star)	1,197	11.0	9,190
Tap (Tri-Star)	585	9.2	15,726
True Believer (Columbia)	897	9.0	10,033
Chances Are (Tri-Star)	1,190	17.0	14,285
Sing (Tri-Star)	864	2.5	2,893
Troop Beverly Hills (Columbia/WEG)	964	10.0	10, 373

$106.0 million

APPENDIX C

Revised Budgets of *Baron Munchausen*
(in millions of dollars)

August 15, 1987	$23.02
September 20, 1987	$26.14
October 11, 1987	$32.90
January 3, 1988	$35.94
January 23, 1988	$38.47
February 12, 1988	$39.49
April 8, 1988	$43.89
May 20, 1988 (revised downward)	$43.31
June 17, 1988	$43.37
July 26, 1988	$44.55
August 28, 1988	$44.56
September 22, 1988	$45.12
FINAL COST	**$46.34**

INDEX

DIRECTING THE ACTION

By Charles Marowitz

Acting and Directing in the Contemporary Theatre

Foreword by Peter Brook

Every actor and director who enters the orbit of this major work will find himself challenged to a deeper understanding of his art and propelled into further realms of exploration on his own. Marowitz meditates on the sacred precepts of theatre practice including auditions, casting, design, rehearsal, actor psychology, dramaturgy and the text.

Directing the Action yields a revised liturgy for all those who would celebrate a theatrical passion on today's stage. Not since Peter Brook's *The Empty Space* has a major director of such international stature confronted the ancient dilemmas of the stage with such a determined sense of opportunity and discovery.

"An energizing, uplifting work . . . Reading Marowitz on theatre is like reading heroic fiction in an age without heroes."
—Los Angeles Weekly

"A cogent and incisive collection of ideas, well formulated and clearly set forth; an important contribution on directing in a postmodern theatre." **—Choice**

"Consistently thought-provoking . . . Sure to be controversial, this is recommended for most theater collections."
—Library Journal

"Stimulating, provocative, sometimes irascible, but always courageous." **—Robert Lewis**

paper • ISBN: 1-55783-072-X

APPLAUSE

SEVEN BY SHANLEY

The Collected Plays, Vol. 1

by John Patrick Shanley

**WELCOME TO THE MOON
DANNY & THE DEEP BLUE SEA
SAVAGE IN LIMBO
WOMEN OF MANHATTAN
THE DREAMER EXAMINES HIS PILLOW
ITALIAN-AMERICAN RECONCILIATION
THE BIG FUNK**

THE DREAMER EXAMINES HIS PILLOW:
"... pungent, though-provoking, original, poetic, and leading by stylized, fantasticated ways to genuinely startling illuminations." — **John Simon**
NEW YORK MAGAZINE

DANNY & THE DEEP BLUE SEA
"... the equivalent of sitting at ringside watching a prize fight that concludes in a loving embrace." — **Mel Gussow**
NEW YORK TIMES

ITALIAN-AMERICAN RECONCILIATION
"... bathed in the same moonlit madness that gave his *Moonstruck* screenplay its savor and flavor ... a lovely play." — **Clive Barnes**
NY POST

paper • ISBN: 1-55783-099-1

THE ADVENTURES OF BARON MUNCHAUSEN
by Charles McKeown & Terry Gilliam

**The Novel, with color and black-and-white illustrations
and
The Screenplay, illustrated with 30 stills**

Baron Munchausen, one of the most famous liars in history, first recounted his adventures over two hundred years ago and since then they have been retold and added to by storytellers around the world. The original *Adventures*, written by Rudolf Erich Raspe in 1785, became an instant best-seller, and was hailed as a comic sensation in the satirical spirit of *Gulliver's Travels* and *Tom Jones*.

To the delight of frivolous adults and serious children who have followed Alice through the looking-glass and Dorothy down the yellow brick road, another most extraordinary adventure beckons. If you can keep up with the Baron and his little companion, Sally, you will ride a cannonball over the invading Turks, sale to the moon in a hot-air balloon, plunge into the bowels of an erupting Mt. Etna, and join the South Pacific Fleet in the belly of a great sea monster.

Terry Gilliam has resurrected the Baron and his comrades in entirely new adventures capturing the Munchausen spirit in a volume destined to be a classic for generations to come.

Novel (paper) • ISBN: 1-55783-039-8   Screenplay (paper) • ISBN: 1-55783-041-X

TERMINATOR 2
Judgment Day
The Book of the Film

**An Illustrated Screenplay
by James Cameron
and William Wisher**
Introduction by James Cameron

A landmark presentation of an action classic.
Special features include:

Over 700 photos

Including 16 page of color
Plus
Altered and deleted scenes
The complete screenplay
The original storyboards
Over 100 detailed production notes

336 pages • ISBN: 1-55783-097-5

A HILL/OBST PRODUCTION FROM TRI-STAR PICTURES

THE FISHER KING
The Book of the Film
directed by Terry Gilliam

**Screenplay written by
Richard LaGravenese**

Terry Gilliam, the internationally acclaimed director of *Brazil* and *Time Bandits*, now investigates one man's attempt to redeem himself from a life of fatal cynicism through his unlikely alliance with a visionary street person.

The Applause Book of the Film includes

- The complete screenplay by Richard LaGravenese in professional screenwriter's format.

- Photographs from the film.

- Extensive interviews with Terry Gilliam and Robin Williams.

- An afterword by Richard LaGravenese detailing the writing and production history of the film.

- An annotated appendix of deleted and altered scenes, illustrating the evolution of the film.

Paper • ISBN: 1-55783-098-3